Crowood Travel Guides are the essential starting point for a holiday to remember – and they'll be the signpost to enjoyment every step of the way. Easy-to-follow, practical advice, combined with a warmth and enthusiasm for the peoples and cultures of the world, mean that they'll be turned to again and again for direction and inspiration.

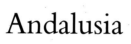

Andalusia

First published in 1991 by
The Crowood Press Ltd
Gipsy Lane, Swindon
Wiltshire SN2 6DQ
© The Crowood Press Ltd. 1991

British Library Cataloguing in Publication Data
Totton, Robin
  Andalusia. – (Crowood travel guides)
  1. Spain. Andalusia – Visitors' guides
  I. Title
  914.680483

  ISBN 1–85223–446–6

All photographs by the author
Maps by Taurus Graphics
Typesetting and page layouts by Visual Image
Printed and bound by Times Publishing Group, Singapore

Andalusia

Crowood Travel Guide

Robin Totton

The Crowood Press

Andalusia

Contents

Cortijo, Andalusia

Foreword

This book divides into three parts.

1. The first section aims to give the general help that may take the time and trouble out of the practical everyday problems of living.

2. A guide to the eight provinces, starting with their principal cities. This part also aims partly at practical help: where to stay and what to see and do and buy. But in it I discuss the things that give me most enjoyment, allowing my own prejudices free rein, while at the same time trying to give reasons for my likes and dislikes, rather than cover all with blanket gush. In this way I hope you may have some basis for deciding what and how much you want to do. I have also supposed that, while you are intelligent and ready to enjoy many things, you are not a tireless zealot for art and architecture, satisfied with nothing less than twenty-five parish churches per day. I simply assume that if you are such, you will use the Tourist Office and Michelin's *Green Guide* and see them all without my help. To my mind, the mountain areas offer at least as much as the famous cities, and to alternate between the pleasures of each makes a well-balanced meal of any holiday.

I do not know where we are going, but I do know this – that wherever it is we shall lose our way.

Práxedes Sagasta

3. The last part, like the first, is designed to be read in the leisure of your hotel, or before you go. It seems to me that you gain more enjoyment and appreciation from what you see if you understand *why* it is so and not otherwise. So I include in this more leisurely section, a brief historical account. For Spain this is more necessary than it would be for France or Britain, and it works in some

surprising ways. Many people seeing the great Mosque at Córdoba, for instance, feel a bit bewildered and only begin to enjoy themselves when they come to the *Mihrab*. They begin to enjoy the rest, only when they know a bit about who the builders were and why it was built in that way. The same is true for that bewildering habit you will find today of giving streets two names. If you do not know why, you put it down to 'Spanish inefficiency'; if you do know about the tact and tolerance implicit in *convivencia*, you cease to scorn, and maybe start to respect and even admire.

In the last section, too, I have put brief accounts of such matters as sherry, bull fighting, horses and so forth – that is to say topics that some readers would like, and others want to leave out, and which would therefore clutter the text if I put them where they might be said to belong. This section also contains the word lists, tables and so forth.

Acknowledgments

When gathering information you can do with friends. Many kind people have helped, of whom my particular thanks go to Juan Pazos of Sandeman's in Jerez and Charlotte Fenn at the Spanish Tourist Office in London.

The Alhambra, Granada

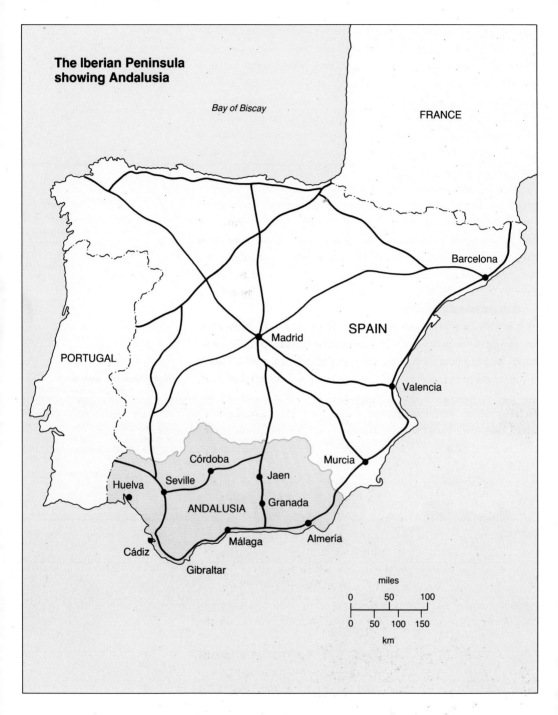

The Iberian Peninsula showing Andalusia

Bay of Biscay

FRANCE

Barcelona

SPAIN

Madrid

PORTUGAL

Valencia

Córdoba

Murcia

Seville

Jaen

Huelva

Granada

ANDALUSIA

Almería

Cádiz

Málaga

Gibraltar

miles

0   50   100

0   50   100   150

km

Introduction
Why Andalusia? The attractions of this region are manifold. There are fine and exotic things to be seen in its cities. The Alhambra in Granada is unequalled in the world; the Great Mosque at Córdoba set a pattern for Islam; Seville is one of Europe's most beautiful cities; Ronda one of its most astonishing towns.

Then there are the four major mountain areas: The Alpujarras, the Serrania de Ronda, and the Sierras of Cazorla and Aracena. All differ in character, each has its own pull that, for me at least, is stronger than that of the cities. They are a delight for botanists, bird-watchers and walkers alike. In their villages, the famous *pueblos blancos* perched on the mountain sides, usually with Moorish castle above, you can find food, a bed and undemonstrative kindness.

There are the smaller towns or more out of the way places: Arcos, Ronda, Baeza, Ubeda and many others, to do what a holiday should do by taking you right away from the usual and the familiar.

And most of all there is the pleasure of being among a different people who have a different way of life and a genius for enjoying it. A people among whom, despite Fax and air-conditioning, rock music and plastic bags, Richard Ford's words still apply: 'Here we fly from the dull uniformity… of Europe, to the racy freshness of an original, unchanged country, where antiquity treads on the heels of today.'

The Spain you see and the Spain you meet
Clearly the visitor who does not speak Spanish will feel he can only belong to the first sort, and most would agree that he is

Relaxations … will be best enjoyed in the Southern provinces, the land also of the song and dance, of bright suns and eyes, and not the largest female feet in the world.
Richard Ford:
Handbook for Travellers in Spain, 1845.

Penelope Chetwode wrote that whenever she didn't understand what was being said to her she found the Spanish word *claro* (clearly) a safe thing to say. Perhaps *vale* might be even safer. This means, literally, 'What you say is valid', but is used for anything from 'OK' through 'Well, isn't that nice, now' to 'I heartily approve'. Together with *claro*, it punctuates most conversation.

11

missing a lot. He is like an outsider looking in through plate glass, taking part in nothing. But I am not sure this divide has to be. I found myself in a position not too dissimilar when I wanted to try the *peñas* in the gypsy quarter of Jerez. A *peña* is a cross between a bar and a club, and I felt hesitant about going in there as a foreigner, like a gawker at a zoo. I was told: 'You are making a big mistake. If you simply go in there because you'd enjoy a drink, and you like the atmosphere, you're not a gawker or an outsider, you're someone who has gone in there for the same reason as everyone else, and you'll be accepted and welcome.'

I did so, and was: my critic was right. I suspect this may well be a sort of paradigm for English people who do not speak Spanish: if you stay conscious of the fact that you are foreigners and outsiders then you will, in a sense, be making it so; you will be cutting yourself off. But if you try to think of others, not as 'Spaniards', but just as other friendly and well-disposed people, who like enjoying themselves and assume you do, too, you will be accepted as just another person rather than as a foreign presence, and I fancy – though I cannot be sure and would like to know – that you will cross the barrier between the Spain you see and the Spain you meet.

Spain on the Move Spain is on the move, and Andalusia at least as much as any other part. After fifty years of being poor cousins – some would say four hundred years – Spaniards at last feel they are on a par with the rest of us in Europe. Statistics deny that they are there yet, but the visitor gains everywhere the impression of optimism and confidence: they know where they are going and that is upwards. This thrust towards a better life is accentuated by the looming of 1992, which means a lot more in Spain than it does in Britain. For in that year Spain becomes a full member of the European Economic Community and, unlike us, they are sure their future lies in Europe; it is the five hundredth anniversary of the discovery of America by Spanish enterprise; the Olympics take place in Barcelona; it is Madrid's turn to be Cultural Capital of Europe and the World Fair takes place in Seville.

The impact of this latter on Andalusia is enormous. Forget what you may have heard about Spanish roads: they are rapidly being transformed, and are already among the best in Europe. They are planning a new railway line for a high-speed link from Madrid to Seville. All airports in Andalusia are being enlarged to

DOMINATOR·HERCULES·FUNDATOR

ANDALUCIA POR SI
PARA ESPAÑA
Y LA HUMANIDAD

The emblem of Andalusia

take increased shuttle services from the international airports. In Seville itself, hotel space for some 10,000 extra beds is under way. And, of course, all this is already bringing work, wages and prosperity to the previously unemployed.

Perhaps most important of all is that, after centuries of relative neglect by the centralist bureaucracy of Castile, Andalusia now governs herself. The future of the Andaluces is to a large extent in their hands, and very many of them now feel they can be proud again and have the chance to forge their own future; meanwhile, the national economy is – under the lead of an Andalusian Prime Minister – forging ahead.

How does this affect the visitor? Firstly, you are unlikely to see all those picturesque little beggar children in rags: you are more likely to find them riding shiny new bicycles on asphalted playgrounds. And secondly, prosperity brings a rise in prices.

13

Given the first, I find I cannot resent the second. Do not worry: the eagles still soar over wild and empty spaces, the gypsies still dance and tell fortunes, the markets still hum, and the Andalusians still turn the evening into a colourful street party.

The Andalusian People Here in the south it is hard to tell what stock the people you see come from: Northern, Celtic, Iberian, Moroccan, Arab, Gypsy or whatever. But the legacy of nearly 800 years of Moorish domination still seems evident in many ways trivial or important, in things you see or in matters of behaviour and attitude.

One of the dominant impressions is of vast stretches of olive groves away over the gently rolling plains, into the hills. This is the land of the Latifundio, the big estate, where the peasant owns nothing while the landowner owns vast tracts of the country, the cause of migrations both seasonal and permanent to the wealthier areas of Catalonia. Andalusia contains the richest and the poorest in Spain. The Regional Government is nibbling away at this inequity, but it will take time.

Most of all it is seen in the domestic architecture, where the house is built round its patio/garden and presents a blind, dingy façade to the street. But the same applies to much of the behaviour, with social life lived in the street and the house kept private and sacrosanct; where good things are tucked away in corners rather than blazoned abroad.

There is the love of flowers and water, the water that makes the flowers possible, but also the water made everywhere abundant in public drinking and ornamental fountains. There are the coloured tiles, the *azulejos*, still everywhere a part of almost every building.

On the Andalusian reputation for an aversion to hard work, I can do no better than quote Joseph Townsend and Gerald Brenan:

The peasants of no country upon earth are more patient of heat, of hunger and of thirst, or capable of greater exertions than this very people who have been accused of indolence.
Joseph Townsend, *Journey through Spain* (1786-7)

The idleness of the Andalusians is a pure legend
Gerald Brenan, *The Spanish Labyrinth*

Nicholas Luard pointed out that the countrywomen around his home near Tarifa wore their headscarves in such a way that a flick of the hand could turn them into the moslem chador.

There are habits of eating and drinking: the concentrated black coffee; the exotically sweet sweetmeats; and *horchata* (an almond milk drink).

I notice the small shops that have little back shops, such as can be found in Morocco, where you can go for a drink and a chat while choosing your wares.

Am I being fanciful in equating a significance attached to numbers with the old Moorish belief in their significance, or even the medieval Jewish *gematria*? You will see people taking considerable care in choosing their lottery tickets, and the buying of lottery tickets itself seems to me part of the same matter. But, more than that, I have heard educated people say 'That is a good number', and on more than one occasion.

In the light of economic statistics, my impression today of booming prosperity may be partly wishful thinking, conditioned by a previous experience of Spain that has made me a convinced Hispanophile. My experience at first was of desperate poverty; more recently only of a country economically backward under the cold grey hand of inefficient autocracy; but always of people whose decency and dignity made them prompt, yes, to say that things are done better in other countries, but never to whinge about their own condition.

Most visitors today are struck by the readiness to help, smile and dismiss your gratitude with an 'es normal', many notice how a shopkeeper or passer-by is, as likely as not, not just to give you directions but to drop his own concerns and go with you to show you. But to me this feels no different from early experiences in the 1940s of, for example, the Colonel's widow and two daughters, living destitute as refugees in France in two attic rooms over a garage, who invited me to tea. One daughter apologized for carrying on with the ironing, but sat down to chat when the other went out to get the tea. Then it dawned on me that they had only three chairs; and that for me to offer mine to the one returning with the tea would be boorishly to destroy the illusion they had so unfussily created of a normal and gracious social occasion. George Orwell, in Spain during the fighting a few years earlier, wrote: 'I defy anyone... not to be struck by their essential decency; above all, their straightforwardness and generosity' and his use of the word 'decency', in this colloquial sense, has come back to me time and again over the years in Spain.

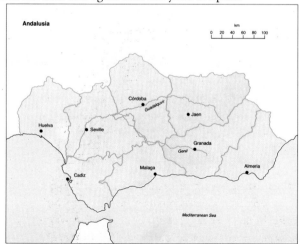

15

Part One: **Planning**

Wayside flowers

When to go It is easier to say when not to go. July and August are too hot, unless you enjoy temperatures in the 40°s (over 100 °F). But even so, it is a dry heat that roasts rather than wilts you.

In April, May, even June sometimes, the whole region is green and bursting with the colour of flowers. The temperatures are going to be in the mid and high 20°s (around 80 °F). Andalusians have inherited a love of flowers from the Moors, and, like them, in the towns they build their house round the garden rather than vice versa; you glimpse the explosion of colour through doors giving on to the inner patio, or spilling out of window frames.

House in Cordóba

Before the leaves come to the jacarandas, whole streets can be a smoke of mauve; bougainvillea spills over the walls to join hibiscus and mimosa and oleander and orange trees. In the countryside there are extravagant stretches of poppy and yellow broom, while the verges are speckled with every colour by bugloss, marigold, speedwell, spartium, snapdragon, thistle, mallow and umpteen others whose names I have been told and forget. April and May are also the time of many fairs and fiestas, though not yet crowded with foreign tourists. *See* the section Events Calendar (page 311) for more details.

September and October are also good times to come, when the heat is beginning to subside, yet geraniums still flower in the patios and window pots. The land now looks wilder and more exotic, with the crops off, the grass burnt brown and the cicadas working flat out. The *campiña* is an endless rolling of shades of every variation from chalk white to tawny, ochreous reds and yellows and dark grey-browns. It is the vast ox-hide land of Gerald Brenan's phrase and, with the temperature still varying

18

between 25° and 30 °C (77° and 95 °F), you appreciate fully, and delight in, the builders' skills in their use of shade and water and cool surfaces.

February and March are good times to escape from the dreary tail end of the British winter, to sunshine and temperatures that average 15° to 17 °C (59° to 63 °F), and are therefore usually warmer in the afternoons in many places. They are also excellent months to visit the great nature reserve of the Coto Doñana. In theory, November and December should be just as good, but when I went in a dry autumn, the marshes were dry and the migrants either had not yet arrived, or else they had gone elsewhere. *See* the Huelva section (page 255) for more detail.

All year round, Andalusia is a relatively dry climate, with the exception of the rainy western slopes of the Sierra de Grazalema, and the semi-desert of Almería which averages one day of rain per year. Indeed, at all times the above generalizations depend on the microclimate: I have driven two hours from shirtsleeves on the coast of Huelva to log fires in the hills of Aracena; and (10 miles) from 40 °C heat to shivering cold on the summit of the Veleta in the Sierra Nevada.

What to pack A light parka or rainproof and one jersey are insurance, and will be needed if you decide to drive up the 11,000ft to the top of the Veleta.

Otherwise, it depends on your plans. You will need a suit if you intend to stay at any Paradors or other top hotels, or attend any functions. On the whole, Spaniards tend to dress informally but never scruffily. Younger women wear jeans, but men tend to abandon them with their teens, unless hiking in the mountains. If you intend to visit churches, headwear is no longer needed, but shorts and bare arms can be offensive and may keep you out.

In most seasons you will want to change your shirt once or twice a day and, except in the best hotels, laundry can be a problem. I make life easy for myself by taking only four white drip-dryable shirts and a couple of metal hangers. It takes only a couple of minutes to wash them before going to bed, and they are dry by morning. It is not worth buying soap to take with you. You can get a small bottle of *Norit* or *Woolite* in any *supermercado* or *droguería* and throw it away on departure. Both makes are good for wool as well as cotton.

19

Shoes: a warning against thin-soled footware for town use, when streets, in towns and villages alike, are so often bruisingly cobbled. For men, for almost all purposes, consider buying when you get there a pair of those Spanish canvas-topped efforts – not the rope-soled *alpargatas*, but the ones with composition soles. They are cool, comfortable enough to cope with cobbles, keep their shape and look smart enough for any time of day, and they cost under £10.

Security: pickpockets are more skilful, and snatchers faster than most people would credit. Yet money-belts in a hot climate can be uncomfortable. For peace of mind, consider attaching a small tab of velcro to the insides of your hip pocket. And for the woman, consider taking one handbag that you do not value much. I deal with this matter under Crime (*See* page 46).

How to Get There

Travelling from Britain Andalusia is 2,000km (1,200ml.) from Britain and it is not far short of the size of England, so unless you propose to backpack and walk, the most practical ways of getting there and seeing it are to fly to Málaga and hire a car, or else to take your own car out.

By Air There are so many flights to Málaga and so many places in the UK to fly from that your local travel agent is likely to know them by heart. The only variable is price. A good travel agent can save you a lot, though unfortunately most do not bother to do the necessary ringing around. You must also bear in mind that the cheapest tickets may leave from places and at hours that involve you in extra hotel and eating costs. The price variation comes because charter flights also serve the independent traveller, and because, by keeping an eye on the newspaper ads you can sometimes make a late booking on a package tour that works out cheaper for the flight alone: that is to say, you book for a week on a package, but desert the party at Málaga Airport, and only rejoin it on departure for home.

Other methods are to consider flights to Gibraltar by GB Airways and Air Europe; or to ring round the reputable (ABTA) operators a week before you go. In this case, it is advisable to try several before you choose, and to check with them for any unmentioned surcharges, airport tax, etc.

On the whole, it is better to arrange the car hire through your travel agent before you leave, especially as there are fly-drive deals that can save you a lot. But there is no problem if you do not. Most of the well-known firms operate in Málaga Airport. In case you intend to base yourself in one place and make sporadic excursions from it, I list the major hire firms under the various cities. The complete list is usually given with the town plan that you should always get from the local Tourist Office in every city.

By Car This involves either driving the 2,000km or using the Motorail to Biarritz and driving on from there, or else taking the car ferry from Plymouth to Santander. Your choice in this will be governed more by personal preference and the time at your disposal, than by the cost, which will not differ significantly between the methods.

I have never costed out the long drive, because I have only done it by roundabout routes, making the journey part of the pleasure. But, even taking the night crossing to Le Havre for a fresh start, you will probably need to add to your petrol costs those of three hotel nights, meals, and hefty motorway charges – about £100 in France alone if you use them as much as you can; and they are not cheap in Spain, although they will be free when the new and rival *autovías* are completed. The cost of coffees and soft drinks alone, over a four-day journey, always takes me by surprise.

The Motorail way will take you and your car overnight across France to Biarritz and should cost £20–£30 less (for two people) than the ferry journey. Details from: SNCF (French Railways), 179 Piccadilly, London W1V 0BA. Tel: 071-409 3518.

The return fare for your car and two people (with cabin) Plymouth–Santander will cost upwards of £600. *Brittany Ferries*, Mill Bay Docks, Plymouth PL1 3EW. Tel: 0752 221 321 – the ferry is modern and comfortable (and, at 23,000 tons, larger than the liner that took me to the antipodes); the journey lasts 24 hours.

Whichever way you choose, I would urge you to consider the western route down through Spain via Extremadura, rather than Madrid and the fast but boring NIV. The latter is so good that you could leave Madrid at lunchtime and sleep in Córdoba. But Extremadura is wild, beautiful and not yet 'opened up' to tourism, though I think that will come soon. And accommodation is not hard to find: There are Paradores all the way down, at Tordesillas, Salamanca, Mérida and the Zafra; or Oropesa and Trujillo, if you take the south-west route from Madrid. Or, if you prefer more moderate stop-offs, even the quite humble Hostales and Pensiones are almost always very clean and adequate. Meanwhile, on the way, towns like Salamanca, the old town in Cáceres, and Mérida are places to be seen at least once in a lifetime.

By Bus The fares will be around £120–£130, not much less than those of a charter flight, and you must add the cost of food on the journey. There are twice weekly buses London –Madrid–Córdoba–Algeciras. Try *National Express Eurolines*, The Coach Travel Centre, 13 Regent Street, London SW1Y 4CR. Tel: 071-730 0202; *Euroways Express*, 52 Grosvenor Gardens, London SW1. Tel: 071-730 8235; or *SSS International*, 138 Eversholt Street, London NW1 1BL. Tel: 071-388 1732.

By Train Whichever train service you take, it is well worth while to buy the *Thomas Cook Continental Timetable*, either at a Thomas Cook agency or by post from the TC Timetable Service at PO Box 36, Peterborough PE3 6SB. Even by the Talgo the overnight journey Paris–Madrid takes 12 hours. For train journeys within Spain *see* page 00. If you are under 26, an Inter Rail ticket will save you money and buy you unlimited travel during its one-month validity. Another possibility is to enquire about reduced fares from: *Eurotrain*, 52 Grosvenor Gardens, London SW1W 0AG. Tel: 071-730 6525.

Travelling from Countries other than Britain

There are, of course, direct flights between Madrid and the US, and I give the addresses of the Spanish Government Tourist Offices in the USA and Canada under Useful Addresses (*see* page 000). But for Australia and New Zealand it makes much more sense to travel via the UK. There are no direct flights to Spain, and although you can get there via Frankfurt or Amsterdam, it will be no easier than doing so from the UK, from which there are more (and often cheaper) flights direct to Málaga.

Travel Documents For the British and Irish, the whole matter is rapidly shrivelling. A passport is needed and that is about all that need be said – except that, as European Community members, you will get into archaeological sites (Itálica, Medina az-Zahra, etc.) free, so you may want to take your passport to these.

Americans and Canadians need no Visa; Australians and New Zealanders do, for some weird reason.

Whatever you may be told, you do not need an International Driver's Licence, either for your own car or to hire one. But the Green Card, as a minimum, and Bail Bonds are still necessary.

Customs The main thing is to pack any metallic object, especially if it has a battery, in your hand luggage. It is in everyone's interest to make it easy for Customs to check out for bombs. The other warning is that if you are coming into Spain from Morocco you can expect a thorough search: this is the main channel for drugs into Europe.

The Airline allowance is 20 kilos (44lb) weight; and you are only allowed one airline bag.

Insurance It makes sense to insure your health, your car, your belongings, your money, and even against missing your plane (especially if you are using Apex). Your bank, travel agent, and insurance company will all be glad of your custom, so it is not hard to get quotations to compare for price and benefit.

When it comes to car insurance, it is worth reminding you at least to enquire into the possibility and costs of Europ Assistance.

Apart from Insurance that covers your health, you should get a form called E111, which plugs you in, as it were, to the Spanish Health Service. You get it from your local DHSS, or data on it from your Post Office. For more detail *see* the following section on Health.

Health

Before you go Your E111, together with passport or other proof of identity, enables you to benefit from the Spanish Health Scheme (*see* under Insurance above). But it would be unwise not to make sure there is enough medical provision in your travel insurance to free you from all worry of both treatment and transport.

The main thing is to know, before you need help, the terms of your coverage (both through insurance and via the E111) and how to operate them.

Chemist For minor matters go to the *farmacia* and see if you can cope with the communication problem. They really are very good, and not considered by doctors to be impinging on their domain. If you need renewal of a regular drug, they can often supply it, when in the UK you would need a prescription. There is always one duty chemist open all night in the towns; a newspaper will give you the address.

Allowances from the Duty-Free Shop
Tobacco: 200 cigarettes or the equivalent (100 cigarillos; 50 cigars; 250g tobacco).
Alcohol: 1 litre of over 22 per cent by vol; or 2 litres fortified or sparkling (under 22 per cent); plus 2 litres table wine.
Perfume: 50g.
Other dutiable goods: to value £32.

Not from Duty-Free Shop
In quantities half as much again, e.g. 300 cigarettes, etc., though 5 litres table wine, and goods to the value of £250.

Doctor If you need a doctor, the Tourist Office will often know which are the English speaking ones. Here you may have to pay his consultation fee, in which case keep the receipt for later reimbursement on your insurance.

Ambulance Ambulances are privately run, so the same payment and reimbursement will probably apply. I say probably because I have yet to come across the E111 in action.

Hospital, Centro de Salud, Consulta I list at least one medical emergency number for each town, though the odds are you will get help from your hotel manager or kind bystander in such cases.

In towns that do not run to a hospital, the Andalusian Government has set up a very useful medical help system. In a small town it will be called a *Centro de Salud*. In it, a qualified nurse or medical assistant will have the facilities to examine you, treat you if she finds it within his or her competence, and help arrange to get you to a hospital if that is the diagnosis.

In small villages there will often be a *Consulta*, which does the same job, but does not have the same facilities.

Green is the standard colour for anything medical, e.g. the signs denoting *Farmacia, Centro de Salud* or *Consulta*.

You are in one of the better countries in the world for medical help, minor or major. The Spaniards are proud of the high standard of their doctors and medical services. (Not chauvinistically, either: most cities honour Alexander Fleming with a street name.) And, personally, I have never found bureaucracy get in the way. On one occasion a badly swollen ankle took me to hospital for X-ray, and manipulation to replace a ligament, and I still do not understand why I never had to sign an insurance form or pay a penny.

Money

Currency The peseta comes in white metal coins up to 50 ptas and yellow metal ones above that – but beware: there is already a small angled coin like our 20p piece worth 200 ptas, and more changes are on the way.

Exchange There are four common ways of getting pesetas:

Travellers' Cheques need no comment other than that it is usually better to take Sterling or Dollar cheques rather than Peseta ones.

Credit Cards are the easiest way. Access/Mastercard, Visa, American Express, and Diners' Club are all widely recognized.

You can pay in before you go more than you owe them, so as to give yourself as high a credit limit as you wish, and then draw cash on any Spanish bank at your convenience. The better hotels and stores also accept them.

Eurocheques cause divided opinions. Within a few years they may become universally easy. For the moment I prefer to wait and see.

Bank Transfer was the method recommended to me by my own bank. They claimed it was a matter of a couple of days. A couple of weeks, at least, would be nearer the mark.

Banks They open in the mornings only. Monday to Friday 8.30 a.m.–2 p.m. (but 9 a.m. is a safer starting time). On Saturdays, 9 a.m. to 12.30 p.m. (or 1 p.m. in winter). Beware of Feast days and public holidays, but do not despair if you are caught out: there are plentiful *Cambios* round the bigger cities, and many hotels will exchange for you, though you may lose a few pence on the deal.

Most of the major banks in Britain and Spain have either started to link up, or are planning to. So if you are happy with your own High Street bank, you may want to know which Spanish one it deals with.

Tipping Deciding how much to tip, if you let it get to you, can be as constant an irritant as gravel in your shoe. I do not find it so in Spain. It may well be true that in important financial transactions, the Spaniard can be as sharp, greedy, grasping and mean (or otherwise) as anyone else. But when it comes to trivial sums, money is a matter for casual disdain. In a shop, if you give a 100 peseta coin for a 53 peseta purchase, your change is likely to be 50 pesetas. The shopkeeper does not think in terms of 'many a mickle makes a whatsit', but rather 'de minimis non curat caballero'. Tips will be casually left and casually received. Thus neither party shows he cares about such things.

Furthermore, the 100 pta coin (so nearly resembling the £1 coin, but half its value) divides conveniently into white metal coins of 5, 25 and 50 ptas. A bar bill of 95 ptas will see a tip left in the saucer of one 5 pta coin; likewise, 85 ptas worth will see three such coins casually left on the saucer. The advantage of this is that you can be carefree: leave little (or nothing) if that is the way you feel; leave more if you are feeling benevolent. The waiter or barman will in either case collect it with indifferent

25

Patio in Córdoba

mien – and whether the indifference is real or affected is his business, not yours.

Safety As a general principle, your things will be safe in your hotel; less so in your pocket or handbag. Take the precautions to protect your credit cards that you do in Britain (number to ring in case of loss), and leave unneeded money, cheque books, passport, etc., in the hotel, or in the hotel safe. But in case I am driving you paranoid, please remember that the vast majority of citizens in both our countries are honest and honourable: the trouble in Spain stems from the problems of unemployment and drugs among the young, and from the fact that as a foreign tourist you are a natural mark for the petty crook. Furthermore, it only applies to cities and to those towns that are much frequented by tourists (*see also* Crime section, page 46).

Accommodation Except for some of the humblest village lodgings, all accommodation is State registered and (in certain respects) regulated. This was done originally under the dictatorship to protect and therefore encourage tourists. But it continues unquestioned today because it is so successful: forty to fifty million visitors per year, many of them coming back and back, are proof of that. You get what you ask for, with no hidden charges, and it is honest value for money. Complaints you read of always seem to concern block bookings by package-tour outfits.

Hotels are in the main still very much cheaper than in Britain. In this book all prices are for a double room in high season 1989. Inflation is running currently at about 7.5 per cent, so that a hotel I list as £25 for a double room will by 1991 probably cost about £30. Maximum and minimum prices (according to the season) are fixed each year in early January, and cannot thereafter be changed. You are always charged by the room, so that singles vary between half (occasionally) and 70 per cent of the prices I list. Breakfast is not normally included in the price, except in the Paradores and most expensive hotels.

Cleanliness is no worry. I have used upwards of seventy hotels in Andalusia, ranging from international down to the humblest £4-a-night places in poor quarters and remote villages. Of the lot, only two (both in cities) were less than immaculate. So your choice really depends on the importance you attach to comforts such as private bathroom, telephone, quiet and air-conditioning, or else to luxuries of that standardized sort you find in hotels that have a sanitized telly in every bathroom, and once inside which, it is hard to tell whether you are in Bangkok or Birmingham.

There are splendid exceptions to this. The *Alfonso XIII* in Seville is one of the world's great hotels. And the Paradores (of which there are seventeen in Andalusia) are, many of them, unique in the world. The Parador is a State-run hotel, originally designed to guarantee a good standard to tourists. But such has been their success that it has become quite common to plan a journey round them, or even to make staying in them the object of a holiday. To get a room at the Parador San Francisco in the Alhambra, you would be advised to book at least a year ahead. But for your £70 a double, you are staying in a beautifully and discreetly adapted medieval monastery, inside the gardens of one of the world's most famous beauty spots. This, however, is an extreme example, and others are easier to get into. At Carmona, for £50, you stay in the medieval castle of Peter the Cruel; at

Ubeda (£50) in a Renaissance palace. The Tourist Office can provide a booklet listing and describing the seventy Paradores of Spain. And you can book them in Britain via *Keytel International*, 402 Edgware Road, London W2. Tel: 071-402 8182.

There are various categories of lodging: Hotel, Hostal, Pensión, Casa de Huéspedes, Camas y Comidas. These are currently being simplified: the Hostal will have disappeared by the time you read this, but I have to mention it as its owners have yet to decide whether to become Hotel or Pension. Meanwhile, if you wish to book ahead there should be no problem addressing them as Hostal. Hotels range from ★★★★★–★, with the variant HR or residential hotel, which has no restaurant, but minor cooking facilities in the rooms. The Pension will come next, with many of them at least as comfortable as a reasonable hotel. The Casa de Huéspedes is, for practical purposes, the same as the Pensión. The humblest category simply advertises Camas y Comidas (bed and meals). These are in villages, and are not Government registered, but I have yet to come across one where the room was not clean, or the meal less than good. Many of them offer *cocina a lo pobre*, poor man's cuisine, which means you eat what the hostess has to offer. But a stew cooked over an open fire, or sardines charcoal-grilled with fresh oregano, washed down with a jug of local wine, this is the sort of stuff that fuels memories.

While I list a selection of hotels for every town, please do not forget that Spain is very rapidly on the move. With the 1992 World Fair coming up, my recommendations for Seville, for example, will be out of date by the time you read this, for there will, by 1992, be some 10,000 more hotel beds available.

Camping The Tourist Offices supply free maps and lists of sites. The *Guía de Campings* is published in Spain every March, setting out the prices for the year. For further information try the *Camping and Caravan Club Ltd.*, 11 Lower Grosvenor Place, London SW1.

Getting About

Car Hire You will probably get the best value with a fly-drive deal via your travel agent. The usual international firms are available (*Hertz, Avis, Budget,* etc.); *Atesa* is a large national company, in fact government owned, and a bit cheaper than the international ones; *Marsans* also operates car-hire deals. There are cheaper local firms that may be good value, but I would not want the onus of checking my car carefully and worrying whether I had not missed something. You must be over nineteen, but do not need an international licence; your national one will be accepted.

Petrol you buy at a *gasolinera*, which in towns will often be an inconspicuous couple of pumps on the pavement. The price is controlled and the same everywhere. If your car is diesel you will have no problem, as they are popular all over Spain. Unleaded is coming in, but not yet as widely available as in Britain, and so far a bit more expensive than leaded.

Except for filling your tank, you do not ordinarily get much service on the forecourt, but if you do, a few 5 peseta coins are an acceptable tip. I find it easier to keep a check on expenditure and mileage by buying my petrol 3,000 pesetas at a time, rather than by the litre (that sum happens to bring my tank from a quarter to full). But at night you must expect to have to do it this way: many attendants do not want to risk carrying change. No Credit Cards.

The word *garaje* designates a place to lock your car up, and not the place to have it repaired. For this you either take it to one of the big makers' establishments, usually on the outskirts of town, or else to a small *taller* or workshop. I have become a fan of these over the years. More than once such local *talleres* have patched up my car for what by English standards is a ludicrously small sum, usually saying it would do to get me home, and sometimes lasting me for years. In the event of a breakdown, if it is your own car, it is worth considering this option, rather than automatically using the full power of your international insurance, when that may involve losing at least a day of the holiday.

Japanese cars have not yet (1989) penetrated the market, so you may not find agencies if you own one.

Car Safety I deal with crime on page 46, but do please note: in the town, never leave anything in your car, not even for a few minutes, and if the car is your own, never leave it on the street at night. My first question after asking if the hotel has a room is do they have a lock-up for the car? Garaging, whether private or municipal, is usually £4–£5 per night (or per 24 hours) and it just is not worth trying to save on it. This applies to towns only; in villages, do not worry.

The cities and towns of Andalusia are often best explored on foot. Driving is best left to the open road

Roads These are already about the best in Europe. Old ones are being not only resurfaced but re-engineered; everywhere work is in progress, building, renewing, widening. The old choice of toll-paying *Autopistas* (motorways) versus single carriageway for free, is now giving way to the brand new *Autovías* which are in effect free motorways. The new NIV, for example, takes you from Madrid to Cádiz via Córdoba and Seville. This thrusting renewal applies to the byways as well as the highways. It is not yet complete, but at present rate it will not take long. Memories of pot-holes and collapsing verges are a thing of the past: over about 6,500km (4,000ml.) of Andalusian roads in 1989, I came across only four or five such surviving.

The various categories are marked, e.g. A1, toll-paying motorway (*autopista* or *peaje*); NIV, free motorway (*autovía*); N34, national or A-roads; C234 or Ma2345, provincial. Even the ones marked uncoloured on the Michelin map 446 are mostly good and never unpracticable.

The improvement in roads is not matched by the driving. As soon as the Spaniard has taken his car into the country to where the lane-lines stop, he reckons the whole thoroughfare is his lane, and has yet to discover the rear-view mirror. My own theory is that by 1993 natural selection will have put this right: the only survivors will have been the quick learners. Until then, I suggest you be wary of contributing to this Darwinian process.

On dual carriageways, both in the country and on the roads out of town, it is no problem to have landed on the wrong road and want a U-turn: just watch for the overhead sign *cambio de sentido* (change direction).

Finding your way by car inside towns can vary from tricky to impossible. One-way street systems have been adopted with what to the driver seems demonic glee. But even a city as large as Seville is best seen on foot, and taxis are plentiful and not expensive. Easiest is to drive straight to your hotel, if it looks accessible, or else straight in towards the centre until you see a garage (the English word 'Garage?' will probably get you there). You can then let your hotel help you over luggage, and forget your car till you want to leave the city.

If you do have to negotiate city streets, however, keep in mind that one-way streets nearly always alternate, and that therefore most city blocks can – just as all city squares must – be negotiated anticlockwise. Add the 'priority to the right' rule and the job becomes simple, if not easy.

Road Rules These are no problem: drive on the right and give way to your right. Otherwise, the signs are the familiar international ideograms, though you may need the following:

Ceda el Paso	Give way
Curva Peligrosa	Dangerous Bend
Despacio	Slow
Desvio	Diversion
Direccion Unica	One-Way Street
Llevar la Derecha	Keep Right
Obras	Works
Paso Prohibido	No Entry
Peligro	Danger
Prohibido Aparcar	No Parking

Seat-belts must be worn outside towns. Speed limits, unless otherwise marked are: dual carriageway 120kph (74mph); other roads 100kph (62mph); built-up areas 60kph (37mph). You are supposed to carry a red triangle for motorway driving, and a spare set of light bulbs everywhere. In the event of an accident you should ring the police emergency number (091); there are telephones spaced along all motorways.

Infringements are treated according to the police force concerned. In towns the *municipales* are helpful, courteous and kindly disposed towards foreign visitors. A parking infringement is likely to be met with a polite and informative note on your windscreen. In any case, Spaniards double- and even treble-park, so if you do not want to be hemmed in, join the fun. But beware of towns where no-parking signs add *grua* or *cepo:* the tow-away and wheel-clamp people are ruthless. On high roads, the *guardias civiles* rule, and are no nicer than road police anywhere. Fines are given, and must be paid, on the spot, and credit cards will not do.

Taxis are plentiful and not expensive. They show they are free with a small green light on the roof at night, and by the sign LIBRE in the windscreen by day. The meter is displayed on the console. There are some supplements: late at night (after 11 p.m.); on Sundays and public holidays (*días festivos*); on journeys to and from the airport, when it is best to agree the price in advance; indeed, they may charge more if you cross the city limits – it has not happened to me, but I may be just lucky. In exceptional cases, there might be a supplement for luggage, but not normally.

Buses City Buses: if you intend to use them much, it is cheaper to buy a *bonobus*, which works for 10 journeys, at any tobacconist (*estanco*). Seville and Granada are the only towns so large that I have been tempted to catch a bus, and they have good networks. But road congestion in Seville meant I could have got there sooner on foot, and I did not repeat the experiment. In Granada, however, you may well find it worth using the buses, so I give details in that chapter. The Spanish for bus-stop is *parada*.

For excursions, or travel round the country, buses are a perfectly reasonable means. They are about as clean, comfortable and slow as anywhere in Europe. And most offer air-conditioning in summer. There are, however, so many different companies, often starting from different places in the town, that this book cannot offer detailed help – certainly not as much as you will get from the nearest Tourist Office or, if you are stranded in a small place, the Town Hall (*Ayuntamiento*).

Trains Contrary to the old cliché about dictatorships ('Mussolini made the trains run on time'), RENFE, the National network, has been getting very much more efficient since the advent of democracy in 1975, and is modernizing fast. Trains are on the whole clean and comfortable, and they are reasonably priced. Your only problem is that the system is extraordinarily complicated: there are umpteen different types of train service, and even more sorts of discount and supplement. However, if you intend travelling by train, do not let me put you off: you can make it fairly simple for yourself.

Stations are usually on the outskirts of towns – indeed, they are sometimes a mile or two outside smaller places, so watch it – but, in the larger towns, there is always a RENFE office in the centre where you can buy your tickets as well as get advice on discounts. Easier still is to buy your tickets from any travel agent who displays the blue and yellow RENFE logo. There is no extra charge.

For long distances, there are three types of train – and there will, by 1992, be four. The TALGO is the most costly, and well worth it. It is probably better than anything in Britain, though not as fast as the French TGV. By 1992, there will be a new line from Madrid to Andalusia, carrying the French TGV, and bringing visitors from Madrid to the World Fair in a couple of hours. The two other superior long-distance trains are called the ELT (*Eléctrico*) and the TER.

The *Expreso* and the *Rápido* are the other two long-distance trains. They are not as speedy as they sound but are fine for overnight journeys with couchette or sleeping-car. They are also the ones you would choose to take you any distance within Andalusia.

All the above have two classes, and you must buy your ticket in advance. This automatically also books your seat, so if you are a non-smoker ask for *non-fumadores*. (Mind you, ignoring rules is part of the Spanish temperament. In most cases this is a refreshing virtue; with smoking, or waiting your turn in a crowd – never a queue – you just accept it).

33

Couchettes (*literas*) are co-ed and 8 to the compartment; sleeping-car berths (*coche-camas*) are more limited in number and gender.

Local trains – such as the *Correo*, *Tranvía* and *Ferrobus* – are fun for lotus-eaters only. It would be hard to get more leisurely They have one class and you can buy your ticket at the *Salida Inmediata* counter (immediate departure) but do not leave it to the last minute.

Discounts are so many and varied that, unless you are a train buff, you will do well to ask RENFE or a travel agent to help you with them – as with the supplements, too, which are fewer but can be heftier. You can buy a *kilométrico* which allows you to travel a total distance and costs a bit less; or a *cheque-tren*, with similar effect; you can do round trips cheaper on *días azules* (blue, or off-peak days) which are more than half the year; and there are reductions for various ages and groups.

Of course, this will all be meat and drink to the railway buff, but whoever you are, if you intend to use the network much, buy the *Guía* RENFE at any station newsagent's. With 200 pages of comprehensive information at less than £1, it is a golden snip.

Traditionally Spaniards have got their protein from pork, fish and beans. It still shows on the menu.

Food and Drink The very best restaurants can give you a meal as delicious as any in the world. And the cuisine will, unless you choose otherwise, be quite unlike any other known to you. It will cost you less than an equivalent meal in Britain, but at least as much as an equivalent one in France. For workaday purposes, there is then a big gap: the medium and cheaper restaurants are usually not good. You can all too easily find yourself in the monotonous grip of a salad, consisting of leaves of iceberg lettuce with tomato and onion rings, followed by a hunk of fried chicken with or without chips, followed by the eternal *flan*, or caramel cream. And do not ask for vinaigrette, since the word means a piquant sauce. So a bit of care and research is needed.

Pay no attention to the number of forks a restaurant boasts in the tourist-guide lists. It tends to bear little relation to the cook's abilities.

Rabo de toro – (ox-tail – the meat, not the soup), every sort of sea food and gazpacho are the typical dishes of Andalusia. Paella, while originating from the east of Spain, is ubiquitous and usually eaten by locals as part of a large or family outing – they know that it is likely to be better when cooked in larger quantities.

Sea-food and tapas, sherry and water: these are among the best things in Andalusia.

Seafood of all sorts tends to be more highly prized than meat, and is accordingly good. I have heard Frenchmen and Americans go further. Indeed, I have a hefty bet on with an enthusiast from Piscataway, NJ (who claimed it was the best in the world) that it is even better on the north coast of Spain and in Brittany. My slight reservations are only because it is usually fried, which does not excite me. But I have no reservation at all about a fresh tunny steak, grilled, or sardines (or anything else) cooked at one of those shanty-like eateries on the beach. Or, indeed, about any fish as cooked in the best restaurants. A visit to the fish market can be a revelation, as well as great fun.

Fish is a popular – and delicious – dish in Andalusia. A trip to the fish market is great fun

Tapas are a unique national institution. The word means a 'lid' or 'cover', and it is supposed to have started in a back-street bar in Seville called *El Rinconcillo*, where they claim to have first served each *copa* of sherry with a slice of mountain ham on top. Today it is no longer free (except, praise be!, in the conservative Alpujarras where one *padrona* told me with a mixture of pity and glee of a Sevillian holiday visitor who, on being presented with a *tapa* with his drink, looked round bewildered and asked 'Is there a wedding?'). In some places you may be given a minute sample free, in which case it is called a *pincho*. Sherry and mountain ham (*jamón serrano*) make as perfect a marriage as port and Stilton, bacon and eggs, or any other classic combination you care to name, and it should not be missed. You will also see the name *jamón Jabugo*: this is mountain ham from a village in the Sierra Morena, that is the best but expensive. In the Province of Granada they will hotly deny that any *jamón serrano* could be as good as the Trevélez ham from the Alpujarra.

The number and variety of *tapas* is endless, but as they are usually all on display you need have no problem choosing the ones that take your fancy. The evening stroll of thousands of citizens that characterizes every Andalusian town is often, in fact, a *tapeo*, that is, a social stroll through the cool of the evening from bar to bar, at each one coming across fresh acquaintances, and at each one trying a different *tapa*. If you can get used to such nibbling, it can make a delicious supper as well as an enjoyable evening.

Eating habits differ so radically from ours that it presents many visitors with a problem, both of timing and content. Not breakfast, which is normally coffee, chocolate or tea, toast (with butter and jam or honey), and often sweet cakes – though the Paradores and more expensive tourist hotels usually put on a vast spread to cater for all European tastes.

But the main meals, apart from being very much later than we are used to, are heavily weighted towards protein, and flavours too rich for many British palates. You will not find meat and two veg. If you like salad with your meat, I wish you luck, for locals have it as a starter, and waiters are conservative. Meat and fish are eaten on their own. There may be an added problem in that modestly priced restaurants are often just as modest in their standards. There are some delightful exceptions, and I recommend the ones I happen to know, but very often the Spaniards seem to hide their good and reasonable restaurants. In this case you are left with the choice: either an expensive one where the food can be as delicious as anywhere in Europe – and as expensive – or else *tapas*. Collecting the latter can come to be a connoisseur's enthusiasm.

The frustrating aspect of this is that the raw materials are gorgeous and plentiful: quite apart from the fish and seafood, or the quantities of beef fillet, the vegetables and fruit are succulent, and of amazing abundance and variety. Artichokes here, for example, are no delicacy – they are so plentiful that they are underrated by local restaurant cooks. The same applies to the fruit: apples do not come up to the standard of Cox or Egremont, but the pears are a joy, so are the greengages (*claudias*) and, together with the familiar melons, figs, pineapples, watermelons, grapes, cherries, oranges, lemons and so forth, there are others less common for us northerners: pomegranates (*granadas*), custard apples (*chirimoyas*), prickly pears (*chumbos*) and many others.

The local market can be a revelation for its fruit and vegetables as well as for its fish. To me, the fruit makes up for the fact that, for dessert, most modest restaurants offer nothing more than ice-cream or *flan* (which is a very unexciting custard cream). I should add hastily that I intend no dismissal of ice-cream: all ice-cream is wasted on me, but I am told the Spanish stuff is delicious. Some people like the Manchego cheese; I find it monotonous.

A pleasant feature of the restaurants is that you do not have to follow the menu: if you feel like a simple, light meal, you can always ask for a Spanish or a French omelette and salad (*tortilla española/francesa y ensalada*), or a scramble (*revuelto*) which you can

Farmers' lunch

have with green vegetables such as beans or artichokes mixed in.

Cakes and sweetmeats show almost more than anything else the influence of 800 years of Moorish rule. I have no sweet tooth, but even I can vouch for *turrón* which is a nougat (almonds and honey) but crisper and lighter than the tooth-pulling, toffee-like stuff from Montélimar. As indeed I can for *queso de membrillo*, quince cheese. Those who like sweet things should visit the *pasteleria*, and keep an eye out for local specialities, for in many places there is a nunnery nearby that makes – and sells at the door – its own special sweetmeat or cakelet to a recipe they must have taken over directly from the Moors. And do not forget the *chocolate*, which is normally taken as a drink. Again, I cannot judge, but I am told it bears little relation to the tinned drink known in Britain.

Picnics have given me some of my best meals, and they are very easy: Spanish bread, if it is from the local bakery (*panadería*), is even better than the French and comes in loaves of all sizes (and, as everywhere, the smaller the village or more primitive the bakery, the better the bread). Beware supermarket bread, which can be as tasteless as ours. *Salchicha* or *chorizo*, which are types of sausage, come in convenient sizes (and keep for several days). A beefsteak tomato (but remember they are best when still a bit green); a variety of cheap and delicious fruit; a bottle each of mountain water

The village fountain is safe to drink from

and wine; a good knife and a mug: and you have a very good meal. Get everything except the bread at the *supermercado*, and you need have no Spanish – pointing is international.

Water I named water, partly because there is so much delicious mountain-spring water around (bottled in Lanjarón, and so named, if you are not in a mountain area), but partly to stamp on an outdated British prejudice: Spanish water is up to Common Market standards; British water is not. You can safely drink out of the tap here. And in the hill towns the water from the village fountain is often delicious. In the restaurant, you will be served bottled water and must state whether you want it fizzy or natural: *con gas* or *sin gas*. Beware the possible confusion: *agua natural* means tap water.

Wine For sherry please *see* the section on it on page 288. It is ubiquitous, and one of the world's great wines.

Montilla-Moriles, from Córdoba Province, is the other great Andalusian wine. I give it its correct name, though it answers to Montilla, except in the Moriles district. It has the nutty flavour that caused *Amontillado* sherry to get its name – the word means 'made montilla-like'. It is matured in the most splendiferous earthenware jars, eight feet high. Do not bother to bring any home: It is now widely available in the UK – my supermarket sells it at £2.50 a bottle which is good value by any standards.

Andalusia produces very little red wine, so do not expect to discover that little local red: if you order it you will usually get

Rioja which is all right (if you pick a good one), or *Valdepeñas*, which is drinkable but characterless. Occasionally, the house wine will be a *Toro* which I much prefer: it has some character, in contrast to the blandness of *Valdepeñas*. There is a sort of rosé in the mountains of the Alpujarra, which is unlike any rosé I have ever tasted and rather good. But you only find it in little village inns and bars, not in tourist restaurants or shops.

Except for the two famous ones, local white wines have until recently been rare. There is a table wine from Huelva Province that is beginning to gain respect, callled *Condado de Huelva*. But recently a number of firms round Andalusia have been making light refreshing white table wines. The best I have tried was a *Viña Verde* from near Córdoba, quite unlike the Portuguese wine of that name, but with a delicate almost flowery flavour.

Sweet wines: the muscatel wines of Málaga used to be as famous in Britain as sherry. Even sweeter is a wine made by fermenting oranges, called *Almíbar de Naranja*, which has about the same strength as sherry.

Beer Spanish beer is a lager and it is very good; the ordinary draught is as good as the bottled, only cheaper; and it is drunk so universally as to have become the national beverage. *Una cerveza* (oona ther-VEtha) will get you a glass of about half a pint; *una caña* (oona CAH-nya) will get you a dainty glassful, although there is some variation on this last according to the Province.

Soft Drinks All the usual soft drinks are available, and a lot more. But curiously, in a land of oranges, fresh orange juice is not offered everywhere. When it is (*zumo natural de naranja*), the sight of the waiter putting two or even three whole sun-ripened oranges through the de-juicer is as mouth-watering as the stuff itself.

Barmen and Waiters They usually work demonically fast – and do not avoid your eye: one glance from them almost always means they will come as soon as they can. And that is faster than my experience of Britain or anywhere else. Add to this that you do not pay until you leave, and it all adds to the pleasure of a civilized way of life. For advice on tipping, *see* page 25.

Shopping
Shop Opening Hours Shops, banks and so forth are open by 9 a.m. and usually stay so until 1.30 or 2 p.m. Thereafter banks stay shut; shops open again at around 5 p.m. and usually stay open

till 8 p.m., though some stay open later. It is a reasonable bet that the smaller the shop the later it stays open.

The major exception to this pattern is the large department store, of which the most ubiquitous and best is the *Corte Inglés*. This and others, such as the *Galerías Preciados*, stay open all day.

Things to Buy Some of Andalusia's most notable products are little use to you unless you happen to bring a van: forged iron-work, wicker and esparto wares, saddlery and tack... Others, such as sherry, are obtainable in England, though you may want to bring back a bottle or two of unusual brand or blend, or of Montilla, as gifts.

To my mind, this leaves leather goods, ceramics and eatables – in increasing order of desirability. On the leather goods in the shops you will judge for yourself better than I could. For the ceramics, apart from the *azulejos*, splendid but not cheap, that I suggest in the section on Seville, my preference goes for the country earthenware you come across in villages, mostly in the mountain areas: presuming I could find it elsewhere and more conveniently near the date of my return, I passed up some very pleasant things during my travels, only to find they were not to be had elsewhere. Grab it when you see it.

Eatables, canned, bottled, dried or downright sticky, can make unbulky, exotic, and inexpensive presents. Saffron (*azafrán*), for example, is about half the price it is in the UK. The gorgeous *jamón serrano* I would keep for myself. But the sheer range of pleasant and unlikely foods is beyond the range of this book or my memory. The trick is to go to one of the many little food shops in unimportant streets, such as the *Casa Moreno* in Calle Gamazo in Seville, which also serves as a bar and which I mention in that chapter. Or choose among the several little shops in, for example, the Acera Canasteros, off the Avenida de la Constitución in Granada.

Where to Get What Most shops correspond with the ones you are familiar with, and indeed are often the same shops (*Benetton*) or the same brands. But there are one or two possible confusions.

The *farmacia,* unlike our British chemist, only sells pharmaceutical products. Medically, Spain is by no means backward, and the *farmacia* is the place of first instance for advice, as well as medication. In matters such as stings, rashes, sprains, sores and the like, I have very seldom found it necessary to go further, and have acquired a hefty respect for their professional skill. But it is not the place to look for toiletry. For this, you go either to the *supermercado*, or to the *droguería*. This latter covers the area from soap and toothbrush to paint and paraffin.

In city kiosks you will usually be able to buy yesterday's *Times, Telegraph, Independent* and *Guardian,* or today's *Herald Tribune* which, since it went out of print in New York, has continued to appear in the Paris and Marseilles edition.

Quality Spanish papers outnumber the tabloids (which are really only sports papers). They are also more independent than English ones.

El Pais (my favourite) has tended to favour González, but then so has the majority of the nation.

El Independiente is possibly a bit less independent and more partisan for the PSOE (the ruling Spanish Socialist Party).

Diario 16 is good, and on the whole manages to be objective, too.

ABC is right of centre and supports Fraga's PP (Partido Popular, officially led by Aznar who, like González, is also an Andalusian lawyer, though Fraga is still the power behind the throne). The PP is the chief party of the Right, but not extreme.

Ya is the organ of the Catholic Church.

El Alcázar is dead. It was the shrill voice of the Army plus the Falange plus the bring-back-the-lash mob, but it went out of circulation a year or two ago for the best of all possible reasons that it no longer had enough readers to pay its way. The extraordinary and nationwide tact and tolerance the Spanish people displayed, even after 23 February, is beautifully vindicated by this natural death of an unpleasant organ.

In case you deduce from the above that I am a doctrinaire left-winger, too biased to be reliable, perhaps I should say that in England I vote Conservative. The Spanish Socialist Party is purely pragmatic, and our notions of Left and Right do not have the same connotations here.

The *estanco* (which is what people call it, if you want to ask), or *tabacalera* or *tabacos* (which is what the sign will say) sells matters of Government monopoly that include postage stamps and cigarettes. The sign will always be written in yellow and brown.

Tourist Offices Spanish local Tourist Offices must be about the most informative and helpful in the world. Go there as soon as you arrive in a town, and you will collect a town plan with every sort of information given on the reverse side. Not only this, but they will help you find a hotel, give you brochures on various possible activities, and others on the things to see in the province. This is the sort of help you come to expect, so that you feel (quite unjustifiably) aggrieved if you get any less. Sometimes you get more: in Seville (one of the very best) they will advise you on prices to agree for carriage rides, or which they think the best flamenco *tablaos*; in Jerez, I had so much active help that I shall go back just to visit them when I am next there. Even in small places that do not run to a *Turismo* there will be someone in the *Ayuntamiento* (Town Hall) with the job of helping the tourist.

Larger cities also have a Municipal Tourist Office which is not to be confused with the *Turismo* and which is of less use to the foreign visitor: it deals more with bus schedules and so on.

Maps Throughout this book I have used and referred to the Michelin no. 446 *Andalucía*. It is by a very long way the best. Its only fault is on the right side: it tends to mark roads as of less good quality than they are. You can buy it pretty well anywhere in Britain and in Andalusia.

If you are driving down through Spain, the Michelin no. 990 *Spain and Portugal* is as good as any.

Photography It is forbidden to photograph policemen or military servicemen. This is not a hangover from totalitarian days, but a protective measure against targeting by terrorists.

Film is rather expensive. The most efficient and rapid developing can usually be had from the department stores such as *Corte Inglés,* or sometimes from opticians (*opticos*), but where I have found especially good service I mention it in the text.

Letters The Post Office, *Correos*, is likely only to be of use for telex or Poste Restante, since you buy stamps from the *estanco*, and make telephone calls from a call-box or from the *Telefónica*.

Post-boxes are yellow. If you cannot find one, ask for a *buzón*.

Postage is currently 25 ptas for Spain, 45 ptas for England. Express (*Urgente* or *Mandato*): Spain 90 ptas; England 125 ptas. This should give you next-day arrival.

Poste Restante is called *lista de correos*. Have yourself addressed: Name, Lista de correos, Town, Province, Spain.

Telephone If coins and language put you off using telephone kiosks, remember every city has a *Telefónica,* where you can get the counter-clerk to put you through, and pay afterwards. This building is always central, and has nothing to do with the *Correos* or Post Office. In Córdoba there is even a special extra one for tourists just by the Mosque, which seems to stay open most of the day and night.

Area codes: Madrid 91; Barcelona 93; Almería 951; Málaga 952; Jaén 953; Sevilla 954; Huelva 955; Cádiz 956; Córdoba 957; Granada 958.

To ring Spain from England: 010 + 34 + area code without the 9-number. Thus, Seville 1234 from the UK is 010-34-54-1234.

To ring England: 07 + 44 + etc. Don't forget to omit the 0 from the STD code, thus to ring Inner London: 07-44-71 + number.

Enquiries: 003. International Enquiries: 9198. The operator speaks English.

To ring Gibraltar from Spain: from Cádiz province just ring the number without code; from elsewhere dial 956 + number. Note the implication of this ...

To make an International call from a payphone: (a) for free information put in a 25 pta piece and get it back when you hang up (b) put in two 100 pta pieces (you will get back one if call is less than 100 ptas).

Public Lavatories They do not exist. If you are American you will not notice a problem, but if you are British you need to know that bars, ice-cream parlours and the like are used to people coming in off the street and using theirs. There is no expectation that you should buy something; and when you find the door locked, ask the barman: he will give you the key. What do you say? Ask for *servicios* even if, when you find it, it is marked *aseos, retretes, wáteres, lavabos,* or merely by an idiotic picture.

Electricity The current is 230 volts, which is all right for our 250v appliances. This is true for everywhere except for a few backwoods or old and humble houses. You can now buy adaptors that actually work, as long as you pick the ones that do not try to be too clever. These latter are usually inefficient and often useless. If, like me, you use electric appliances a lot, you may find it helpful to pack a length of three-core flex with a socket on one end.

In Spain, you can buy a plug for pennies: *enchufe* (En- *choo* -fay). All plugs are two-pin, and of the same size and shape, but if you ask for it earthed (*con toma de tierra*) you will get one with a metal earthing strip set in the side of it. If you feel impractical, take your flex to the shop and point to the three bare wires. It should do the trick – and save you the bother. Come to think of it, showing your bit of wire to a passer-by should even find you the shop.

Adjusting to Spanish Hours Short exchange with a garage hand: 'The car'll be ready at noon.'
'Very well, I'll come back at twelve, then.'
'No, señor: In our country noon is at two o'clock.'

It is worth trying to adjust to Spanish hours. Kicking against the pricks, means trying to eat before the restaurant is open. It means the frustration of finding museums closed – indeed, finding whole towns apparently deserted and dead, if you try to visit them between 2 p.m. and 5 p.m. If you make the effort to adjust, things are available when you want them. The siesta not only avoids the heat of the day, it means you can enjoy the late night spectacles without feeling drawn the next morning. Spanish hours are not only practical and sensible for the climate, they also suit the Andalusian habit of playing as hard as one works.

Dress Anywhere round the town and of an evening, one point is universal: Spaniards may dress informally as to jacket and tie, but the clothing will be spotless and apparently freshly ironed. Anyone looking a bit creased and sweaty is likely to be a foreigner – and, alas, most likely British. Except among the drop-outs, this applies just as much to the young: if you see jeans and T-shirt, the T-shirt will be immaculate. Spaniards in a crowd almost always give the impression that they have just this moment emerged from the bath and just this moment put on freshly ironed crisp clothing.

Manners Obviously, courtesy can be recognized anywhere. But one or two slight differences may be helpful to know.

The Spaniard is much more sparing than we are with the 'Sorry', 'Please', 'Excuse me', 'Thank You'. You may find him rather offhand (he may think you rather gushing). Patient courtesy can get you further through red tape, officiousness, or distrust here in Spain than in most places. George Borrow and Richard Ford both commented on it in the early nineteenth century; it is just as true today.

Spaniards do not share tables: in the café, the chair at another table may be free and takeable, but not the place.

Spaniards are in the main a reserved people, but unlike us in one significant respect. In Britain, if you happen to catch a stranger's eye the common reaction is for both to look quickly away, as though you were guilty of something vaguely shameful; in Spain the usual reaction is a smile of friendly politeness. Outside the town, such eyeball contact between strangers commonly elicits a 'Hola, buenos días'. Indeed, in the country a 'Buenos días' is normal when you pass a stranger – and comes better from you since many a countryman has never met a foreigner and does not want to appear inquisitive. One need never feel shy about addressing a stranger in Spain, though back-slapping familiarity is at least as obnoxious there as here.

The generation gap seems to show when Spaniards take the cool of the evenings – the older generation tend to walk in pairs, the younger more often go in couples.

At this point, a word about the Spaniard's views on alcohol. For the Spaniard, teenager or adult, alcohol has no macho associations. The concept of taking your liquor like a man, or of the rugby club booze-up, or the teenage feeling that drinking will make the hair grow on your chest – all these are Anglo-Saxon or, at least, northern ideas. In a group of youths, the boys are as likely to be drinking soft drinks as the girls. Any sign of intoxication is viewed with pity, and left alone at the earliest polite opportunity: it is for the inadequate and the drop-outs.

A Seville doctor gave Richard Ford, the nineteenth-century travel writer, a recipe for Unto del Hombre or Man Grease: 'Take a man in full health who has just been killed, the fresher the better, pare off the fat round the heart, melt it over a slow fire, clarify, and put it away in a cool place for use.'

Customs The difference between Spanish customs and ours are so many that a paragraph or two would be quite inadequate, and I attempt to deal with such things as they crop up. But a word about children. The Spaniards' love for their children entails keeping them with them, at all hours and on most occasions. The shocked Anglo-Saxon often assumes that such late hours must be detrimental to health. I would not know, though I can detect no obvious evidence of it. Perhaps the siesta makes up for all. What is often noticed, however, is that the children run no risk of psychological deprivation from being left alone. In the evening stroll, the 8 p.m. *paseo*, the children of even the most modest families are dressed up as for a party, and the constant and manifest demonstration of parental love brings about, so I am told, a considerable and helpful self-confidence in later years. I point out the phenomenon merely, leaving the truth of the matter to those who know more about it than I do.

When smuggling of cigarettes from Gibraltar got going in a big way recently, the crime statistics for La Linea showed a perceptible dip. The local youth had found an alternative source of income to bag-snatching.

Crime The problem, such as it is, lies less in the likelihood of your being a victim (London has as bad a record), than in the fact that apprehension can spoil your enjoyment. How can you be carefree if you keep worrying about the safety of your handbag, your wallet, your necklace or your car? The answers are simple, and the precautions well worth taking. Please note that this applies only to the cities, where unemployment, drugs, a long tradition and careless tourists are all factors.

Never leave anything in your car by day, however trivial: a smashed quarterlight still costs money and delay. By night, keep it in a lock-up or supervised parking place. At traffic lights, a handbag on a lap is within reach of a sneak-thief on a motorbike.

Men: Keep your car in a garage and your wallet in a sealed pocket.

Women: In the street, do not wear a necklace or earrings that could be (painfully) snatched. Carry a handbag you do not treasure, with enough money in it to cover the day's possible needs, but leave behind in your hotel all those credit cards, passports and treasured photos of little Willie. Thereafter forget all care.

Please do not be worried by these apparently hideous and lurking dangers. Actually, the risk is slight. When you take out travel insurance you do not get worried by all those clauses that tell you how much money they will pay you for the loss of one eye or two fingers. Consider these precautions as insurance. They are well worth it. I have been robbed and I know that the upset, the lingering anger and the corrosive destruction of your pleasure are quite disproportionate to the triviality of the loss. So do take these precautions, even though the odds are that at the end of your stay you will wonder why you bothered about it.

The Policía Nacional If you need them in a hurry, ring 091 from any telephone in Spain.

Police There are three police forces. In towns the *Policías Municipales* wear blue. They are there to regulate traffic, look after bye-laws, and help you.

The *Policía Nacional* wear khaki (at present), are responsible for crime, and work out of the *Comisaría* which is where you must go to report theft or breakage – not only by law, but also to validate your insurance claim. If you need them in a hurry, ring 091 from any telephone in Spain.

The Policía Nacional will shortly be changing their uniforms again to one less military looking: it will be white shirt and navy

46

trousers – which will mean they will only be distinguishable from the Municipales by their shirt. The reason seems to be part of a long and deliberately gentle process: originally they had grey-green uniforms and were the Armed Police plus the Secret Police – the hated *grises* (greys), all very much part of a totalitarian state; then the two were merged and went into khaki; now, they will be even less military and more bobby-like. The tactful intention behind such slow change does not seem to be working: my impression is that they feel they are being emasculated, with their hands so tied in the fight against crime that they are despondent, and sometimes just go through the motions.

The ones in grey-green are the road police (also responsible for crime outside the city). These are the old *Guardias Civiles* of the patent-leather hats. They used to have a reputation for being both stupid and trigger-happy and were to be avoided. But they had to change their image (and uniform) after one of their Colonels gained international televised notoriety, and nationwide odium, by holding Parliament at gunpoint at the start of the failed military putsch of 23 February 1981. *El 23 febrero* is a date that will not be forgotten in Spain.

Part Two: **The Region**

Seville

Plaza de España

Seville Córdoba (mainly, though not solely) for its Mosque; Granada (mainly, though not solely) for the Alhambra; but Seville for Seville. It seems to have more vitality to the square yard than anywhere else. It has a perfectly redundant theatre, and it is building itself an Opera House: goodness knows why it bothers, when the whole city is a theatre, every street, every square, every palace, every church an operatic backdrop for one massive, non-stop, over the top production with a cast of 680,000. Yes, there are buildings and districts that deserve to be seen in their own right, and which it would be a pity to miss. There are many others, too, which you might well judge gaudy or grandiloquent if you look at them without taking them in their Sevillian context, though you would be the loser if you did so. But, more than anything else, Seville is a good place just to be in, whether as audience or participant or, as the Sevillanos seem to prefer, both at once.

It is a large city; it is down in the plains and hot; it has a reputation for petty crime against the person and against cars: these things put me off and delayed my first visit. Within a couple of days of arriving I was kicking myself for having needlessly deprived myself of the pleasure. As for the crime, pickpockets, bagsnatchers and cut-purses are as active here as anywhere and, being Sevillians, probably operate with more panache than most. I saw none but know of people who have been victims, so I would urge you to take the precautionary measures I outline in part 1 (*see* page 46) and having done so, leave all care behind, with your valuables, in your hotel.

For a minority (that includes me), a second possible shadow on one's pleasure is the feeling of being a bit bewildered and dwindled and disorientated by a big city. Part of the charm of towns like Ronda, Arcos, or Baeza is that you feel you can grasp and comprehend them almost as soon as you enter them. They have a flavour, not a whole mass and mess of flavours. In a metropolis, I feel at the start that I do not know which way to turn, what to look for, how to get my bearings. If this does not apply to you, then I am wasting your time with this paragraph. But it explains my aim in the following ones: to help you get hold of the pattern of this city, as well as its atmosphere, and some of its particular sights.

The city plan printed here is necessarily quite inadequate for finding your way round the streets, and I assume that, here, as everywhere, your first act is to visit the Tourist Office to collect a town plan and other helpful stuff. The first thing to see is that Seville goes by extremes: either its avenues are vastly wide with great open spaces and gardens; or, as if to compensate for that prodigal use of space, it is tightly crowded together. It has the same modern, unsightly, noisy, traffic-laden surrounding shell that uglifies every Spanish city; but in Seville it is only a half shell – from north to south round the eastern side. On the west bank of the Guadalquivir you are out of the city within minutes.

If you try to leave out of consideration this hideous modern half-shell, then for tourist purposes Seville reduces to three main areas. South of the Avenida da la Constitución, in the area round the old Tobacco Factory (now the University) and the Plaza de España, it is all airy spaciousness. North-west of the centre, on the other side of the river, are 540 acres more of airy spaciousness, that should continue to be so even when the site is fully developed for Expo 92. In between these two lungs, the heart of the city is tightly compact. It is bounded round the east side by

See Seville in style

Menéndez Pelayo round to Resolana Andueza; and on the western side by the river together with the districts of Triana and Remedios on the west bank. Actually, the city is in practice even more compact than this, since most of what you may want to visit lies in the southern part of this centre, say in the area bounded on the north by a line running east from the railway station. Beyond that (unless you are a fanatic for churches), you may want only an occasional foray.

If, within this limited area, you now take as your north-south axis the Avenida de la Constitución and the pedestrian Calle Sierpes that continues it (with the Plaza Nueva and the Town Hall as the hub of this axis), you will see that life becomes relatively simple. It is not that you will not get lost among the maze of narrow streets to either side of the axis. Of course you will, unless your name is Clark Kent. But you will be lost-and-enjoying-the-exploration, knowing that we should be heading in *that* direction, as against lost, bushed, bothered and bewildered. The thing about this axis is that the two streets are immediately

52

Above
Casa de Pilatos

Left
Plaza de España

recognizable when you hit them, and above all very well known indeed to Sevillians, whom you ask for direction. Both streets figure in the Holy Week processions, and both have been famous in literature since Cervantes described them. So 'Sierpes?' or 'Constitución?' will put you in the right way. It is a bonus for the struggling foreigner that Spaniards do not bother to say (and often do not write) 'Street', 'Avenue' or whatever.

When your wanderings take you through maze-like narrow streets, in the areas of the Casa de Pilatos, for example, or the Fine Arts Museum, or the Maestranza or almost anywhere except the Santa Cruz district, you may get an impression of dinginess. Do not be fooled by it: the patios inside the buildings are less visible here than in Córdoba, but an occasional glimpse through an open street door is likely to reveal that here, as throughout Andalusia, houses are inward-looking, private, shut off from the world – and often far from dingy. It is the Moorish legacy. The slightly run-down appearance of dusty walls and eyeless windows in narrow streets seems to say, 'My private life, my means and my comfort, are none of your business'. I imagine that Spaniards living in England – particularly since the post-war mania for massive picture-windows turned our houses into public aquariums – may often suffer from agoraphobia, or have the nightmare impression of being in the street with no clothes on.

Today, Seville is an especially good place to be. More than most places in Spain, there is here a resurgence of life, a driving optimism. For the last three hundred years Andalusia has been treated as the poor relation by Castilian government. And Seville is essentially a metropolis, a capital city: it has been so since the end of the Caliphate in the eleventh century; it was so for five hundred years when Madrid was still a muddy village; and especially during the two hundred years after the gold of the Indies started pouring in. And now, since 1982, it has become so again – the capital in reality of an autonomous Andalusia. This is not just a fancy: I have found it reflected in the conversation of people of all walks: once regional autonomy came, they felt their fortune was in their own hands; the climb out of need and neglect was now their own business. They did not even have to bother to overcome the Castilians' stereotype image of them as southern, fun-loving lay-abouts; they simply had to set about thrusting up to prosperity. And that is what has happened.

It has happened all round Andalusia and all round Spain, of course, but perhaps more consciously in Seville, where they also feel the city is at last taking the place it should hold as a capital city. For there is about the Sevillanos a touch of the arrogance you find in London or Paris or Rome: the metropolitan assumption that everyone else is bit of a hick.

Luckily for you, the visitor, they also take pride in their mastery of the art of having a good time. As one rather successful Sevillano put it: 'We know how to work as hard as anyone, but we reckon we know how to work in order to live.' The emphasis was on the word 'live', and the significance was in the word 'but'.

What to See I have not, in this guide, stressed buildings to be seen (If you want wall to wall culture, I assume you will follow the Tourist Office's yearning to drag you round every church and museum). The small area that includes the Cathedral, the Alcázares and the old quarter called the Barrio Santa Cruz, is clearly a prime attraction and worth while, indeed, unique. But

for me one building in Seville, the Casa de Pilatos, ranks ahead of all the rest; it is a personal opinion, perhaps an idiosyncratic one, but it is one that urges me to say: 'Don't miss it'.

The scene of Seville's last great fair, the Plaza de España and the María Luisa Park, are worth a visit for more than one reason. So are various other buildings and districts of the city. There is too much to cover in one or even two suggested walks. So, except where a route is clear, I shall simply list the things I most enjoy, leaving you to make your itinerary on the town plan according to your selection.

When to Go The April Fair, Holy Week, Corpus Christi: these are the high points of the year, and the first two especially would need planning and booking far ahead.

But, apart from them, May sees the May Crosses and the feast of Saint Ferdinand (on the 30th); July has a whole week (14 – 21) of celebrating St James and St Anne in Triana, August is Mary's month, especially the Assumption on 15 August; Michaelmas (29 September) is also important and has a fair; and, if you happen

Left
Barrio Santa Cruz

Above
The Alcázares

to be here in December, the feast of the Immaculate Conception is almost a private preserve. They were arguing for the doctrine here two centuries before it was adopted by Rome as dogma. But the city does not fall asleep between these festivals, far from it, and every church has its patron saint to celebrate.

In 1992, between 20 April (Easter Monday) and 12 October (Anniversary of the discovery of America) you come to Seville for Expo 92 and would be crazy to try to come for any other reason.

Hotels Please remember that by 1992 there will be something upwards of 90 more hotels available, or 10,000 extra beds. Of these roughly a half are planned as permanent (the others being designed for conversion to flats and other purposes). So that even after the Fair is over, Seville's hotel accommodation will be up by some 5,000 beds. Thus, with one or two exceptions, any recommendations of mine are provisional, to say the least.

Please note also the price guide: to stay consistent I always give the high season price for a double room. But in Seville the high season price for Holy Week, the Feria and the following two months, is disproportionately more than the low season one, so I give below both the maximum and minimum prices for 1989.

H. *Alfonso XIII*★★★★★, Calle San Fernando, 2. Tel: (954) 22 28 50. (£130–£75) – nothing provisional about this recommendation: it is one of the world's great hotels, owned by the owners of the Danieli and the Griti Palace. When it was restored a few years ago to bring it up to modern standards of comfort, that did not involve modernizing the furniture: It is mostly period stuff. You are paying for spaciousness and service, and the site is also ★★★★★.

H. *Gran Hotel Lar*★★★★, Plaza Carmen Benitez, 3. Tel: 41 03 61. (£90–£46) – nothing special but it does have a garage and is immediately off the easily accessible Calle de Recaredo.

HR *Doña Maria*★★★★, Calle Don Remondo, 19. Tel: 22 49 90. (£80–£43) – successfully aims at seeming like a town mansion. Right behind Cathedral. Roof-top swimming-pool with best view of Giralda over the road. No garage.

HR *Murillo*★★, Calle Lope de Rueda, 7. Tel: 21 60 95. (£40–£24) – more than central: it is in the middle of the Barrio Santa Cruz, the medieval quarter abutting Alcázares and Cathedral. No garage because the streets are too narrow for cars.

56

HR Internacional★★, Calle Aguilas, 17. Tel: 21 32 07. (£40–£23)
— I give it for harassed drivers because it does have a garage and
is accessible from the Calle Menendez Pelayo via Calle
Esteban. Narrow street by Casa Pilatos.

HR Sevilla★★, Calle Daoiz, 6. Tel: 38 41 61. (35—£23) — close to
shopping, Fine Arts Museum and Casa Pilatos; fifteen minutes'
walk from Cathedral; has been strongly recommended to me.
No garage.

H. Simon★, Calle Garcia de Vinuesa, 19. Tel: 22 66 60.
(£28–£17) — very good value, but therefore known and may
need booking ahead. An old mansion, complete with patio and
fountain, just down the street from the Cathedral. Rooms vary
in quality. No garage.

Restaurants There are a dozen or more expensive
restaurants, recommended by Sevillians, that may tempt you for
one reason or another:

La Dorada, Calle Virgen de Aguas Santas, 6, in Remedios — the
most highly reputed, especially his fish baked in rock salt. I
wonder if it is better than the same dish cooked at Paco's
rather cheap restaurant in Alhaurín (*see* Málaga, page 161).

La Albahaca, Plaza Santa Cruz — go primarily for its site and for its
most elegant rooms.

Rio Grande, Calle Betis near the Plaza de Cuba — go for its terrace
and view.

One of the more memorable meals of the past year, in Spain or
anywhere else, was for me one I ate at the *Oriza*, which is also a
pleasant tapa bar, at the end of Calle San Fernando, opposite the
corner of the Tobacco Factory: *Oriza*, Calle San Fernando, 41.

I have not managed to make any discoveries, in the middle or
lower price range, but I enjoyed eating at the very humble *Atún*,
Calle J. Guichot, just off the Plaza Nueva and 30 metres from the
expensive Becerra. It is an ordinary café, and the dining-room at
the back is not attractive. But he is proud of his grilled fresh
tunny, *atún acebollado*, the taste of which bears no relation to the
tinned stuff. He also does good steak and salad, and seems
genuinely pleased if you like his food.

Cathedral I start with it because its site, its size and the
Giralda make it the natural hub of Seville, and a good starting
point, not because I think it the most worthwhile thing to see.

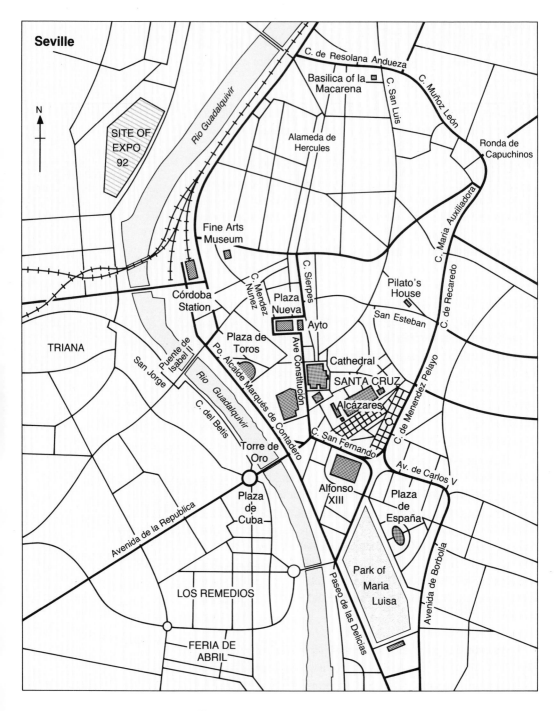

Seville

N

Rio Guadalquivir

SITE OF EXPO 92

C. de Resolana Andueza

Basilica of la Macarena

C. San Luis

C. Muñoz León

Ronda de Capuchinos

Alameda de Hercules

Fine Arts Museum

C. Maria Auxiliadora

C. de Recaredo

C. Sierpes

C. Mendez Nuñez

Pilato's House

Córdoba Station

Plaza Nueva

Ayto

San Esteban

TRIANA

San Jorge

Puente de Isabel II

Río Guadalquivir

C. del Betis

Plaza de Toros

Po. Alcalde Marqués de Contadero

Ave Constitución

Cathedral

SANTA CRUZ

Alcázares

C. de Menendez Pelayo

Torre de Oro

C. San Fernando

Av. de Carlos V

Avenida de la República

Plaza de Cuba

Alfonso XIII

Plaza de España

Avenida de Borbolla

LOS REMEDIOS

Paseo de las Delicias

Park of Maria Luisa

FERIA DE ABRIL

It is the third largest church in Europe, and the biggest Gothic building in the world. This is because its chapter determined to build a church 'so large that future generations will think us mad'. If you aim for the *Guinness Book of Records*, you are unlikely to win a beauty prize. ... But the whole concept is very Sevillian and that is how you should view it. The reredos behind the High Altar, for instance, would reach to within 20 feet of the vault of Salisbury Cathedral, and it took eighty years to build and mould and carve and paint and gild. How long you take to look at it is your affair.

Everything is devoted to exuberent excess: you will come across here a bronze candlestick and there a golden custodia of brobdignagian proportions, both of them proper to this Cathedral, and even more so when you realize they are used in Holy Week and for Corpus Christi processions. Of course: they belong to the street theatre in which Seville has always made Cecil B. de Mille look rather flashily provincial. Here, things are by no means flashy; they are fitting, right for the city's combination of exuberance and fervour. My sober northerner's search for proportion, for the articulation of space and light and form, which makes me react with immediate sympathy to Moorish architecture, however lavish and exotic its decoration, is here simply misguided. It is mistaken to seek proportion where the builders aimed to be disproportionate; either shrug and dismiss it, or else look at it and let it colour the way you see the rest of Seville.

The Capilla Real (Royal Chapel) which occupies the apse behind the High Altar is worth seeing at any time, but it was riveting when I first saw it, at night during a televised society wedding that tipped the Renaissance style over into the richest Plateresque. When walls are lined, not only with marble, but also with rising tiers of silver and crystal and silks and lilies, when you add rich priestly vestments and the Cathedral choir singing Palestrina, and flood the whole with television lighting, the impression is of a world of swansdown and chased silver. Busby Berkeley, eat your heart out.

In the cooler light of day it contains the silver urn-tomb of Fernando III, who was a saint but no bigot. He called himself king of the three religions (though it did not stop him conquering the Moors here and at Córdoba), and he had his epitaph inscribed here in Hebrew and Arabic as well as Latin and Spanish. It also contains the tomb of his heir and successor Alfonso the Learned, who was responsible for the emblem of Seville which you may have noticed on buses and many other places: the rebus of a figure-of-eight knot, flanked by *no–do*. In a rebellion fomented by Alfonso's son, Seville stayed loyal to him, and he is reputed to have declared 'It deserted me not'. In Spanish *'No Me Ha Dejado'* gives *no* and *do* on either side of *madeja* (a hank or tangle) – well, nearly anyway.

The wooden statue over the altar is the Virgin of the Kings who rivals the Virgen of the Macarena, from the north part of the old town, and the one known as the Hope of Triana, in the number and fervour of her devotees in the Holy Week processions.

Some people find the main part of this (as any other Spanish) Cathedral a bit baffling, although we are more used to it than the French are. For Spaniards tended to keep on in their cathedrals the monastic habit of isolating the clergy from the common herd by walling off the choir. We did, too, but kept the choir to the eastern end of the church, or at least, as in Exeter and others, gave the congregation a full vista of the vaults. In the much wider, squarer ground plan of Spanish cathedrals, the choir leaves less space to the western door, and instead lets the congregation flood round the sides. This may have been what blinded the builders of Córdoba Cathedral in their destructive Philistinism.

When you get round this central block, in the south crossing, you find the socking great tomb of Christopher Columbus. Imposing, if not beautiful, it dates from 1899, the year after perhaps the most traumatic date in Spanish history (and, after 1492, the best-known one). 1898 saw Spain lose Cuba, the last of its colonies, and find itself having to face the truth that it was no longer the head of an Empire, that it was just another country – a trauma we are in a very good position to understand. So Columbus's remains travelled again. They had already been moved a century before from Dominica, when it was thought the French might get them. This tomb was built, and they came to rest here. Or most of them: it seems that part of the poor chap may be still in Havana, so he shares with Saint Teresa the fate of being in various places at once. At least, unlike her, he has avoided being in part the personal possession of Franco.

There are paintings and other works in the two dozen or so chapels round the walls, but none that are in a light or a condition to be seen properly. The three chambers in the south-east corner, the chapterhouse (Sala Capitular) and two Sacristies, contain work by Murillo, Zurbarán and Goya, as well as various treasures.

What remains to be seen is the Giralda and the Patio de los Naranjos, and both deserve attention.

The Giralda The Giralda is much better than just Seville's most famous landmark. It manages to be both massive and elegant, the classical balance of an art at its peak. It was built in 1184 by the puritanical Almohads who had come over from Africa and taken over Al Andalus, and it has a near twin at Marrakech. The surface decoration of diaper brickwork, together with the twin embrasures, delicately balconied, manage to lighten what would otherwise seem a heavy fortress tower. But I found that it took a few days before I began to appreciate quite how good it is. As a minaret, it was topped with large gilded balls which, so they say, when they hove in sight, informed the traveller he was one day's march from the city. The Christian belfry added to it in the 1560s manages, uniquely in Andalusia, to harmonize with the rest. It tapers gently, like all such towers, Moorish, Mozarabic or Mudéjar, starting from a base 16m (54ft) square with walls 2.5m (8ft) thick. If you want the view from the top, the climb is made easier by there being a spiralling ramp inside, of reasonably gentle slope, rather than steps. Its name ('the Weathervane') stems from the figure at the top, which represents the True Faith – weirdly, considering she veers with the shifting wind.

The Patio de los Naranjos The Patio de los Naranjos beneath, was the *sahn* or courtyard of the Mosque. Most of what you see in it has been added or remodelled since the seventeenth century, and as a tourist attraction it relies somewhat on the orange blossom, and the wooden model that replaces a stuffed crocodile presented by some mediaeval Egyptian potentate with a sense of humour. However, the basin in the middle of the court has seen the lot: it was the baptismal font of the Visigothic church, that was replaced by the Mosque; and the place for ablutions of the Mosque, replaced by the Cathedral.

Two details of the outside of the Cathedral may amuse. A heavy iron chain link fence runs part way round the Cathedral.

The fence posts are Roman columns picked up either at nearby Itálica, or closer to. For though Itálica, just up the road, gave birth to two Roman emperors, Seville (Hispalis) was also a Roman city, visited by Julius Caesar and declared an assize town by him.

More recently, the raised step or plinth along the west front served, when Cervantes described it, exactly the same purpose it serves today: as a good post for sneakthieves and cut-purses on the look-out for a mark. Cervantes had been in the army, fought in a sea battle, travelled Italy, spent five years in a barbary prison, and over twenty years here in Seville, three months of it in prison. Out of this biographical chip of irrelevance come two most relevant points. Firstly, that he really knew his crooks first hand; and secondly, that he developed an overwhelming urge to find some way of putting to use the rich experience of his own hardships and set-backs, and so give value to what he felt would otherwise be a wasted life. He succeeded: out of that urge came *Don Quixote* and the short tales or novellas that he called the Exemplary Novels. If you are interested, the Exemplary Novel called *Rinconete and Cortadillo* is about the Sevillian underworld. Cortadillo means Little Cut-purse; nowadays they do it by motorcycle, but not much else has changed since 1598.

The Alcázares Just south of the Cathedral, across the Plaza del Triunfo, the Alcázares is a complex of palace buildings and gardens that spans seven centuries. The main part is a splendid and exotic-looking palace built for Peter the Cruel in 1364 by Mudéjar workmen who clearly knew both the Alhambra and the Caliphal art of Córdoba. If you intend to see the Alhambra (or, better still, if you have already seen it), the comparisons and contrasts are intensely interesting. The workmanship here is no less fine, but this is a palace commissioned by a Christian potentate. For such a one, grandeur takes precedence over delight and surprise; regality and regularity are more important than water and flowers; and public display, more than private pleasure. Here, all the detail and decoration of Spanish Islamic art are authentically recreated by Islamic craftsmen who knew the Alhambra and the Great Mosque. But little or none of the essence.

There is also considerable interest in the comparison with the Casa de Pilatos a quarter of a mile away. Both marry Moslem to Christian art: In the Casa Pilatos, with total success; in the Alcázares, successful perhaps in parts.

The Alcázares

A word about Peter the Cruel (reigned 1350–69). This is not the place for a history, but it might be helpful to make a couple of points. You will come across plenty of legends, especially in Seville which he made his capital and loved. Some of them may even be based on fact, though he is unlikely to have deserved his sobriquet any more than other rulers of the time, and the Sevillanos knew him as Peter the Just. But chronicles get to be written by the winners. Peter was murdered, and his throne usurped by his bastard step-brother Henry of Trastámara, who comes out of it all smelling of roses. Yet he had to pay for power with privileges granted and greeds assuaged in ways that must have contributed indirectly to the horrific pogroms of 1391. The moral is, do not believe what you read in the press – at least until you know who owns the paper.

My own instinct is to drift round a place like this for the impressions, uncluttered by knowledge. If by any chance you are like me, I should skip the rest of this section. I would only remind you that here, as in all Moorish and Mudéjar work, it is unwise to forget to look at ceilings and tile-work.

You enter by the Lion Gate (King Peter's emblem stands inset above it). This takes you into a series of three courtyards all properly called the Monterías after the royal mounted guard. But the third and largest, which you reach through a triple arch, is usually known as the *Lion Court* because a caged lion, the gift of a Moroccan Potentate, used to be kept in it. Here you see King Peter's palace in all splendour ahead of you. To your right the court is enclosed by the *Contratación* (1503), built to regulate trade with the Americas. To your left are areas not open to the public, including the *Patio de Yeso* which, together with a few bits of wall and a Court of Justice, is the only survivor from the previous twelfth-century Almohad palace, but is at present under restoration.

The *Vestibule* gives a good introduction to the wealth of glazed tiles (*azulejos*) and wooden ceilings (*artesonados*) that you will find throughout. The narrow and tortuous passages that lead out of the Vestibule are about the only structural element that is genuinely Moorish. Turn left and follow round to the *Patio de las Doncellas* ('the Maidens' Court'). This is the main centre of King Peter's Palace, giving access to the Public Rooms. It is mostly 1364, but

The Alcázares

PLEASE NOTE: The diagram is not in proportion, and is for finding your way round only.

1. Entrance. The Lion Gate. Arms of Peter the Cruel over (1364). Walls date from 12th c.
2. & 3. Courts of the Monteria, or Royal Guard.
4. Court of the Lion. So-called from a caged lion once kept there.
5. Main Entrance & Façade: Inscriptions give date 1364, and in Arabic 'God alone conquers'.
6. Vestibule.
7. Maids' Court (Patio de las Doncellas). 14th and 16th cs.
8. Room of Charles Vth or Salón del Techo (i.e. ceiling). Both ceiling and tiles 16th c.
9. Maria de Padilla's Chambers. Peter the Cruel's mistress.
10. Ambassadors' Hall. 14th c. but heavily restored 19th c.
11. Philip II's dining room.
12. Philip II's bedchamber.
13. Patio de las Muñecas (Dolls' Court). So-called from tiny faces in spandrel of one arch.
14. Isabel the Catholic's bedchamber.
15. The Prince's room. Her son born here.
16. Bedchamber of the Moorish kings.
17–20 Part of the Casa de Contratación, or Chamber of (American) Commerce set up in 1503.
17. Audience Chamber.
18. Chapel.
19. Fans.
20. 19th c. bedchamber.
21. Stairs to upper floor: Royal apartments 16th to 19th c. Not at present open to the public.
22. Patio del Crucero, sometimes known as Patio de Maria de padilla. Mainly 18th century reconstruction.
23. Tapestry Hall.
24. Emperor's Hall 16th c.
25. Chapel. Originally 13th c. but mainly later.
26. Fish pond (18th c.) and gardens 16th–19th centuries.
27. Apeadero i.e. place for dismounting, or alighting from one's carriage. 18th c.
28. Patio de las Banderas (Court of the Flags). 18th century enclosed square, now government offices and grace and favour residences.
29. Passageway to the Barrio Santa Cruz.
30. Area closed to the public which contains the Patio de Yeso (Plaster Court) dating back to the 12th c. Also the Justice Hall of 1345.

the columns and upper gallery are mid-sixteenth century. I do not think the blend is as disastrous as others seem to. The patio manages to be pleasing in itself, though I do not know what it looked like before, and it certainly does not compare with its counterpart in the Casa de Pilatos. But this is the heart of the palace and I doubt if you will feel disappointment on seeing it.

On the north side (that is, backing on to the Vestibule) are chambers known as the *Dormitorio de los Reyes Moros* ('The Moorish Kings' Bedroom'). Goodness knows why, but then almost all the parts of this palace have names attributed to them at much later dates. It may be best to return to the courtyard and continue your visit at the opposite (south) side, so as to see the public chambers before the private ones. The first long chamber on the south side is the *Salón del Techo* ('Hall of the Ceiling'). Both ceiling and *azulejos* are of the sixteenth-century. Beyond is a suite of rooms for *María de Padilla*, Peter the Cruel's mistress.

On the west side of the courtyard, the grand main chamber is the *Salón de los Embajadores* ('the Ambassadors' Hall'). One is surprised to learn, in the face of such exotic splendour, that the cupola was built by a Christian in 1427. It is hard to imagine a Christian court having quite the sartorial pizazz to compete with such surroundings. The great ruby in the crown of our own dear Queen is reputed to have come from a Moslem potentate murdered for his jewellery by King Peter. Could it have been the need to live up to these surroundings that prompted the naughty deed?

Once inside this Hall, one's first impression is that it is an echo of the Alhambra, except for those consciously oriental peacocks that belong to a nineteenth-century restoration. But the portals are clearly inspired by the Caliphal art of Córdoba, either the Mosque or the Medinat az-Zahra palace. And the doors themselves are the work of Toledo craftsmen. It would seem that King Pedro was an eclectic admirer of Moorish art, wanting the best from all over.

Behind the Ambassadors' Hall is the long chamber known as *Philip II's Dining Hall*. Both this and the Charles V Hall (on the south side) are also known as the Hall of Ceilings: indeed, the cedar-wood ceilings here are more worth your attention than the pictures.

At this point the private part of the palace begins to take over, with *Philip II's Bedchamber* on the north side of the Ambassadors'

Hall. These private chambers are grouped round the little Patio de las Muñecas or Dolls' Courtyard, so called because of two little faces carved in one of the spandrels. The upper part dates from 1856 when Isabel II used the palace (and had a music room upstairs). The long chamber behind the Patio is known as the *Salón del Príncipe* after the only son of Isabel the Catholic who gave birth to him in this palace. From the Dolls' Patio a narrow passage will bring you back to the Vestibule.

There are many additions to the palace complex. In the Contratación, to your left as you leave the Vestibule, you can see the Admiral's room, and chapel, as well as a collection of fans and a nineteenth-century bedroom, though all the upstairs apartments are closed for restoration at the time of writing. To your right as you exit the Vestibule, a passage in the centre of the courtyard takes you round to the more modern additions. There was a medieval palace here but little remained after earthquakes, especially the great one of 1755 that destroyed Lisbon, Huelva and so much else. Thus, even *Charles V's tapestry Gallery* and the *Patio del Crucero* date from the eighteenth century. María de Padilla's baths here are currently closed for restoration. If they reopen them, you will inevitably hear the Susanna and the Elders-type legends that attach to them. To my mind the best of what remains are the gardens and one more courtyard.

The *gardens* were made at many periods and show it. They need no commentary, unless you want the dry facts that the fish pond is eighteenth century; the attractive central pavilion was built for Charles V; and the gardens are an ideal place to sit for a moment and rest after all this unadulterated 'kultur'.

The Gardens

Barrio Santa Cruz

On your way out you pass through the elegant eighteenth-century *Apeadero* (i.e. alighting point for those arriving by carriage) and come to the Patio de las Banderas (Court of the Flags). This is now a busy yard with cars and 'grace and favour' residences and government offices, and I like it. As you emerge into it, in the nearest right-hand corner, you can take a covered passageway that leads direct into the Barrio Santa Cruz.

The Barrio Santa Cruz This is Seville's old Jewish Quarter, corresponding to Córdoba's *judería* and Granada's Moorish Albaicín. Like them, it has survived largely unchanged since the Middle Ages. It is a pleasure to wander at random through the maze of narrow alleyways and miniature squares. Unlike them, it is a small quarter, of a dozen streets or so. And, quite unlike them, parts of it erupt in the evening when thousands of University students and others make the open street sound more like those parties where conversation has to be conducted at a scream.

Even in the heat of day this is a good place to wander, for the streets are mostly too narrow to let the sun bake them – no accident this – and the shaded squares, the flowers in the windows, the whitewashed walls picked out in ochrous yellow (almost Seville's signature)... all these things tend to counter the heat. Although I do not lead you on a guided walk here, I would recommend you include in your stroll the alley (called Agua) that runs along the edge of the Barrio by the high garden wall of the Murillo Gardens. Also, the Plaza Santa Cruz to which it will lead you. Of an evening, if you want to avoid the noisy part, but still would like a café, there is one in the quiet Plaza de la Alianza where you can sit outside in peace, while a music student plays classical guitar as little as he can and tries not to be heard. But avoid the coffee – it is the powdered stuff.

The *Hospice of the Venerables*, in the square of the same name just left from the exit from the Patio de las Banderas, is a Baroque church which acts as a museum of objects used in the Holy Week.

The nexus of buildings round the Plaza del Triunfo (between Cathedral and Alcázares) is completed by the Lonja or *Archives of the Indies*. It is not an attractive building, but it has since the eighteenth century served to hold the archives, the richest

Barrio Santa Cruz

House of Pilatos

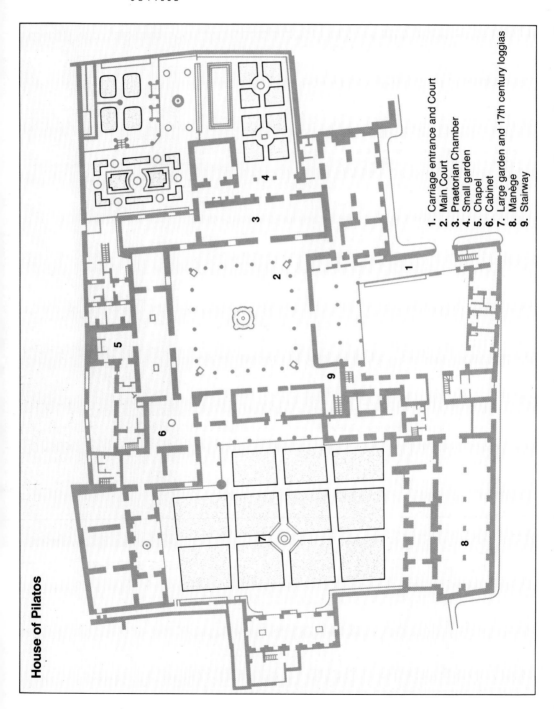

1. Carriage entrance and Court
2. Main Court
3. Praetorian Chamber
4. Small garden
5. Chapel
6. Cabinet
7. Large garden and 17th century loggias
8. Manège
9. Stairway

collection in existence, and which has yet to be fully explored. You can see the occasional document on display, but the archives are not available, except to accredited scholars.

The Casa de Pilatos This I consider the most memorably good single building in Seville. Built for the Rivera family, and still the property of the Dukes of Medinaceli, it dates mainly from the early fifteen hundreds. It is the work of Christian architects who not only appreciated Moorish architecture but, much more importantly, understood its aims. They were also understanding enthusiasts for the New Learning.

It has the lightness and grace of the best of the Italian Renaissance; it marries this perfectly with the rich surface textures of Moorish art; and to this it adds the Moorish delight in gardens and water, in making flowers and trees and the sound of water, as well as its sparkle, an integral part of architecture. And, on top of all this, its walls are covered in the finest *azulejos* I have ever seen.

When everywhere in Andalusia you see the depressing consequences of the Christian reconquest, especially whenever

Casa de Pilatos

The Azulejos

Casa de Pilatos

Isabella the Catholic had a hand, despising, desecrating and destroying a culture so much finer than their own, it comes like a draught of cooling water to see these architects learning, appreciating, mastering – and then marrying it to the best of their own culture.

Azulejo is a word of Arabic origin meaning 'coloured tile'. I state the obvious because many people assume they ought to be blue, the Spanish for 'blue' being *azul*. But the words are unconnected. Here in Pilatos they are almost all of them made of five glazes; white, black, brown, green, blue. Looked at from close to, they amaze by the endless variations of patterning in these five tints; you have to search far to find duplication, and

72

even when you think you have found it, in most cases you are mistaken. Looked at from a bit more distance, they amaze by the rich variations of colour – it does not seem possible that the mere juxtaposing of five colours should give stretches of wall of such delicate and rare shades of purple, viridian, and countless other subtle tints.

Again, seen from close to, they seem busy; from further off they are not. They are tranquil and unfussy, but they blend with the patterns of light and shade of the Mudéjar plaster carving, to produce walls of rich and opulent texture. In colder climates, carved panelling, and tapestry or fabric gave the walls of palaces their rich textures. Here, in the burning heat of summer, tile and marble and plaster are more suitable. Every now and again there are panels of tiles with metallic glaze forming abstract patterns, that seem to belong more to 1930s' Art Deco, but they were in fact an early form of Moorish *azulejos*.

The main court in the Casa Pilatos achieves something else again, at least for me. Roman statuary has always left me cold. But here, standing in the corners of the patio, the Roman sculpture (from nearby Itálica) sets off the court and is set off by it. The statues blend with the other forms and surfaces, masses and textures, and are held by the patterns of light and shade, in a harmony that stays vividly in the memory. I do not think it is a question of focusing on anything or scrutinizing anything, but just the pleasure of being here, lingering. As with the Alhambra (but unlike the Alcázares here in Seville), this place may have been built for a grandee, but there is nothing grand, nothing of awe, just sensory pleasure that seems to enhance your feeling of being alive, as well as make you feel that man, some men at least, have improved the world.

The Azulejos

However different the feel and style of their work, I have the impression that the English builders of the eighteenth century, almost alone, share with the medieval Moors this concept that masonry and gardens intermingle and set each other off. But whereas the English eighteenth-century architects saw plants and gardens as a setting and a backdrop, the Moors brought the garden inside the dwelling. Instead of surrounding Gibbs or Kent with Capability Brown, they wove the two together; instead of placing pavilions in the greenery, they brought the greenery into the building. To compare Pilatos with Stourhead might seem a silly paradox. But there are many strange parallels and affinities between these pleasure-loving southerners and us ulcer-seeking Britons. One of them is the importance of decorated surfaces in architecture: from the Alhambra through Plateresque to Churriguerresque; from Earl's Barton through Castle Rising to King's College chapel (a shoe-box laid on its side, but what rich surfaces...). Mind you, before I get too carried away, maybe I should remember that another common trait is a love of fried fish.

Do not forget the gardens at both ends: while delightful in themselves, their chief pleasure lies in their being all part of the building, acting in a vague sense rather as a conservatory does in an English country house. They are also different worlds, one from the other, largely thanks to the differing light they receive and the different architecture they are made to interact with. While you saunter round in them, look up and see what pleasure they must bring also to the upper apartments of the house.

When you have drifted round downstairs, you can if you wish take a conducted tour round the public apartments upstairs. These would have been used in winter (as with the Alhambra). The interest here will be more in furniture and family history, and the effect they have on me is to make me wish I could see (or, better still, stay in) the much more extensive private apartments used by the present members of the family. But whether or not you visit it, do not fail to look at the stairway: the dome over it is worthy of the building.

Museo de Bellas Artes This is the second largest collection in Spain, but will not be reopened till 1992. Meanwhile some of the major works are on show next door in the Convent of the Merced. It contains the great Spanish painters – Velázquez, El Greco, Zurbarán, Ribera, Murillo, Goya – and most of the ones of second rank – Alonso Cano, Valdes Leal, Pacheco, etc. – as well as Lucas Cranach, Rubens, Titian, Van Dyck and others. With a large assembly of good Murillos, it may well be the best place to decide whether you like him or find the mixture too rich.

If you are a keen connoisseur and are spending some time in Seville, and if you do not have occasion to see the Prado, then this is a fine picture gallery. If one or another of my 'ifs' does not apply, then I suggest there is so much else to see and do in Seville that cannot be seen (or done) elsewhere. Whereas for the visitor to Madrid, once he has seen the Prado, I am inclined to agree still with Richard Ford's verdict of the 1840s: 'Madrid itself is but a dear second-rate inhospitable city.'

The Hospital de la Caridad A Baroque charity hospital, it attracts a lot of tourists, perhaps because guides plug the spurious story that its founder, Mañara, was the original of Don Juan (apart from any intrinsic unlikeliness, Don Juan predates Mañara); perhaps because it contains a couple of paintings of death that are reputed to have made Murillo say you have to hold your nose to see them; perhaps because it does contain a very good Murillo – one in which he shows that when not at the mercy of the demands of his patrons, he too can paint real people with that same almost visionary intensity that characterizes the other great Spanish painters; perhaps because it is close to the Cathedral and all, and so can be taken in, with the rest, in one lightening tour.

There are many other churches and museums. I give these last two as a token obeisance to the guide-book writer's obligations. But I think that much more is to be gained, and with more pleasure, by sauntering round one or two areas of the city. Two places I will mention here, although neither would count as a major attraction in itself. The *Ayuntamiento*, especially as seen from the calm Plaza de San Francisco, is an example of Plateresque architecture that I find very pleasing to the eye. The pleasure is partly because the squares on either side give it breathing-space and the Plaza San Francisco itself is handsome.

The busy, noisy side of the Ayuntamiento, the *Plaza Nueva*, does not have the same charm. Nevertheless, if you are passing that way, as you will if you go shopping, or to the Fine Arts Museum, take the trouble to look at the cobble-stones in the centre. It is just a cobbled paving being laid still as I write this, by just ordinary city workmen, but with every square a different pattern, created by the workmen themselves, without recourse to supplied models; pictures and patterns of all sorts created at the will and whim of the paving workers.

Suggested Walks
The Riverside and Triana In the late afternoon, an hour or two before sunset when the heat is off the day, the slanting light can give a view of Seville like a Canaletto straight from the

75

brush. You do not have to start down at the Torre de Oro. Like so many fortified buildings, it is better seen from a distance, adding what painters call an accent to the landscape. With its warm sand-coloured walls, it makes an accent indeed.

Start anywhere: the quayside is a promenade, clean and tree-lined, where the shipyards used to be. For until the Guadalquivir started to silt up and meander, Seville was Spain's busiest port for the maritime links with the Americas. Before that, in the days of the Almohads, the Golden Tower and a twin across the river were linked by a chain defending the port from invasion – citizens of Norwich will recognize the device from their own version. But now it has all gone, long ago; sudden flooding persuaded the city to cut the river and by-pass the town with a canal to the west. Today they are planning to open this branch of the river again so as to create an island on which to hold Expo 92, and create sailing and rowing areas. But meanwhile the traffic on the east bank is set well back and the riverside makes a pleasant walk.

Between the Torre de Oro and the Triana Bridge (officially the Puente Isabel II), the Maestranza or bullring is an elegant and colourful addition to the townscape. It is the earliest in Spain, and as important in the making or breaking of reputations as any. The name Maestranza, applied to this and the other very early one at Ronda, comes from the origins of modern *corridas*: originally it was a nobleman's sport and done on horseback, often using a town square. When the modern ring, and fighting on foot evolved, an organization of gentlemen called the Maestranza (i.e. 'Mastery') regulated it – a sort of eighteenth-century Jockey Club.

It is from the Triana bridge itself that you get the best view back over Seville. And now you have a choice according to your purpose. First right over the bridge is a short and widening street called San Jorge. At the end of it, facing you is the Santa Ana pottery, as good as any of the many in Triana. For this quarter has been producing pottery since late Roman times. In the Santa Ana shop there is a vast stock on sale of *azulejos* and ceramics of various kinds, from the beautiful to seaside resort kitsch. Try to get them to let you see the workshops behind. It depends on the assistant and his mood, and there is no reason why they should let you explore. But if they do, the workshops are out of Dickens, except that they are several hundred years older: an ancient labyrinth with all the old methods; massive bits of millstone turn to mix the glazes, a sudden warmth from a side room makes you realize it is not a room but a kiln that has recently been used – its brick door broken open. Men in dusty attics paint Virgins in glaze on tiles or else stylized rabbits, deer, bulls that you recognize from the early sixteenth-century ones set in the floor of the Pilatos palace gardens. Here, as elsewhere, you stand more chance if you do not try it on Monday. Reserve Mondays for the country: nature does not close.

If your choice is not for seeing or buying pottery, then this quarter of Triana is worth a stroll in itself. It is traditionally where the gypsies live, and figures much in their songs. It is no hostile ghetto, and a pleasant part of town. You can head back down the riverside by taking Calle Betis, once the docks but now a pleasant walk. I suggest the *Restaurant* and *Café Rio Grande* in Calle Betis just before you reach the Plaza de Cuba is an excellent place to sit out on the terrace and watch what the late sunlight does to the Maestranza, the Torre de Oro and the Giralda peering over the top – or indeed a good place to sit out for supper in the cool of the night. Beyond the Plaza de Cuba the Remedios quarter begins, all modern, but containing many of the fashionable restaurants and tapa bars. At its southernmost side is the vast area where the Spring Feria is held.

The Plaza de España and María Luisa Park This might well be better done as a carriage drive. Do not be afraid of sharks: the horse-carriages of Seville and Córdoba operate under the eye of the Tourist Office who will help and advise you on routes and prices. Do not forget the Office is a few metres along from where you hire the carriages in the Plaza del Triunfo, outside the Alcázares entrance. The main thing is to make sure you agree the price before you start. Such a drive (or walk) takes you past the Alfonso XIII Hotel, itself almost a tourist attraction, past the San Telmo Palace and the huge Tobacco Factory, now the University, along spacious, gracious tree-lined avenues, in spring a haze of mauve jacaranda blossom, past the massive Plaza de España and down shady rides through the María Luisa Park. Such is the best way of seeing the buildings you pass: they lend themselves to the grand perspective rather than detailed scrutiny.

The Tobacco Factory is one of the largest buildings in Spain and dates from the eighteenth century, but that is all that needs to be said about it. Carmen was invented by one Frenchman and popularized by another, and between them they did much to create the legend of *la España de panderete* (tambourine Spain), the whole compost of passionate gypsies with a rose between the teeth, dancing to castanets while proud boyfriends kill bulls to the rhythm of the fandango. Well, at least they set it in the right place, for the various ingredients that make up this scenario are most nearly true in this corner of Andalusia, between Seville and Cádiz – the ingredients, not the scenario.

The Plaza de España, together with the Hotel, the Opera, much of the lay-out of the park, and the museums at the far end of it, are all the result of the pan-American Fair held here in 1929. The other pavilions were temporary, but these survivors stand as proof of achievement, and serve as a very good omen for the coming Expo. The Plaza de España is a good piece of architecture that served its original grandiose purpose then, and serves another purpose today, to wit that of being a colourful, pleasant and thoroughly theatrical adjunct to these surroundings. Children play, take boat rides and donkey rides in the vast safe space; visitors from Spain and abroad come to see it or ride in the carriages past it; and it is all very happy and Sevillian. And now, with the success of this as a background, they are working to achieve, on the other side of town, another and bigger international Fair: Expo 92.

Expo 92 This also intends to leave in its wake a permanent improvement to the city, another airy space of trees and water and buildings that will remain when the temporary pavilions are pulled down, and the captains and the kings of industry have departed. To be precise and statistical, 538 acres of space for air, 350,000 trees and shrubs for shade, and 40 acres of lake, fountains, waterfalls and channels which, as the Moors knew a thousand years ago, not only make you feel cooler, but actually do lower the ambient temperature.

The theme of it is 'The Age of Discovery' and, with some 80 countries represented as well as international organizations, the future is likely to dominate. The discovery of America of which it is the 500th anniversary, is likely to be restricted to the first pavilion out of more than 100. This being Seville, they are determined to make it a six-month fiesta as much as an exhibition. So amphitheatre, concert theatre, play park, planetarium, cinema, boating, canoeing, circus, gardens, overhead car tours and the like are to be backed by some 140 restaurants, cafeterias and cafés, and a further 100 shops.

They are expecting 18,000,000 visitors and 36,000,000 visits, not because of their own thinking (wishful or otherwise), but because this is the figure spewed out by the computer of the BIE in Paris, the international regulatory office that builds on data from all such previous international occasions since the war.

One of the 80 countries taking part will be Israel, despite the irony that for them must be savage: this fifth centenary of the discovery of America is also the fifth centenary of the expulsion from this country of a whole people, for whom it had been home for longer than the expellers – upwards of 1,700 years...

But if the planners and builders succeed in their aim of creating a place of pleasure by the interplay of water and buildings and greenery, then the futuristic and popular Expo 92 may even manage to reflect the ancient and royal Alhambra, echo it across the width of Andalusia, and over a chasm of 700 years.

Eighteen million people in six months means an average of nearly 100,000 per day. Even the addition of 10,000 hotel beds to the present 20,000 still means that most will visit from outside Seville. Hence the dramatic improvement of Spain's road system, the new motorways, the extending of airport runways for shuttle flights, and the projected new railway line from Madrid to take the French-designed TGV. What with the little matter of the Olympic Games at the other end of the country...

Some other things to do

Flamenco As throughout Andalusia, this is bound to be commercial unless you have friends locally who know where and how. But commercial does not mean it is badly done.

Tablao de Curro Vélez, Calle Rodó, 7, (between the Cathedral and the bullring – probably as high quality as anywhere. Perhaps more for the *aficionado* than the visitor wanting an evening's entertainment. (Please get the name and exact address right: I would hate to have you think I recommended another that is nearby but...).

79

Los Gallos, Plaza Santa Cruz, 11 – if Curro Vélez is more for the *aficionado*, the Gallos is clearly out to give good entertainment. They make a thoroughly good professional job of it, the more admirable because they have to work to entertain a puddingy, unresponsive audience and warm them to appreciation, and yet still put a lot of themselves into the dance, and at times manifestly succeed in losing themselves in it. You pay 2,000 ptas for entry and one drink (of your choice), and for that you get a two-hour performance. I went with little expectation of seeing anything genuine, and less desire to stay for two hours. Two very enjoyable hours later, I emerged full of admiration for their professionalism, and convinced of their quality as genuine flamenco dancers.

Flea Markets They are all in the mornings, i.e. starting when they start and winding up at about 3 p.m. Thursdays: (it is called the *Jueves*) in Calle Feria. Second-hand goods and antiques. Sundays: *Alameda de Hércules*. Not far from the Jueves and selling some of the same goods, but mainly trinkets, crafts, etc.

Pet and Bird market, Plaza de la Alfalfa, (between the Ayuntamiento and the Casa Pilatos).

Stamp and coin market, Plaza del Cabildo – elderly men and young boys in earnest debate. The Plaza del Cabildo is worth seeing for itself: you get to it through the passageway of the Seises, opposite the Cathedral.

Triana market, Calle San Martin de Porres.

El Tapeo... or doing the round of the tapa bars. Londoners at least are now used to them, but it is not quite the same thing. In London you order your tapas and make a meal of them as though you were in a restaurant. Not so, here in Seville. The idea is to have a nibble in one bar and a bit of a chat with any acquaintances there. Then to the next bar for another nibble, and another few friends. At the end of an hour or two (or three), you have met up with and chatted to a very large number of acquaintances, and meanwhile the constant nibbling at umpteen different things has both satisfied your appetite and kept you sober. It is not like going to a cocktail party every night (which would be pure hell) because there is no social obligation: If you do not feel like the company of Jack and Jill just now, you move on to the next person or the next place.

Seville claims to have invented the tapa, specifically one bar, the *Rinconcillo* in Calle Gerona, 42, (Shut Wednesdays) and they have not changed their décor since then. In the 1920s they first thought of serving sherry with a slice of mountain ham laid over it like a lid or *tapa*. The place dates from 1670, when Nell Gwyn was active. It is not far from the Casa Pilatos, if you happen to be that way…

Everyone has their favourites, and to some extent it goes by fashion, so you may well choose to go to the most frequented on the grounds that there must be a reason for their popularity, or else to the less frequented on the grounds that you would rather be able to hear yourself think. Of the ones hotly recommended to me I would only pass on one or two for the variety:

Bodega Morales, Calle Garcia de Vinuesa – it is next to a *Freiduría* (or fried-fish shop) so buy your cornet of fried fish, take it in, and eat and drink under the metaphorical shadow of the 2.5m (8ft.) high *tinajas* (earthenware jars, – I was going to call them Ali Baba-ish, but they would each hold three Frank Brunos.)

Casa Morena, Calle Gamazo. It is not a bar but a tiny shop selling ham and delicatessen. Through the back is the narrow store-room heaped from floor to ceiling with every sort of sauce, spice, herb and conserve – even HP Sauce and Camp Coffee – but there is just room for four or five people to drink a *fino* from the barrel. And meanwhile you can choose presents to take home: tins of baby clams in piquant sauce, or giant capers, or saffron, or olives, or turron nougat, or mountain ham, or any of a hundred or so other things.

If you have a *very* sweet tooth try the *naranjo* or orange wine (as strong as port or sherry) at the Tasca Juan on the right as you go up Calle Mateos Gago behind the Cathedral.

Casa Manolo, Calle San Jorge, in gypsy Triana near the Santa Ana church, and with his restaurant next door.

El Morapio, Calle Pelay Correa, in Triana – to combine tapas with a genuine flamenco ambience.

Bullfights These are held daily during the April Fair, and also during the September Fair, otherwise on Sundays, April to October.

Holy Week and the April Fair Holy Week is certainly an experience, but hardly what could be described as a tourist attraction. The fervour and devotion that are inspired by the figures of Christ and especially the three images of the Virgin – the *Macarena*, the '*Virgin of the Kings*', and the *Esperanza*, (i.e. 'Hope') *of Triana* – either drag you in, or shock you by their paganism. One of the oldest manifestations of Andaluz song, the *Saeta*, will burst and wail out from time to time as the Virgin passes, carried by sweating struggling penitents and devotees. Nowadays these *Saetas* are sometimes not spontaneous but sung by professionals; but there is nothing unspontaneous about the cries of *Guapa*! ('Pretty!') as She passes.

The April Fair is another matter. Even the vast space of the Prado San Sebastián, behind the Tobacco Factory, has long since become inadequate, and a much greater space has been allocated in the Remedios Quarter on the right bank of the city. Here *casetas*, or frame-built tents, are set up, many of them private for week-long parties, but many more public for the same purpose. The pride of it all is the horse, ridden, bestridden, and flaunted in the grey *traje corto* by the men, with the girls up behind in flamenco dresses. And the rest is mainly song, dance, food, drink and socializing in one massive week-long celebration. Most foreigners, like myself, find the *Sevillanas* dance as memorable as anything, with its gracefully smooth swirling and twirling of hands, arms, bodies and brilliant, long flounced dresses.

By the time this book comes out, the tragedy of the horse plague will I hope be only a sad memory. It was checked almost at once, and stopped altogether within a few months. Vets came from all over Spain, and specialists from Africa, to defeat it, and because its urgent seriousness was at once recognized, it was confined to a very small area. But because of that same seriousness, the precautions still ban all horse movements now a year later. It has been sad indeed to see the Feria without horses (and just as sad to see the Jerez Horse Fair without horses). But it is precisely that rigour which may have saved the Andalusian horse – and possibly even the horses of Europe – from catastrophe. I say '*may* have saved' because breeders need to sell, and the stock is in danger if they are prevented from selling.

Shopping Except for the ceramics in Triana which I describe a couple of pages back, I think all the shopping you might want may be found in the area bounded by Plaza Nueva,

Calle Mendez Nuñez, Plaza del Duque de la Victoria and Calle Sierpes. This also contains three large Department stores of which the best is *El Corte Inglés* in the Plaza del Duque.

Possibly the best book and guitar shops are both in Mendez Nuñez. I mention the latter because people sometimes want to bring a guitar home as a present, and *Viuda Ramón Delclos* sells only good ones; but I have some mental reservations since, if you are not expert, the Japanese ones available in England are, price for value, probably the best bet except at the topmost end of the range.

For fans, go to *Casa Rubio* in Calle Sierpes, 56. For mantillas and lace try *Feliciano Foronda*, Alvarez Quintero, 52.

If you are staying long enough to want to develop your photos, I have found *La Casa Sin Balcones* in Calle O'Donnell the most careful and reliable.

When you have finished your shopping spree, if you have a sweet tooth or sore feet or both, *La Campana*, at the top of Calle Sierpes has (according to my informants) 'a yummy line in goodies' to go with your cup of chocolate or coffee or tea.

Useful Addresses

UK Consulate: Plaza Nueva, 8. Tel: (954) 22 8 75.
Canadian Consulate: Avenida Constitución, 30-20. Tel: 22 94 13.
Tourist Office: Avenida Constitución, 21. Tel: (954) 22 14 04.
Post Office: Avenida Constitución, 32.

Pottery from Seville makes a good souvenir

Telephone: Plaza Nueva, and booths in many places.

Police: Plaza de la Gavidia. Tel: 22 88 40.

First Aid: Red Cross emergencies. Tel: 35 01 35.

First Aid Posts: Calle Jesus del Gran Poder, 34.

Calle Marqués de Nervión.

Calle San Jacinto, 23.

Calle Torreblanca.

Travel

RENFE: Office, Calle Zaragoza, 29. Tel: 41 41 11.

Córdoba Station, Plaza de Armas, for Córdoba and Madrid. Beware: they may have moved this for the Expo 92.

Cádiz Station, Calle San Bernardo. For Cádiz, Jerez, Málaga and Granada

Air Iberia: Calle Almirante Lobo, 3. Tel: 22 89 01. They are agent for all other lines.

Buses: Main station, Calle Manuel Vázquez Sagastizábal. But ask in a travel agency: many leave from the Prado de San Sebastián; the Huelva buses from Calle Segura, 16; and airport buses from the Iberia Office.

Car Rental: Avis, Constitución, 15. Tel: 21 65 49. (Airport: 51 43 14).

Hertz, Avenida, República Argentina, 3. Tel: 22 88 87. (Airport: 51 47 20).

Europcar, Calle Recaredo, 32. Tel: 41 95 06. (Airport: 51 61 11, Ext. 131).

Atesa, Plaza Carmen Benítez, 7. Tel: 41 97 12. (Airport: 51 47 35).

Museums and Galleries

Fine Arts Museum, Plaza del Museo. Tel: 22 18 29. Closed till 1992, but selection of works in next-door church of Merced.

Archaeological Museum, Plaza de América. Tel: 23 24 05.

Contemporary Art, Calle Santo Tomás. Tel: 21 58 30.

Folk Arts and Customs, Plaza de América. Tel: 23 25 76.

Maritime Museum, Torre de Oro. Tel: 22 24 19.

Hospital de la Caridad, Calle Temprado.

Seville Province From the city of Seville you can visit Jerez and Arcos, in the Province of Cádiz, and the Coto Doñana and the Sierra de Aracena, in the Province of Huelva – though, as a tourist who carries his home in his suitcase, I do not think it a good idea, when you can more easily stay in these places. But in this Province itself, there are really only the Roman ruins of Itálica and the town of Carmona.

Itálica The town is 6km (4ml.) out of town on N630 Mérida road. Turn left into Santiponce and then right. Entrance is free to members of the EC, so take your passport (although I was not asked for proof).

It was a whole city, with Temple at the top end and Amphitheatre at the bottom, founded by Scipio Africanus, he who fought the Carthaginians (Hannibal and Hasdrubal were down the road in Murcia). Both the Emperors Trajan and Hadrian were born and brought up here. So in a vague and indirect way, this was the source of the only and partially successful attempt to keep the Scots out of England.

For the most part, only foundations remain. I would say it is interesting to those interested in Roman history, or archaeology – for example, you can see the municipal drainage system (vaulted tunnels still complete); the lay-out of the houses, complete in many cases with their mosaic floors, one at least of them amusing, in a seaside postcard sort of way; the tunnels through which wild beasts or Christians were brought into the arena; and how the floor of the arena could be adapted for water or whatever.

Up at the top, near where the comic mosaics are, stands one of the few remaining statues, a marble figure with a cloak over his

Itálica mosaics

Roman remains at Itálica

shoulder (or perhaps it is his toga). They have painted the cloak red, and it is rather jolting and thought provoking. Suddenly it brought back to memory a reflection Richard Ford made here in Spain, although it cannot have been in Itálica:

'A marble statue never deceives; it is the colouring of it that does, and is a trick beneath the severity of sculpture. The imitation of life may surprise, but like… Madame Tussaud's waxwork figures it can only please… children of a large or small growth, to whom a painted doll gives more pleasure than the Apollo Belvedere.'

Whether he is right or not, I cannot think of a better place for putting it to the test, and finding out what you believe. For in Seville you can see two fellows to this statue in the main court of the Casa de Pilatos; and you can put them and this one against the rather disquieting image of the Virgin called the Macarena, complete with pretty dress, and colouring and tears on her cheeks.

Here in Itálica nothing spectacular remains. This is no Herculaneum; and Mérida offers more. And yet I enjoyed it. It was sunny, and not crowded, and I could stroll round and feel once again, as so often in Andalusia, the *presence* of the past. The Romans lived here and now they have gone, as you might say the Jones's lived here and now they have gone: last Thursday... during the war... two thousand years ago...

I am no historian, but in Andalusia history is now. This sense of slipping in and out of time pervades every aspect of life. In England there is nothing to remind us that 'Goodbye' is or was 'God be with ye'; nor do I find '*Adiós*' makes me conscious of that original meaning. Yes, but here you just as often hear them say to you '*Vaya Vd con Diós*' ('Go with God') – and suddenly the past is there, beside you. I am conscious of a different set of ancestors breathing over my shoulder when I hear someone say '*Ojalá*' which is a Spanish word meaning 'I hope so', but which is very clearly 'Inch Allah' ('May Allah will it'). Why should this consciousness be so much stronger here in Andalusia than in Paestum or on the Acropolis? Why?

Carmona is a sleepy town, 30km (20ml.) out of Seville on the Córdoba and Madrid road. It has a Roman Necropolis just outside it, and the western gate into the old town is a massive and very complete Roman one with Moorish additions and improvements. But unless you are a historian, all of that is nothing beside the eastern or upper part of the town. Here, you come through the crumbling Renaissance gate to be met by a piece of Spain hardly touched since Richard Ford passed through in the 1830s: whitewash, cobbles, sun-bleached tiles, an occasional scratching dog, shuttered façades with large doors from which a gentle stable smell seeps out to explain their size. No doubt a determined tourist might with much persistence persuade somebody, sometime, to open some doors. I felt, on all three occasions I visited, not that I was the wrong Prince, by simply that Sleeping Beauty was even better left asleep.

Up at the top of the bluff on this eastern edge of town is Carmona's chief attraction: the Parador built inside Peter the

Seville Province

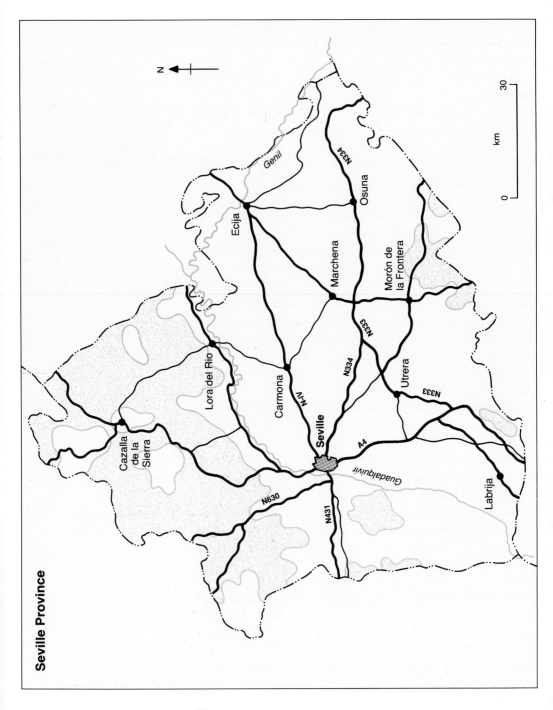

Cruel's castle, with a magnificent view eastwards out over the whole *campiña*, the rolling lowland countryside that stretches from here to Granada, richly green in spring and early summer, a symphony of pale browns, chalky greys and ochres in late summer and autumn. Up here the thick walls give coolth indoors, while out on the terrace you catch the breezes. Sevillians use it; and in the times of crowded festivity it is filled with those visitors who prefer not to stay in the city.

Parador Nacional Alcázar del Rey Don Pedro★★★★, Carmona. Tel: (954) 14 10 10 . (£53). Garage.

Alcázares entrance court

Cordoba

Córdoba The Province of Córdoba has little to offer the visitor; the city, a great deal. It was, in its heyday (in the ninth and tenth-centuries), the first city of Europe, with half a million inhabitants, rising to nearer a million by the year 1000, at a time when London and Paris were, by present-day standards, little more than villages. Ambassadors returned from it to the rush-floored courts of their rulers, wide-eyed with tales of the splendour of the city and the magnificence of the Caliph.

In Europe, only Rome and Constantinople could compare. It was already a city under the Romans (you can see the large late Roman temple now being restored at the bottom of Claudio Marcelo Street), and it became important under Moorish rulers after AD 711. But its greatness came with the arrival in Spain in 759 of Abd er-Rahman I, the sole survivor the the Umayyad dynasty of Caliphs, ousted and massacred by the Abbasids. He and his descendants set up a vastly powerful Empire that lasted 250 years, with Córdoba as its capital. After the eleventh-century it steadily declined into sleepiness until, when Richard Ford

Plaza del Potro

described it 150 years ago as 'a decaying place… dying of atrophy', it had about 50,000 inhabitants. It has revived in the last thirty years, though even today, with 280,000 inhabitants, it is less than half the size it was a thousand years ago.

To outsiders – not just tourists, but writers such as the Andalusian poet Garcia Lorca and others – Córdoba seems a brooding city, self-absorbed and locked into its past. For sure, it does not give the impression of extrovert liveliness that makes Seville a permanent street theatre. But I think much can be explained by the unusual division of the city into old (tourist) area, and modern town. They hardly interpenetrate at all. There are a Renaissance palace, a couple of towers, a fistful of convents and various churches dotted around the modern part; otherwise, pretty well everything worth seeing is near the river, grouped round the great Mosque, with as limits the Alcázar, the Almodóvar Gate, the Plaza del Potro, and the Plaza de la Corredera. Most of the hotels are within these limits, too, although I mention a couple outside it for other reasons.

91

What Córdoba has to offer, uniquely, is: the Mosque (*Mezquíta*), one of the oldest and largest extant; the *judería*, or Jewish quarter round the Mosque – there is one of these ancient quarters in each of Granada (*Albaicín*), Seville (*Santa Cruz*) and Córdoba, but they are so different that each is unique; and I would add the Plaza del Potro with its sixteenth-century inn. Of course, there are other things thoroughly worth seeing, and I shall discuss them; and, just as certainly, whole areas of the city have an atmosphere all their own; but the three things I mention are the ones which on their own justify a visit to the city.

When to go The month of May is the very best, but also therefore the most crowded. At the very biginning of the month is the festival of the Crosses (*Cruces*) when families and neighbourhoods rival to produce the most splendidly decorated cross; flowers are everywhere, and of course the whole thing is an excuse for general celebration. Almost immediately after that comes a competition to produce the most beautiful courtyard, the *Fiesta de los Patios*. However, the love of flowers in patios and window-boxes and on walls that the Andaluces inherited from the Moors goes on being in plentiful evidence through into the autumn. At the very end of the month comes the May Fair which is Córdoba's answer to Seville's famous April Fair, with pageantry, dress, horses, flamenco, eating, drinking, singing and noise.

Access If you want to spend half an hour or so getting lost in narrow, crowded one-way streets, then by all means drive into Córdoba: you will probably manage, eventually, and even get out again, as long as you speak Spanish, and can understand the broadest Andalu'. For this reason alone it is a good idea to stay at a hotel in the old quarter near the Mosque (*Mezquita*). It is easy to find as long as you stay on the NIV (Madrid–Cádiz) until you get to it: Do not let the signs saying 'centro cuidad' lure you. Turn in towards the city centre (i.e. away from the river) only when you get to the Arch (like a failed Marble Arch). It is unmistakable because it stands beside an equally bad column, with th Archangel Raphael on top trying to escape the ugliness of his pedestal. Turn in beside the Arch and you will see ahead of you the massive dingy cube of the Mosque. You must go anticlockwise round it.

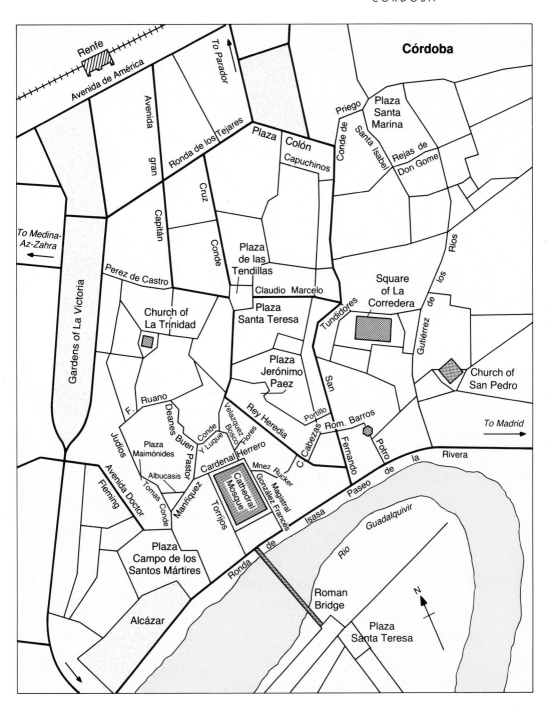

Hotels
Luxury

The Parador La Arruzafa ★★★★, Avenida de la Arruzafa. Tel: (957) 27 59 00. (£50) – is on the northern edge of the city, none too easy to find, and with Parador comfort but nothing alse to recommend it that I can detect. However, it does have the slightly cooler air (outdoors, that is: inside, all but the cheap hotels have air-conditioning) of suburban trees.

The Melia Córdoba ★★★★, Jardines de la Victoria. Tel: (957) 29 80 66. (£60) – is one of those international chain hotels with all comforts identical to its clones in Cairo or Toronto. Its main advantage is that it is easy to find: Where the NIV (Madrid–Cádiz) road crosses the Guadalquivir, you turn off it and the Melia stands ahead of you in the middle of the broad boulevard. Its other advantage is that it is within walking distance of the old quarter – that is, if you succeed in crossing the street first.

If you decide to stay in the old city (where most of the other hotels are) then, for high quality and price, try:

The Maimonides ★★★, Calle Torrijos 4. Tel: (957) 47 15 00 (£55) – easy to get to, right beside the Mosque. By car, go anticlockwise round three sides of the Mosque. Ahead of you will be the entrance of an underground car-park (the only safe place for your car at night), and the hotel next door.

Medium-Priced Hotels

The Gonzalez ★★, Calle Manriquez, 3. Tel: (957) 47 98 19. (£30) – single rooms are half that, instead of the frequent two-thirds. This is my preferred lodging in Córdoba: it is spotless, its mod cons and lift work, and it has air-conditioning. That is all I want. The desk porter speaks English. The waiters in the restaurant are pleasant, too, but do not let that lure you: eat elsewhere; the cook should have been a navvy. The hotel is behind the Maimonides, therefore one minute from the Mosque, but it is tricky to get to. Best to park and walk, arranging with the desk porter about your luggage and garaging the car (same garage as the Maimonides).

The Marisa★★, Calle Cardenal Herrero, 6. Tel: (957) 47 31 42. (£28) – go two sides round the Mosque: Calle Herrero runs along the top of it. They have garaging at about £3.

The Albucasis ★★, Calle Buen Pastor, 11. Tel: (957) 47 86 25. (£34) – they have parking for 5 cars only, and Buen Pastor is one of the maze of narrow streets in the *judería*, so I do not recommend this unless you are going by taxi.

Cheaper Hotels

Boston (now Hs ★★, but likely to become H★, Calle Málaga, 2. Tel: (957) 47 41 76. (£16) – the hotel is, in fact, slap on Tendillas Square, which is the hub of the city. It seems popular with backpacking young Americans who tell me it is clean and satisfactory.

Personally, I would choose for a budget place any of the little Hostales that abound in the old quarter: They are clean; it is quiet at night: and what you lose in modernity you make up in the traditional, Moorish style of houses, for every one that I saw was built round a patio, with its *azulejos* and flowers, while the grille doorway to the street means that, today just as in the Middle Ages when this pattern of house evolved, your things are safe in your room. Or, at least, any theft in such a house can only come from the other tourists staying there.

Hs. M. Rucker ★, Calle M. Rucker. (£20) – is an example, just off the Calle Magistral Gonzalez Francés which runs up the E side of the Mosque.

There is a place that looks good, though I cannot vouch for it, which is well sited down beside the charming Plaza del Potro:

Hs. Maestre ★★, Calle Romero Barros, 16. Tel: (957) 47 53 95. (£20) – it has garaging, and the street contains a *peña* or club bar which is at once typical of modern Andalusia and a good place for a late evening *tapa*, with the possibility of guitar music. And yet, from the street, it is hardly heard – so, no disturber of sleep.

Restaurants There are two restaurants I would recommend strongly: The *Churrasco*, Calle Romero – one minute from the Mosque, is of medium price. Its policy is to use only first-class ingredients, prepare them relatively simply, and serve them well in a pleasant environment. It succeeds. Simple preparation means a chef who prefers flavour to impressing the victim with exotic recipes or the complexity of his sauces; the service is discreet and good; and the place – a patio, open or covered with the traditional *toldo* (awning) according to time and temperature – is as much part of the pleasure as the service or the food. It is also patronized by locals, many preferring to dine by the bar off *tapas*.

My second recommendation is the best-known – and best – restaurant in Córdoba: *El Caballo Rojo*, in Calle Cardinal Herrero. It is expensive and I was not going to recommend it, since my policy has been only to name restaurants when I found something of exceptional vaue for money. But never mind the policy: I ate here one of the more delightfully delicate, light and subtle dinners I can remember. Spanish cuisine, at its best, resembles neither French, Italian nor any other. And it bears not the remotest relationship to the paella, gazpacho and fried chicken familiar to the traveller. I can remember what the dishes were called, that is to say, what their basic ingredients were, but I left in such a vague haze of well-being that I cannot recall what the chef did to them – only what he did to me. Please take this paragraph in lieu of the lyric poem I do not know how to write.

Suggested Walks The *judería* lies all round the Mosque, and is best enjoyed by simply strolling where your feet take you, rather than searching for this or that feature.The streets are narrow the houses whitewashed, flowers peep out at you and everywhere you catch glimpses of inner courtyards with their play of sun and shade, masses of flowers, *azulejos* of endless variety, and all this usually seen through a delicate black tracery of forged iron. Do not feel you are intruding on privacy by peering through these doorways: the Cordobese are proud of them, and taking a photo shows, after all, that you admire their efforts. Many of these streets are inaccessible to cars – though, in any case, the Spanish pedestrian is much less cowed than we are by the motor-car, and in all but main thoroughfares makes it wait its turn.

No. 6 Calle Albucasis

1. If you would prefer specific guidance in your stroll, starting at the Calle Judería, (*see* map page 97) which leads off from the north-west corner of the Mosque, turn left down Calle Manriquez and into Plaza Judah Levi. Calle Albucasis leads off it and contains a particularly pretty patio at no. 6. Turn right into Calle Tomas Conde to Plaza Maimonides. Here is the Museo Taurino in the fifteenth-century House of the (Papal) Bulls. It is not so much a museum as a shrine to famous bullfighters, and a revealing indicator of attitudes to them. Amusing, perhaps;

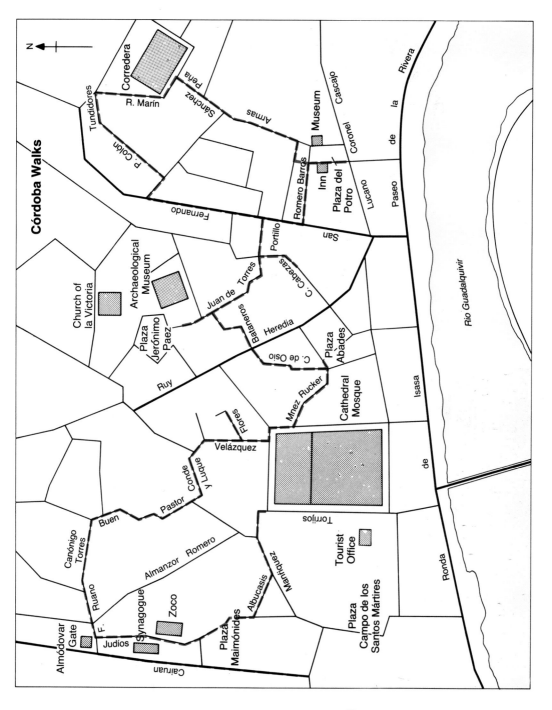

Córdoba Walks

N

Corredera
R. Marín
Tundidores
Sánchez Peña
P. Colón
Armas
Museum
Inn
Coronel Cascajo
Romero Barros
Plaza del Potro
Lucano
Paseo de la Rivera
Fernando
San
Portillo
C. Cabezas
Juan de Torres
Bataneros
Heredia
Archaeological Museum
Church of la Victoria
Plaza Jerónimo Paez
Ruy
C. de Osío
Plaza Abades
Mnez Rucker
Cathedral Mosque
Río Guadalquivir
Isasa
Flores
Velázquez
Conde y Luque
Pastor
Buen
Canónigo Torres
Almanzor
Romero
Manriquez
Albucasis
Torrijos
de
Ronda
Tourist Office
Plaza Campo de los Santos Mártires
Ruano
F.
Synagogue
Zoco
Judíos
Almódovar Gate
Plaza Maimónides
Albucasis
Cairuan

The Judería

though laughter might be offensive. Just by it is a crafts centre worth a visit to see its beautiful patio, even if you do not want to buy anything. They call it the Zoco (i.e. Souk or Market), but you may notice that the streets all around still have their old signs, and were all called Zoco.

Continue up Calle Judíos. Almost at once, Plaza Tiberiades has a modern statue to Moses ben Maimon (or Maimonides, as he was known to the Christian West). He was, indeed, one of the great doctors and philosophers of the first, twelfth-century, Renaissance. Ten metres further finds, on your left, the Synagogue (1315). It is the only one in Spain to have survived as a synagogue because it became a shoemaker's centre, then a private house store, and was only recently cleaned out and restored a bit. Open: mornings 10 a.m.–1 p.m. Before you reach the end of Calle Judíos, on your right is a bar, the Bodega Guzmán, which I hesitate to recommend simply because it is, so far, unpolluted by tourists. Nevertheless, it is a good place to try a tapa of *jamón serrano* with a glass of cold *montilla*. Almost opposite is a charming patio whose owners, if you happen to see them there, will willingly invite you in to photograph it.

At the end of Judíos, to your left, is the Almodóvar Gate. It is part of the Moorish city walls, which were themselves an update of the Roman wall, The name is modern: the Moors called it Bab-el-Yahud (Gate of the Jews), which is just one of the constant reminders you get in Andalusia that enmity between Moslem and Jew is a twentieth-century phenomenon. There was no paradox in having the Great Mosque and the Caliphal Palace in the Jewish quarter.

From here, at the Almodóvar Gate, you can either be tempted to walk back down the outside – pools, statues and city walls – or just look back that way, then turn in again along the Calle F. Ruano, and let yourself drift back via Calle Almanzor or Calle Buen Pastor, left into Calle Conde y Luque, and right down Calle Velazquez Bosco. The point of this last is to see the tiny, flower-laden *Callejuela de las Flores*. It is pretty, but to my mind not to be singled out from many another, less tourist-sought, that can be discovered in the quieter maze of alleys to the east of the Mosque.

2. This brings me to my second suggested walk. The Mosque and the Judería are the most famous tourist attractions in Córdoba, but

The Almodover gates and walls

when a friend came to visit, the walk I chose was to the Plaza del Potro and the Corredera (*see* map page 97). In this part of the old city, at once quieter and more varied, you will see a few old houses of the nobility and wealthy burghers, with open loggias and arcading at the top-floor level, which was their place for sitting out taking the cool of any stray breezes – their equivalent of the Moorish *azotea* or flat roof as part of the living area. Most of these houses have now decayed, at least in social status, if not literally.

Again, taking the Mosque as departure point, go eastwards. And again I suggest that the random stroll, with your own discoveries, is best, but if you prefer guidance try taking Calle Martinez Rucker to Plaza Abades; then left up Calle Osio – on your left here is the alley known as Pañuelos (kerchiefs) because if you bought one, the width of the alley made a fair test for size. At the end you come to the rather decrepit Convent of Santa Clara and Calle Rey Heredia. The convent bell-tower is about the only original minaret remaining and dates from about AD 1000. If you are interested in buildings, a little way up this street nos. 29 and 13 are worth a look, the latter being one of the umpteen palaces of the dukes of Medinaceli. But, personally, I find that if you try to see and enjoy every building of note on a walk, it ultimately spoils the pleasure of the stroll.

This applies also, when you have crossed Rey Heredia and walked up Calle Bataneros: you have the choice of either just savouring the square at the end, before turning right down Calle Juan de Torres; or else visiting the Palacio de los Paez which is the Archaeological Museum, and also a Renaissance Palace, with a Plateresque façade that matches the sixteenth-century square. In fact, for me the building gives more pleasure than its contents – the patio with its garden and fountain, make an aristocratic contrast to the ones you have been seeing in the *judería*. If you do visit it, I would not miss the Moorish section on the top floor: It includes a model showing what the Mosque looked like before the Christians mucked it up. Open: 10 a.m.–2 p.m. and 5–8 p.m. Sundays: 10 a.m.–1.30 p.m.

Go down Calle J.R. de Torres to Calle Cabezas. Down this on the left, the house of the Marquis of Carpio is partly medieval, and round at the back (Callejón de los Arquillos) its garden wall is Roman. The plaque tells you that Gonzalo Gustios, Lord of Salas de Lara, was imprisoned here with his window giving him a view of the impaled heads of his seven sons, who had come to beg his release. This is not tourist-oriented guff: the whole story of intrigue and treachery, and of Gonzalo's ultimate – posthumous – revenge, is told in a series of powerful ballads, so if it is invention, the invention is a thousand years old and the written record of it, more than half that. Incidentally, if you feel in need of refreshment about now, try no. 17 in Calle Cabezas.

Back opposite Calle Juan de Torres, take the short Calle Portillo: It leads you through one of the old city gates, This is a curiosity in that Córdoba was divided into *two* walled cities by a wall running down what is now Calle San Fernando, and this gate passes through that wall. Cross Calle San Fernando and turn right, then left into Calle Romero Barros. This leads into the Plaza del Potro, but if you are thirsty there is a pleasant bar-cum-club on the left before you get there. It is call the *Sociedad de los Plateros*, or Silversmiths' Club.

Plaza del Potro The Plaza del Potro ('Colt') attracts so many because it is a pretty well unspoilt sixteenth-century square, smiling and small scale. The fountain, whose little statue gives it its name, the old Charity Hospital with its façade of golden stone, and the inn opposite it are today much as they were when

Cervantes described them. Try to get there when the inn (*Posada del Potro*) is open: it has a charm that makes you wish just one of the hundreds of coaching inns in Britain might have survived without having been first modernized and then 'ye-olde-ied' again. By the well, you can see the *tinajas* or amphora such as Penelope Chetwode describes as still in use in up-country inns in 1960, and which have not changed since the ancient Greeks.

Provincial Art Gallery The old Charity Hospital opposite houses the Provincial Art Gallery, together with a collection of the local painter Julio Romero, whose pornographic bent is offset by his dullness. There are supposed to be one or two Zurbaráns, Riberas and Goyas in the museum, but they were not on show when I went. As for the building itself, little remains but its Plateresque façade.

The lower end of the Plaza is more modern, and a pleasant, cheap and cheerful place to sit out, eat, drink, chat, doze or loll. Back at the top end of the square take the Calle Armas (with its guitar-maker's at no. 4) which continues as Calle Sanchez Peña and brings you to the Corredera.

The Corredera This enclosed square is, at the time of writing, dingy, decrepit, almost derelict and altogether splendid. Except for an ugly modern building beside you as you enter and the old prison, the Pósito, in the left-hand corner, it was built all of a piece in 1688, though it had been a market, orginally outside the Walls, for centuries before that. It is also easy to imagine it in its use as a bullfighting arena in the old days, before the modern rules were evolved and special rings built. Come back by moonlight, when it is deserted, and it has as much atmosphere as you can take, or come back on a Saturday or Sunday morning for the flea-market.

If you would now like a *tapa* and a drink, leave the Corredera by the north-west corner (top left hand, as you came in), walk the few yards up the street and turn left into Calle Tundidores: the *Taberna Salinas* has kept its décor from sixty years or so ago and is a good place for *tapas*. Though do not count on it too much: there is a rumour that it is going to close down. From here back to the starting point, go left out of the café into Calle Colon, down to Calle San Fernando, turn right under the Portillo again, and so retrace your steps.

The Mosque - La Mezquita

Knowing that this is one of the great buildings of the world, you may find at first, as many do, that you are thrown off balance, and wonder what the fuss is about. From outside you see a drab cube, large no doubt for the year AD 1000, but not wonderful to look at. However, if you have already seen the Alhambra or other Moslem work, you will be aware that in all their building, they tended to prefer private architecture that reveals nothing to the passing stranger. So you go in, expecting revelation inside, expecting the eye to be spatially organized and focused by the building, and instead you get a bewildering mix-up of obstructed views and apparently endless vistas dimly perceived in the half-light, like a forest of palm-trees with marble trunks and red and white fronds. It is impressive, but it seems formless. To enjoy a building, the eye and mind need some organizing principle, either of focus or of understanding or both. What follows is an attempt to supply this. Any historical data I give is not for its own sake, but to explain the how and why.

The form of a Mosque is dictated by no liturgical need other than that of showing the direction of Mecca. Thus there is one at least, in North Africa, that consists of a row of stones marking a rectangle on the ground. Of the Five Pillars of Islam (that is, its essential demands), only the one that requires five times daily prayer facing Mecca is helped by having a mosque to pray in, though the injunction to wash before prayer makes a fountain almost universal. But Moslems soon began to model their houses of prayer on Mohammed's house, the place where it all began: an open forecourt with a fountain or well, and a rectangular roofed area. This latter is a single space so that all may be together in prayer, facing the *Qibla* (the Mecca-facing wall). Communal prayer required no ritual, no celebration, no music; just a roof overhead, a smooth clean floor to prostrate yourself on, and grateful shade conducive to quiet. Other features evolved: the Minaret tower; in the case of a royal mosque (as here) a *Maqsura*, or area by the *Qibla* reserved for the potentate and his family; a *Minbar*, or pulpit for the prayer leader (*Imam*); and, most importantly, a *Mihrab*, which is a niche or alcove in the centre of the *Qibla* wall, in which the Koran is kept, and which is made as beautiful as possible.

The Mihrab

The columns of the Mosque

Until the Christians moved in, that is what you had here: the courtyard with its fountain, leading straight into the shaded vastness of the hypostile hall with, dimly glowing at the far end, the jewelled richness of the *Mihrab* and surrounding area. There was no wall separating courtyard from hall (although there may have been a lattice screen) so that the transition was gradual from blazing sunlight, to shade, to deeper shadow. The two sides were unencumbered with chapels; the Cathedral was not there; the combination of a vast and simple space, quiet cool, restful shadow, and the endless wealth of column and arch must have been stunning – without being ostentatious or distracting. The only anomaly here is that they built this mosque with the *Qibla* not facing east to Mecca, but south. Perhaps Abd er-Rahman I, yearning for his lost Kingdom, wanted it built with the same orientation as his mosque at Damascus.

Into the middle of this, the Christians brutally plumped a dynamic, thrusting building, all verticals and business and raw daylight. Not content with this, they made the sides busy, too,

View to the maqsura

104

with fussy chapels. Then they walled off the hall from the courtyard, and finally replaced the minaret with an ill-proportioned Baroque belltower. Well, I suppose, after all, we did bomb Dresden… and the analogy (of war) is not too inaccurate, though we did not destroy Dresden *after* the war was over: the outrage here was continued and repeated over two or three centuries.

When the Emperor Charles V saw the Cathedral he is said to have said: 'You have destroyed what can be seen nowhere else, and built what can be seen anywhere'. This was unfair in two ways: he had personally given the go-ahead for the building despite opposition from the townsfolk; and, leaving aside its outrageous site, the Cathedral is far from commonplace. It is the equivalent in wood and stone of a piece of triumphant Bach, played all stops out on the organ. Its dome is a Christian echo of the splendid Moorish ones over the *Maqsura* and the Villaviciosa chapel; its carved choir stalls, a Christian equivalent of the richly decorative effect of the Moorish *ataurique*, or carved surface work.

The dome

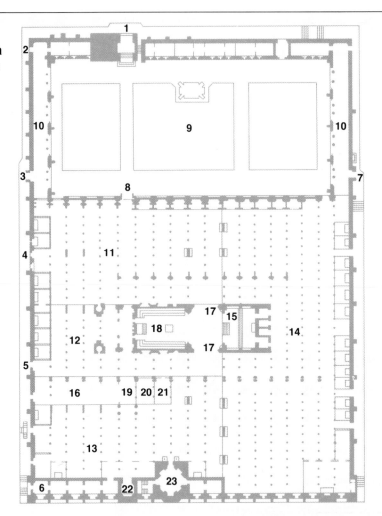

Córdoba Mosque

1. Belfry (old minaret) and Pardon Gate
2. Milk Postern
3. Deans' Gate
4. St. Stephen door (originally entrance to Visigothic Church)
5. St. Michael door
6. Postern door to palace
7. St. Catherine Gate
8. Palms Door
9. Patio de los Naranjos, or Sahn
10. Cloister, originally Court of Justice (E) and School of Philosophy (W).
11. 1st Mosque of Abd er. Rahman I
12. Extension of Abd er. Rahman II
13. Extension of Al-Hakem II
14. Extension of Al-Mansur
15. High Altar
16. Earlier Cathedral
17. Lecterns
18. Choir
19. Villaviciosa Chapel (Al-Hakem II)
20. Royal Chapel (Mudejar)
21. St. Paul's Chapel
22. Mihrab
23. Chapel of St. Teresa and Treasury

Its high altar is an uninhibited flourish of Baroque grand opera, all the way down to the strangely writhing bull of St Luke holding up the gospel lectern, in a pose mysteriously identical to the one carved on the tympanum at Moissac five hundred years before. In fact, it is one of the best cathedral buildings in Andalusia: it just should not be here.

The Courtyard (Patio de los Naranjos) This was originally planted with cypress, olive and laurel. The surrounding walls were arcaded but otherwise uncluttered. If you enter by the Puerta del Perdón (a later, Christian, reworking done by Mudéjars) the wall to your right was where philosophers such as Averroes taught, and on the opposite, east side the Qadi judged civil cases. As the Koran gives not only religious guidance, but covers all matters, legal and social, just as the Pentateuch had done for the early Jews, it is easy to imagine this courtyard as the heart of the city's life, with the cool shade of the *Haram*, or hall of the Mosque, open and inviting before you, but reserved for prayer. The pool for ablutions was put there by Almanzor in the tenth century, when he widened the Mosque. All the doorways to the Patio date from the Christians, including the little Postigo de la Leche (Milk door) to your right, so named because it was there that unwanted babies were abandoned for the Church to raise.

The Mosque Hall The entrance corresponding to the Puerta del Perdón, is called Puerta de las Palmas and brings you into the central line or nave that runs straight through the length of the first three buildings to the *Mihrab* 32 bays away. It only became off-centre when Almanzor widened the Mosque in the fourth building phase. Following roughly down this central nave is probably the best way to see and understand the building.

The first 12 bays are the original Mosque of Abd er-Rahman I, dating from AD 785. These early Arab architects had no style of their own – they were after all mainly a tent-dwelling people – but they were ingenious, good engineers, and ready to adapt to whatever they found. So, if you feel this building is typically Islamic, that is because it set the pattern from which the style evolved: The horseshoe arch was already common in Visigothic Spain, before the coming of the Arabs; the system of support by a double arch, they found in the Roman aqueduct at Mérida; and alternating red brick with white stone also came from the Romans in Spain.

The materials, too, are Roman and Visigothic. Because the columns were of varying lengths they set them into the ground rather than base them on plinths. Their shortness required a second pillar on top, and so a lower shoring arch, and an upper arch to support the roof. If it feels unfamiliar and exotic to you, this may be because all western architecture from the Greeks onward has tended to move from heavy at the base to lighter towards the roof. Here, it is the reverse: The columns are graceful and slender; the pillars and arches above are thicker. Technically it is sophisticated: a column, with a capital, then an inverted truncated cone to support the relieving arches, a pillar topped with double springer, and finally the supporting arches, holding up the roof. The result was so pleasing that it was kept to over the next two hundred years of enlargements.

The next 8 bays (bays 13 to 20) were added by Abd er-Rahman II in 833, with no innovation, though there are signs that his *Qibla* and *Mihrab* would have been more orientally ornate than his ancestor's. Hardly anything remains of this, though it is worth looking at the last pair of columns in the slightly wider 'nave' before where his *Mihrab* was: They are still Roman (some of the others in this part were made for the job) but fluted and of fine translucent alabaster, as befits an approach to the *Mihrab*. At this point, too, Christian interference makes things a bit messy: two bays of columns were removed and the ceiling vaulted (to your right) for a fifteenth-century church, that was pulled down when the present Christian erection began. But this pulls your eye less than the start of the next addition to the mosque: ahead of you, it is all glory.

The years 912–76 saw the Caliphate at its greatest. Abd er-Rahman III was one of history's great rulers, and his son al-Hakam II a cultured patron of learning, art, and religion. Between 961 and 970 he added the last 12 bays – again in the same style, though with regular columns alternating blue-black and pink, topped by alternating Corinthian and composite capitals. But few people would bother to notice them, sandwiched as they are between the splendour of his Villaviciosa chapel and the even greater splendour of the *Maqsura*. The three great bays of the

Maqsura were echoed at the start of al-Hakam's addition by three bays enclosed by polylobed arches of which the central one remains. It is known as the Capilla Villaviciosa or Lucernario. The western one got swallowed by the church, and the eastern one was rebuilt by Mudéjars working under Christian rule, and is called the Capilla Real. I think the Villaviciosa may have been completed after the *Mihrab,* for the dome looks like a refinement (which is not necessarily an improvement) on it. This system of dome construction with ribs that do not meet at the centre, did not originate here (it probably came from Christian Armenia), but the prestige of the Córdoba Caliphate meant that it spread from here up through Spain and into France – if you have visited Le Puy you will have seen the results of its bishop's admiration for Caliphal art.

Moorish plasterwork

The *Maqsura* and *Mihrab* also became a model in Islam, though I am told there is none more splendid. Al-Hakam sent to the Christian Emperor of Byzantium asking him (according to the Arab chronicler *ordering* him) to send a mosaic artist. The Emperor did, and added a gift of 320 quintals of bits of glass for the job. If that is true, and my dictionary right, that makes 16 tons. If it is not true, it's a happy thought. The austere forest of the Mosque here becomes a sumptuous jungle with these great polylobed arches, with this glow of jewel-like colour, and with the richly textured carving of every surface not covered in mosaic – no plaster here: the panels are marble. And yet all is order, perhaps emphasized by the delicate and slender marble columns, the pair on either side of the *Mihrab* taken from Abd er-Rahman II's *Mihrab,* but those of the arcades inside and above the *Mihrab,* at least as fine. The domes of the *Maqsura* are not only splendid in themselves, but serve to let in the light, bright but indirect, that draws the rich colour from the mosaics. Inside the *Mihrab* itself is a small dome of a single slab of marble, carved out as a scallop shell, which adds a curiously classical, un-Islamic touch.

The last addition to the Mosque was made by Almanzor in 987. He widened it by 8 aisles, and the *Sahn* (courtyard) accordingly. This of course sets the *Mihrab* off centre, but gives the building back something like its original proportions. There is a certain deadness to Almanzor's addition. His horseshoe arches (slightly pointed) are not of alternating brick and stone: The red is painted on. The capitals are thinner; the walls, too. Somehow

even the light seems more lifeless here. I find this fitting for the work of a dictator who combined power-lust with Puritanism – he started the destruction of Madinat az-Zahra by burning many of the books in al-Hakam's unique library. It is hard to associate book-burners with anything good.

The Doorways Apart from the little Postigo de la Leche and the Puerta de los Deanes (Deacons' Gate) all the doors on the west side are, or were originally, of the period. Going south from the Puerta de los Deanes, the first is the Puerta San Esteban. This is the oldest and most interesting. When the Moors first came to Córdoba, they shared with the Christians the Visigothic church of St Vincent whose west door was here. This went on for seventy odd years. Then Abd er-Rahman I bought the Christians out and built his Mosque on the site. It is likely some of the columns in that first part were re-used from the church. What is sure is that the bit of wall surrounding this door is the Visigothic original. The door itself, as you see it, is as restored by the Emir Mohammed in 855. The behaviour of the Moors towards the Christians they had conquered, first sharing and then paying to take over their church, compares uncomfortably well with that of our co-religionaries. Whenever I come to Andalusia, I am reminded of Mahatma Gandhi's reputed comment that he might have become a Christian if it were not for the Christians.

The next door is the Puerta San Miguel, which belongs to the extension of Abd er-Rahman II. Originally it was the Emir's private entrance direct through from his palace to the *Maqsura* of his Mosque. Incidentally, in case you are confused by my use of Emir and Caliph, Abd er-Rahman I became independent Emir (Commander/Governor) in 756; it was only in 929 that Abd er-Rahman III declared himself Caliph, or Successor (i.e. to Mohammed, and therefore supreme spiritual leader), though Art Historians refer to the whole period as Caliphal.

Next after the San Miguel door come three doorways from the third (al-Hakam II) part of the Mosque. The centre one, the Puerta de las Palomas, was adapted to fifteenth-century Gothic, as the entrance to the early Cathedral. At the end there is an undecorated wicket door that leads direct to the Caliph's doorway into the *Maqsura*, to the right of the *Mihrab*. On the east side of

**Opposite
9th century doorway to the
Mosque**

111

the Mosque are the over-restored doorways of Almanzor's part, where the designs are applied, not carved or constructed.

Other things you may wish to see

The Alcazar (Open: 9 a.m.–1.30 p.m. and 5–8 p.m., night-time tours 10 p.m.–12 a.m.). Despite its name, it is not Moorish: It was built as a royal palace in 1328, a century after the Reconquest, was *not* used by Ferdinand and Isabella, despite the plausible story that she could not sleep for the noise of the Moorish water-wheel and ordered it to be destroyed, thus destroying the Moorish irrigation system that fed the gardens. Christopher Columbus did not sleep here. The gardens probably date from one of the Bastard Trastamara line of the fifteenth-century, though Michelin hopefully claims that the kitchen garden dates from the Moors. There are some Roman mosaics and a sarcophagus to be seen.

As for the building, it is like most castles, more impressive from a distance than when visited. Unless you are keen on Roman remains, its main attraction may be the view of the river and Moorish mills you get from the towers, or the fact that the gardens are a bit cooler than the city. Or, if you have normal (that is to say, bloodthirsty) children, the fact that it served as a prison for the victims of the Inquisition, when added to battlements, passages and imagination, may produce a worthwhile visit.

Besides it are the Royal Stables, and that is frustrating, since at the time of writing they are seriously at risk of being disbanded. The 1989 outbreak of horse plague, though quickly dealt with, has led to a ban on the sale of any Andalusian stock. And breeding for sale, together with stud fees, are their life-blood. The stables (*caballerizas*) themselves are worth seeing, though I fear they may be henceforth off limits.

La Torre de la Calahorra (Open: 9.30 a.m.–2 p.m. and 5–7.30 p.m.; History of Córdoba slide-show shown at extra cost at various times; Shut Sundays and Mondays). It stands at the south end of the Roman bridge (of which little that is Roman remains visible). As with the Golden Tower of Seville, it was strategically important in days when the Guadalquivir was more navigable. The present structure dates from the fourteenth century. The museum is dedicated to the golden age of Córdoba under the Moors.

More worth while, to my mind, than either the Alcázar or the Calahorra, if you have an afternoon or evening to spare, would be a stroll round the northern part of the city, taking in a selction of the following:

The Palace of the Marquis of Viana (Open: 10 a.m.–2 p.m. and 5–8 p.m.; Shut Wednesdays and weekends). This is the best of the noble houses in Córdoba, and worth a visit. It is mainly sixteenth century, with no less than 14 patios, a noble staircase, and a good collection of ceramics, silverwork and Córdoban leather – the stuff that gave us the word 'cordwainer'. It is privately owned, and has belonged to a number of families, one of whom seemed so keen on large *rejas* (window grilles), that the square and palace are popularly named after him.

Plaza Santa Marina This is an old and peaceful backwater in the Calle Santa Isabel, not spoiled by the Manolete memorial. One side of the Square is taken up by the blank wall of the Convent of St Isabel. You cannot visit, but you can buy their confectionery. It is strange that the Moorish taste for very sweet sweetmeats has been perpetuated in Andalusia by the Christian nuns.

The Church of Santa Marina de las Aguas This was one of the first churches to be put up by Fernando III after the reconquest in 1236, and like all the Fernandine churches it is notable for its tact: None of them, except where later rebuilt, has the statuary you would expect of a Gothic façade. To Muslims, images of the human form, especially on a religious building, would have been idolatrous and profoundly shocking; and after 500 years of Muslim civilization it is likely the Córdoban Christians would have acquired the same feelings. If these Fernandine churches interest you, the ones that have survived with least remodelling are San Lorenzo (my favourite, and only a short walk from the Viana Palace), San Miguel (most other people's favourite), and San Pedro. Little more than hundred yards from here…

The Cristo de los Faroles (Christ of the Lamps) It stands in a mainly seventeenth- and eighteenth-century square, the Plaza de los Capuchinos. It is evocative after dark, when the lamps are lit, and perhaps a place to come if you wish to try the horse-drawn carriages.

Just round behind, in the Plaza Colón, *El Convento de la Merced*, is now the seat of local government. It is eighteenth century and its coloured façade makes it typical of Andalusian style. The cloisters are used for exhibitions, but are more worth seeing, at times, than what it contains (Open: 10 a.m.–2 p.m. and 6–9 p.m.).

Museums and Galleries

Archaeological Museum (Museo Arqueológico), Calle Jerónimo Páez, 7. Tel: 22 40 11. Open: 10 a.m.–2 p.m. and 5–8 p.m., Sundays 10 a.m.–1.30 p.m., Shut Mondays.

Provincial Fine Arts Museum (Museo Provincial de Bellas Artes), Plaza del Potro. Tel: 22 13 14. Open: 10 a.m.–2 p.m. and 6–8 p.m., Sundays 10 a.m.–2 p.m., Shut Mondays.

Museo Julio Romero de Torres, Plaza del Potro. Tel: 22 13 14. Open: 10 a.m.–1.15 p.m. and 5–6.45 p.m., Sundays 10 a.m.–1.45 p.m., Shut Mondays.

Bullfighting Museum (Museo Taurino), Plaza de Tiberiades. Tel: 22 51 03. Open 9.30 a.m.–1.30 p.m. and 5–8 p.m., Shut Mondays, and weekend afternoons.

Torre de la Calahorra (History of Córdoba), Open: 9.30 a.m.–2 p.m. and 5–7.30 p.m., Shut Sunday afternoons and all Monday.

Alcázar (Antiquities), Plaza Campo de los Santos Mártires. Open: 9 a.m.–1.30 p.m. and 5–8 p.m.; garden tours 10 p.m.–12 a.m. nightly.

Palace of the Marquises of Viana (Córdoba Crafts), Calle Rega de Don Gome, 2. Tel: 25 04 14. Open 10 a.m.–2 p.m. and 5–8 p.m., Shut Wednesdays.

Shopping Córdoba is traditionally known for leather goods, silver filigree, and also wrought metal and pottery. If you are looking for local handicrafts, stay in the *judería*: the *Zoco Municipal de Artesanía*, next to the Bullfighting Museum in Calle Judíos, mainly for pottery; *Carlos Lopez Obrero Mairóns* in the Callejuela de las Flores, for leather and wrought metal, or *Sicilia Forja*, Calle Juan de Mena, just south of Tendillas square, for ironwork.

Otherwise, you will find most things in the area between Tendillas Square and the Ronda de los Tejares. Take Calle Cruz Conde as your main axis, and try branching off right and left. For clothes and accessories, apart from the individual shops you find in Cruz Conde, the one called *Don Algodón* is a successful chainstore mainly for the young, and in the Ronda de los Tejares you will find *Cortefiel*, a major chain store, and others. Also in Tejares,

Neichel and *Juncal* and been recommended to me by (well-dressed) aquaintances, for women's clothes and things.

Flea markets are held in the Corredera on Saturday and Sunday mornings.

Food and Drink *See* my section on it in part 1 (*see* page 34). For lovers of sweet things, add the *Convento del Cister*, Calle Carbonell y Morand, to the *Santa Isabel Convent* I have already mentioned. Carbonell y Morand is about half way between Tendillas and Santa Isabel, so you could make a glorious hog of yourself in one outing.

Photography Best is *Studio Jimenez* on the corner of Calle Cruz Conde and Ronda de los Tejares: in fact, they were more careful than any other studio I found in Andalusia.

Jewish Music, Pottery, Books *Librería Sefarad*, Calle Romero, in the *judería*.

Guitars *Reyes*, Calle Armas 4, (between the Plaza del Potro and the Corredera). It is the workshop as well as the shop, so it makes an interesting visit.

Useful Addresses

Tourist Office: Calle Torrijos, 10. The Municipal Tourist Office (useful for catching buses, etc.) is in Plaza Juda Levi, which is off Calle Manriquez.

Post Office: Calle Cruz Conde, 21. Tel: 47 82 67.

Telephone (Telefónica): Plaza de las Tendillas. There is also a useful one in Calle Cardinal Herrero at the end of Calle Torrijos.

Police Headquarters (Comisaría): Avenida del Dr Fleming, 2. Tel: 47 75 00/01.

First Aid: Avenida de la República Argentina, 4. Tel: 23 46 46. Night-time nursing assistance (Angeles de la Noche): 24 24 50.

Travel

RENFE: Office: Ronda de los Tejares, 10. Tel: 47 58 84.
Station: Avenida America.

Air Travel: Iberia, Ronde de los Tejares, 3. Tel: 47 26 95.

Car Rental: Avis – Plaza de Colón, 35. Tel: 47 68 62.
Europcar – Avenida Medina Azahara, 7. Tel: 23 34 60.
Hertz – Glorieta del Conde de Guadalhorce (i.e. at the Railway Station). Tel: 47 72 43.
Ital – Calle Condes de Gondomar, 6. Tel: 47 82 12.

Córdoba Province For touristic interest, the city of Córdoba dominates its province. To the north lies the Sierra Morena, pleasant hills, unspectacular waves of pasture, cork and holm-oak. To the south lies the gently rolling Campiña, the 'yellow, ox-hide land' of Gerald Brennan's phrase, stretching far into the distance with its crops of grain, olive and grape.

This is not to say that there is not a great deal that might well hook your interest and fascinate you, providing only that you had the leisure to explore unspectacular places, and get to know them. Some of my more memorable moments have resulted from turning aside off the road to somewhere in order to have lunch in some ordinary, whitewashed, red-roofed, sun-roasted village in the Campiña.

It takes very little distance from the main road for you to come across a place where tourists – outsiders of any sort, Spanish or foreign – are strangers in the strict sense of the word: strange people. The initial reaction of the locals is often to pretend you are not there: it is the reaction of a courtesy that does not wish to

Cork oak in the Sierra Morena

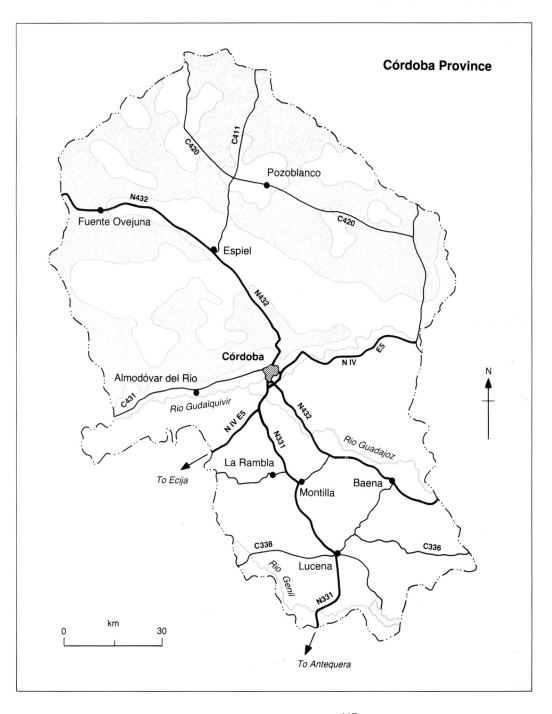

Córdoba Province

gawp. But is is never hostile. The slightest thing will release friendly, open interest. In one such place, it was my visible delight at the taste of a humble bar offering: kidneys fried in lemon-juice. I had never liked kidneys till then and used my hunk of bread to wipe from my plate the last smidgen of taste. This pleased the cook so much she lost her shyness, the whole café followed suit, and I spent a pleasant and sociable hour. Decent folk of good will are always a pleasure to meet. This is the common denominator in the writings of all those English people (more commonly Irish people) who have got hooked on Spain, or on Spaniards: Walter Starkie, Gerald Brennan, George Orwell, Richard Ford, V.S. Pritchett, Laurie Lee, Jan Morris, Penelope Chetwode, Rose Macauley, and many more. 'Everything was rotten in Spain except the hearts of the poorer people,' wrote Napier in his history of the Peninsular War, and has been echoed by others ever since.

But I suppose a brief holiday implies more purposeful travelling. So I recommend three places: Madinat az-Zahara, Almodóvar, and Montilla.

Madinat al-Zahra When Abd er-Rahman III declared himself Caliph – that is, Successor to Mohammed and supreme leader of Islam – he decided to build himself an appropriately splendid place. You will see it spelt in various ways, but they all mean 'City of the Flower'. It was, indeed, more a city than a palace, like Versailles though seven hundred years earlier, on a comparable scale, and housing numbers as huge. It was built from scratch from 936 onwards, using not only stone and brick, but marble, glass tesserae, porphyry, ivory, ebony, gold, and gem-stones. It was the wonder of the western world. And it lasted barely 75 years.

The Berbers, those warlike mountain people from the Atlas, destroyed it in a civil uprising. And the Caliphate disappeared with it. For centuries even its memory vanished; folk thought the bits of ruin must have been the old Roman Córdoba. But modern archaeology is bringing it back. There is still a long way to go, but already it is well worth a visit.

It is about 11km (7ml.) out of Córdoba. You leave the city by the Avenida Medina Azahara, which is the C431 Almodóvar road. After 8km (5ml.) turn right (signposted) and you will see it a couple of miles further on, terraced on the first slopes of the Sierra Morena. It opens from 9.30 a.m.–1.30 p.m. and from

118

Palace of Madinat Al-Zahra

The audience chamber

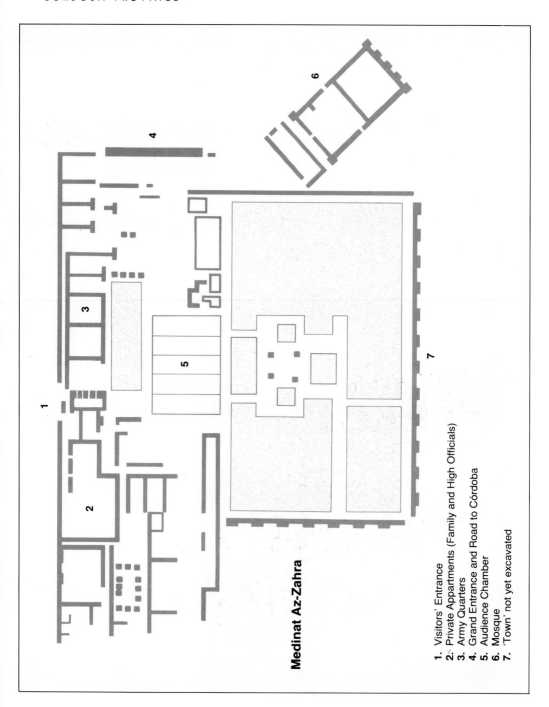

Medinat Az-Zahra

1. Visitors' Entrance
2. Private Appartments (Family and High Officials)
3. Army Quarters
4. Grand Entrance and Road to Córdoba
5. Audience Chamber
6. Mosque
7. 'Town' not yet excavated

The guards' quarters

4–7 p.m., Shut Mondays; free to members of the EEC, so take your passport.

As you enter by the northern (upper) gate, you see it spread out beneath you in three terraced levels. The upper one housed the royal family, attendants, and guard; the second level contains, among other more uncertain things, an audience chamber, and a garden with pavilion and water cisterns distancing the court from the common herd; the lowest level has the Mosque, and the rest of the 'city' which is yet to be unearthed. This sounds quite clear. It isn't: the three levels only add to the impression of maze-like chaos that is quite clearly deliberate. There are no axes of symmetry; it is an oriental sprawl. It is easy to see, even in this excavated complex, the embodiment of oriental texts of the period that conjure up a multitude of chambers, dark passages, bare corridors emerging into dazzling halls, opulently decorated.

The Upper Level You cannot yet visit the royal apartments (probably for visiting dignitaries and important members of the Court), but you can see that they are all built with their rooms round patios, on to which they open. About the first area you come down to is the *Dar al-Djund* (the military quarters), a splendid chamber that the blurb describes as 'austere' though its columns are topped by capitals deeply incised by Byzantine carvers, and as rich in effect as the ones in Justinian's church of San Vitale in Ravenna. There is ample space around, water for the horses, and stabling to your left as you face the Dar. To your right, the ramp begins for the cavalry to ride down to the great portico, the triumphal entrance to the Medina. To the left of that Portico as you come down to it, was a large area, again for the military, but of which little remains.

The Second Level Here, facing on to the garden, was the Caliph's palace. What remains is impressive enough: it is a great chamber, presumably the audience chamber. It has been well restored. Until quite recently these intricately carved walls were lying in thousands of small pieces on the floor. Perhaps it was here that the Caliph kept a great marble dish, filled with mercury, on which light was made to fall from above, so that when the bowl was gently rocked reflected lights flashed round the walls and amazed the poor visiting envoys. One of them was so overcome by the magnificence of it all that, on backing out of the Caliph's presence, he felt compelled to abase himself before the empty throne in the next room.

The ceilings and roofs would have been some of them domed, probably rather as the *Maqsura* of the Mosque, but most would have been wooden and flat: the builders aimed at a static architecture, creating atmospheric rather than structural effect. The outside walls then, as today all over Andalusia, were lime-washed to a dazzling white. The Moslem historian who is the source of all the commonly quoted statistics on Madinat al-Zahra mentions the bringing of 400 mule-loads of whitewash and lime-mortar per day. But as he was writing two hundred years later, I take it he was simply telling us that this was a jolly big place with an awful lot of people in it. In any case, Arab chroniclers liked giving precise statistics that were quite spurious, though this has not prevented the hand-out (and indeed many books) from repeating them as fact. But we do know it was whitewashed because of a fragment of poetry written by a prisoner here. He describes his cell as 'so dark that, while white al-Zahra shines all around, it seems like ink in an ivory standish'. What with that and the white almond blossom of Spring…

The Lowest Level Except for the foundations of the Mosque, this has yet to be excavated and has little to show. The great Portico is worth a look; from here two roads connected the complex with the city, one of them more or less following the present one.

Incidentally, you can return to Córdoba, by way of pleasant variety, by carrying on up the hill and keeping to your right. Or else you can drop back to the C431, turn right, and go the extra 10 miles to Almodóvar del Río.

Almodóvar del Río I suppose it is just one more of those many hundreds of castles in Spain that stand dominant on their rock protecting the sleepy white township that huddles below. But it is one of my favourites. The rock rises massive from the river bank; the castle stands out against the mountain backdrop, its five towers silhouetted against the sky; and the sleepy town beneath is about as sleepy as it could get. Perhaps it is all a thumping great cliché, but if so it is an uninhibited one and I like it.

The castle was Moorish. It was rebuilt in the fourteenth century by a Christian king. The township is unspoiled by tourism or industry. Its sleepiness vanishes on the second Sunday in May when they have the Romería de la Virgen de Fátima.

Montilla The town lies just off the main Córdoba–Málaga road some 40km (25ml.) from Córdoba, and your reason for going there is the wine. I do not think it matters much which Bodega you choose to visit, so you can take one of the ones on the main road, or else turn into the town, especially if any of your party have become hooked on Convent-cooked goodies: the *Convento de las Madres Clarisas* in Calle Benedicto XIII sells a well-known form of gingerbread called *alfajores*.

Apart from the two Bodegas beside the main road, you will find the *Bodegas Cruz Conde*, Calle Marquez, 3; *Bodegas Navarro*, Avenida Antonio y Miguel Navarro, 1; *Garcia Hermanos*, Avenida Marqués de la Vega de Armijo, 4; *Perez Barquero SA*, Avenida Andalucia, 31; and *Tomás García SA*, Llano de Palacio, 7.

The wines are similar in style to sherry, and not totally dissimilar in process. But the *tinajas*, the vast Ali Baba jars containing the wine, are unlike anything else. If you get the chance, try also the young fruity wines (*vinos jóvenes*).

You may be interested in local pottery, in which case it is worth calling at La Rambla, 8 or 9km (5 or 6ml.) west of here, where they make those spouted drinking jars called *botijos* and, increasingly nowadays, more touristy articles. It is worth while making the short detour to the village potteries, though the wares are sold on the main road.

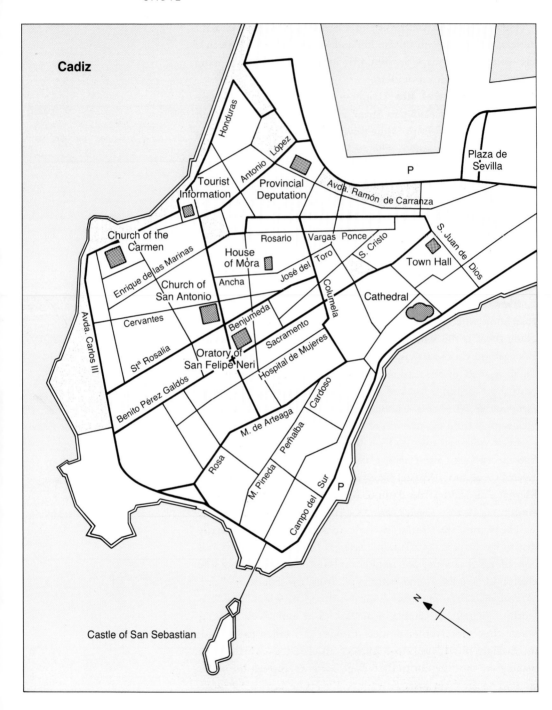

Cadiz

Honduras

Antonio López

Tourist Information

Provincial Deputation

Avda. Ramón de Carranza

P

Plaza de Sevilla

Church of the Carmen

Enrique de las Marinas

Rosario

Vargas Ponce

S. Cristo

S. Juan de Dios

Town Hall

House of Mora

José del Toro

Church of San Antonio

Ancha

Columela

Cathedral

Cervantes

Avda. Carlos III

Benjumeda

Sacramento

Stª Rosalía

Oratory of San Felipe Neri

Hospital de Mujeres

Benito Pérez Galdós

Cardoso

M. de Arteaga

Peñalba

Rosa

M. Pineda

Campo del Sur

P

N

Castle of San Sebastian

Cádiz and its Province The Province of Cádiz has a lot
of good things to offer the visitor, of which the city itself is not the
most important, though it is worth a quick visit. There are Jerez
and the other sherry towns, Sanlúcar de Barrameda and Puerto
Santa María. There are the splendid mountains of the Serranía de
Ronda, together with Arcos de la Frontera and a whole chain of
other 'White Towns'. There are the coastlands between Cádiz and
Tarifa. And (according to the Spanish telephone exchange) the
Rock of Gibraltar is also a part of Cádiz Province.

In our English imagination, Cádiz looms large because of
Francis Drake and Trafalgar and all those sea-shanties where it
rhymes with 'Ladies' when it should be 'Laddies'. But it is in
reality a hemmed-in little place, sitting as tight as an egg on its
isthmus, brilliant white against the blue Atlantic, with oodles of
atmosphere but nothing specific to see. It is the provincial capital,
but not even the largest town in its province. It can claim the
longest history of any city in Spain, or indeed the Western World
– it has been a city continuously for three thousand years, since
the Phoenicians – but little of that history is visible today thanks
to earlier English visitors who put it to the torch in 1596.

The way in by road is disproportionately long because when it
had to expand, it could only do so by a single spaghetti-like
extrusion down the narrow neck of the isthmus and beyond on
the almost equally constricted causeway between marshes and
salt-pans. So if you go by car, the tarmac and concrete and traffic
seem to go on for ever.

The most pleasant way to visit the city is as an excursion from
Puerto de Santa María across the bay – the one where the King
of Spain's beard got singed. The ferry, known locally as the *vapor*,
leaves the Puerto at 11 a.m. and returns at 2 p.m. It is a 45-
minute crossing, so you have a couple of hours in Cádiz, and the
trip there, across the waters, becomes part of the pleasure. If you
miss the return ferry, there are frequent trains to Puerto de Santa
María and Jerez.

The light is blinding, somehow more so than anywhere else in
Andalusia; it is one's dominant impression and memory. The
town turns its back on the south-west and the glare of the sea. On
the north-east side, where the bay waters sparkle without the
same glare, are the parks and avenues – a strip of park and a single

avenue, like a thin coating on the egg. Apart from atmosphere, what you have is a tightly packed grid of streets, so narrow that many are now pedestrian ways, with the buildings mainly eighteenth and nineteenth century, enclosed by an eggshell of modern construction.

A random saunter down these streets is a pleasure. Somehow the inhabitants give the impression, not just that they belong, but that they belong thoroughly and happily. This is not quite any Spain I know; nor is it African, like Tarifa; it is as far away, as foreign to me, as Kurdistan or the days of Good Queen Bess. In the eighteenth- and nineteenth-century parts, the houses, curiously enough, share a characteristic with those of Santander and other towns on the north coast of Spain: they have narrow glassed-in balconies (*miradores*) all up the façades, and this gives them a certain delicate elegance, a lacy quality. In the slightly

older bits, the streets are even narrower (if possible) and shadier. And there is one little corner, the *Barrio del Pópulo*, which survives from the Middle Ages, unburned by the English, with access through archways.

This is not a place that tarts things up for the tourist trade. The city, the streets, the bars and the restaurants are the way they are because that is how the Gaditanos want them. You feel that here, as much as or more than anywhere else in Spain, the notion of the *patria chica* (the little homeland, as against Spain, the *patria grande*) applies: that Spanish phenomenon that must be understood by every foreigner who comes to live or work in this country, whereby patriotism is felt, and very strongly, for your village, your town, your province – and only after that for your country. A Gaditano, for instance, will feel he is a Gaditano above all, and only then a Spaniard. This phenomenon may well help to account

127

for the Spaniard's keenness to join an integrated Europe. He cannot feel any fear of loss of identity; he is politically linked already to such people as Castilians and Catalans, without feeling the slightest loss of his integrity as a Gaditano (or as an Andalusian), so what difference can it make to extend the links to include Britons and French and Germans?

If my impression of these people is correct (and I think it is), then it goes some way to explain why they were the only city in Spain to defy the French rule imposed on them by Napoleon: they held out against Marshal Victor's troops until a British relieving force arrived, and so stayed independent of French rule throughout. What is more, during that period they formulated the Constitution of 1812, known affectionately as the *Pepa:* It was not only the most liberal and democratic of such documents in the nineteenth century, it added the word 'liberal' to the world's political vocabulary. Furthermore, together with the Gaditano example of defiant independence, it inspired the Latin American thrust towards independence from Spain: If you look at the façade of San Felipe Nero in Calle Sacromonte, where the Constitution was formulated, you will see the plaques put up in tribute by other cities of Spain and by Latin American nations.

My advice to visit Cádiz from across the bay is given on the assumption that you speak no Spanish. As the drift of these last paragraphs implies, the main attraction of this town is its people, so that if you cannot communicate with them, a diurnal visit will give an impression of the place without great loss. If you do have some Spanish, you would need to stay overnight. For this is a nocturnal city. As anywhere in Andalusia, it is deserted in the afternoon. But unlike other places (or, at least, more than other places) when they come out in the evening they stay out: Cádiz is noted, even in Spain, for its ability to enjoy life. The Carnival has no rival this side of Brazil. Not even Franco, who banned it everywhere else, was able to stop the Gaditanos holding it. But the Carnival is just the year's highpoint: almost anything will be cause for festivity; and festivity is what they are best at. If you do stay, take a good siesta to prepare for an evening that may last most of the night...

When to Go Carnival, but only if you have made sure of board and lodging well in advance. Holy Week and Corpus Christi. June 23 and 24 for midsummer bonfires and much more.

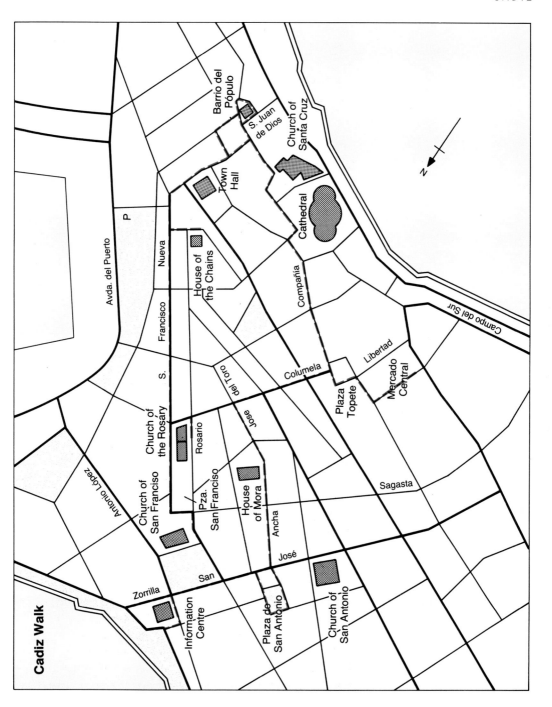

Cadiz Walk

During June or July there is a Flamenco Festival. From July to early September you can take an evening trip round the bay (departures at 10.30 p.m.).

Hotels

Atlantico★★★, Parque Genovés, 9. Tel: (956) 22 69 05. (£50) – a modern Parador in all but name. Fine site.

San Remo★★, Paseo Marítimo, 3. Tel: 25 22 02. (£33) – on the Victoria beach; has air-conditioning.

Hostal Imares★, Calle San Francisco, 9. Tel: 21 22 57. (£17).

Hostal Manolita★, Calle Benjumea, 2. Tel: 21 15 77. (£7).

Eating Obviously, fish from one of the numberless *freidurias* (fried fish shops) to take into the neighbouring bar. Try the Calle Zorilla – the choice will be enormous. The town's best restaurant, according to the locals, is *El Faro*, Calle San Felix, 15. It is not cheap. There are plenty of reasonably priced places around the Plaza San Juan de Diós.

Suggested Walks Assuming you start from the Tourist Office in the Plaza de Mina, where you have picked up your city plan, all four directions will be of interest. (*See* page 129.)

At the north-east corner (by the Tourist Office) is the Calle Zorilla which is a good street for *tapa* bars.

At the north-west corner, the Calle Calderón de la Barca takes you to the agreeable promenade round the city's edge, via the Comillas gardens and then the Genovés Park. In fact, it does not take long to do a complete circuit of the town, with the post-card view of the Cathedral when you get round to the south-west. (If the Cathedral were in Paris, it would beat even the Sacré Coeur for sugary kitsch, but here under the bleaching sun, this distant view is exotic.)

On the opposite or south-western side of the Plaza de Mina from the Tourist Office is the Arts Museum. Of the various Spanish painters represented, the most notable works are the Zurbarán series of saints; Murillo, Ribera and Morales are also represented. The ground floor is an archaeological museum with some Phoenician and Roman statuary; the top floor has some fun puppets – a local speciality.

Lastly, from the Plaza de Mina you can drift pleasantly through the town, for example Calle San José as far as Calle Ancha, with a glance at Plaza de San Antonio to your right before you turn. Calle

Ancha is pedestrian, and the name, believe it or not, means 'wide'. When you get down to Calle Columela, turn right because it takes you to the Plaza Topete and the market. The Plaza Topete, is memorable mainly for the name: it marks the site of a Phoenician Tophet, a temple that specialized in sacrificing first-born babies. The covered Market just beyond is well worth it, if it is in action. All Spanish fish markets are a revelation; this one is a few metres from the fish-rich Atlantic. If you can name half the creatures you see, in any language, you are an expert. But even if you are not there during market time, you should be lucky because in and around Topete there are no less than six open-air markets a week.

From Topete it is a short walk to the Cathedral. If you walk a short way down the quayside from the Cathedral, the second street is Calle San Juan de Diós which runs alongside about the only survival of the British taste for arson: the so-called Barrio del Pópulo, a small bit of thirteenth-century survival. From here it is a short step across to the Plaza San Juan de Diós, with its large and ugly City Hall, and from there into the Calle San Francisco Nueva. This is one of the main shopping streets and takes you straight back to the Plaza de Mina. On the way you can try to see the Goya frescos in the Santa Cueva in Calle Rosario: I would put the odds against it being open at about 100 to 1.

Museums

Arts, Plaza de Mina. Tel: 21 22 81. Open: 10 a.m.–2 p.m. and 5.30–8 p.m. (weekdays), 10 a.m.–2 p.m. (Saturday). Shut Sundays.

Cathedral Museum, Calle Arquitecto Acero. Tel: 28 61 54. Open: 10 a.m.–2 p.m. (Monday–Friday). 11 a.m.–2 p.m. (Saturday). Shut Sundays.

Oratorio de la Santa Cueva, Calle Rosario. Tel: 22 22 62. Open: 10 a.m.–1 p.m. and 4–6 p.m. (Monday–Saturday). Shut Sundays.

Useful Addresses

Tourist Office: Calle Calderón de la Barca, 1 (actually on corner of Plaza de Mina). Tel: 21 13 13.

RENFE Station: Plaza de Sevilla. Tel: 25 43 01.

Buses: for Puerto de Sta María and beyond: Comes Co., Plaza de la Hispanidad. Tel: 22 42 71 (just beyond Pl de España) for Tarifa coast: Amarillo Co., Avenida Ramón de Carranza, 31. Tel: 28 58 52.

Car Parks: No problem: there are three underground parks, all on the major avenues surrounding the city. Whichever way you go round, you will hit one of them. They are in Cuesta de las Calesas (immediately to your right as you enter Cádiz under the Gateway); Paseo Canalejas (a bit further round, opposite the Passenger harbour, and the nearest parking to the centre of town); and the Campo del Sur (on the seaward side).

Cádiz Province

Jerez de la Frontera With 180,000 inhabitants, Jerez is the largest town in the Province. It is a mixture of pleasant open boulevards, a twisty narrow – and attractive – older quarter, and massive, dominant Bodegas, looking like factory warehouses, which is what they are. Nowadays people may come here because of the Grand Prix circuit just outside town, or because of the magnificent horses of the Royal Riding School, or even a few because of the clocks in the clock museum. But for most people the obvious attraction is the sherry. Seventy-five per cent of the population earns its living from the sherry industry, and the town is prosperous.

If you can, I would spend three days or so here, and make sure one of them is Thursday. This is because Thursday is a special day at the Riding School: you can watch the horses being exercised on any weekday, but on Thursday they give a display such as you will not find this side of the Spanish Riding School in Vienna. You could combine this with a visit to one of the Bodegas. One day would be for touring the vineyards and the other two major sherry towns, Sanlúcar de Barrameda and Puerto Santa María. And it would be another day's worth at least to manage some of the other things worth doing here: have a look round town itself; visit the Clock museum; if flamenco interests you, then go to the gypsy quarter and hope for luck in one of the little bars, *tabancos,* or *peñas* there, as well as visit the Flamenco Foundation; and do any shopping.

You could, at a pinch, give it only one day: look round a Bodega; look round the Riding School; and leave to spend the night somewhere else. It would be a pity. Like all the best Andalusian cities, it has an atmosphere all its own, patrician, even élitist perhaps, courteous and welcoming certainly. It is nothing like anything you know in Britain, yet it has something

132

to do with an English ingredient, by which I mean English of an older style. All the great sherry families are related by marriage, so that with them adjectives such as 'English', 'Irish', 'Spanish' have little significance, and in any case the casual visitor is unlikely to be seeing the town in terms of messrs Domecq, Sandeman, and co. Yet somehow it is as though an affinity existed between the good manners of the merchants who set up here and the dignity and courtesy that are indigenous, and that this came to colour the whole town.

Jerez

Here, in contrast to Granada (for instance), the gypsies are a part of the community, and a valued part at that, and they can be just as patrician in their courtesy as any of the great names. Even as I write this, I am aware that it sounds like tourist-guide guff. How much do I really know of it? But I stick by it because, as far as my small experience goes, it is true, and it is the only way I can find to convey the attraction of Jerez. Perhaps the miniature facsimile of Big Ben standing in the town centre says something...

133

Access The one-way system is second to none – even Hampton Court Maze. The Avenida Alvaro Domecq is easy and where you are most likely to arrive. If you are staying at a hotel elsewhere in town, drive down Alvaro Domecq and continue round left into the Alameda Cristina, a broad and elegant avenue. Towards the end on the right is the Tourist Office. Park near it, illegally and without worry: the Municipal Police are as courteous as the other Jerezanos, and instead of a fine, leave a civil note on your windscreen telling you where to find a car park. In the Tourist Office ask for both a town plan and, above all, help to find your way to the hotel: Jerez shares with Seville the prize for the most helpful Tourist Office I have come across. Still assuming a car, Jerez is also as good as any other Spanish town for its criminal classes: cars emptied, boots forced, almost while you wait. But like Cádiz, (and unlike Seville, Córdoba and Granada) it has municipal underground parking, under the Alameda Cristina itself, in Calle Madre de Dios, and in Plaza Monti.

Hotels

H. Jerez★★★★★, Avenida Alvaro Domecq, 35. Tel: (956) 30 06 00. (£75) Garage – all of five stars plus cool gardens.

HR Avenida Jerez★★★, Avenida Alvaro Domecq, 10. Tel: 34 74 11. (£34) Garage.

HR Avila★★, Calle Avila, 3. Tel: 33 48 08. (£25) Garage nearby.

H. Serit★★, Calle Higueras, 7. Tel: 34 07 00. (£32) No garage, parking nearby – it looks nothing, in fact it has modern air-conditioning, and a friendly family run it.

H. Torres★★, Calle Arcos, 29. Tel: 32 34 00. (£18) Garage next door – some air-conditioning. Old, with patios.

Hs. Gover★, Calle Honsorio, 6. Tel: 33 26 00. (£10) Garage.

Restaurants There are plenty of expensive restaurants, of course, but I would urge you to try the Cocheras, Plaza Cocheras, 3. Tel: 33 32 26. It is almost as if they wanted to keep it to themselves: like some of the best houses in the town, it is tucked away in unpromising surroundings. From the Tourist Office go round the corner and walk up Calle Por Vera until you come to the section of the old Berber Ramparts. Turn left down Calle Chancillería. If it is still daylight, turn right into Calle Cid and look through the grille of the gateway 20 metres up on the left. Everything around is shabby. But through the gate is a beautiful

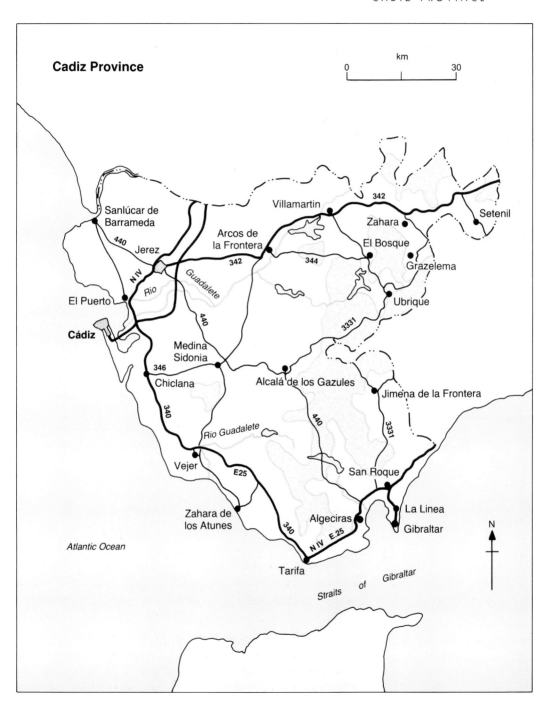

Cadiz Province

km

0   30

Sanlúcar de
Barrameda

Villamartin

342

Zahara

Setenil

440

Jerez

Arcos de
la Frontera

El Bosque

342

344

Grazelema

N IV

Rio

Guadalete

El Puerto

Ubrique

Cádiz

440

3331

Medina
Sidonia

346

Alcalá de los Gazules

Chiclana

Jimena de la Frontera

340

440

3331

Rio Guadalete

Vejer

E25

San Roque

Zahara de
los Atunes

La Linea

Algeciras

N

Gibraltar

Atlantic Ocean

340

N IV E.25

Tarifa

Straits   of   Gibraltar

garden and a splendid house. It is the Moorish legacy of hiding
fine things behind a drab exterior. Now backtrack up Chancilleria
and turn right into Plaza Cocheras. It is the same phenomenon: all
around you, seedy garages but, unannounced, one of the old
coach-houses has been turned into a very good restaurant – and,
incidentally, very reasonably priced. I only ate a light two-course
meal, but a *fino* with a *pincho* (appetizer) of fresh tunny pâté, a
gazpacho, and Pimientos de Piquillo (stuffed with seafood and
served with a rich tomato-based sauce), together with a half bottle
of Rioja and coffee set me back £9.

Otherwise, as usual, I prefer to live on *tapas* and sherry. But, if
your budget is tight, or you want a bit of local colour, there are a
couple of old barn-like places in, or just off, the Calle Medina,
that are quite fun and a revelation for speed of service.

The Sherry Bodegas I have written a brief account of the
Solera system (*see* page 290) because the brochures are a bit too
brief to be clear, and it is rather hard to take it all in while you are
being shown round. The same applies to the nature of the
differences between one sherry and another: a little information in
advance enables you both to appreciate better the differences in
taste, and to ask the right questions. So here I merely give some
suggestions about visiting, and take a look at the Harvest Festival.

You can visit a number of the Bodegas, and if you have your
own favourite brand you will presumably want to see them.
Remember only that several well-known sherries are blended for
shippers who are not producers, while in a couple of instances old
shipping firms have only recently set up as producers: Harvey's
was until very recently a firm of Bristol shippers, buying from the
producers and making their own blends. Both they and Croft's
have now set up their own Bodegas, the Croft one a long way out
on the edge of town.

If you do not mind which one, the Domecq and the González
Byass Bodegas are the biggest, while the Sandeman and the
Williams and Humbert ones are close to the Alameda Cristina. I
do not know the Domecq Bodegas. Avoid González Byass: they
explain nothing and show nothing; you are simply made to traipse
past endless barrels while they tell you how good they are. I
would urge you to choose either Sandeman's or Williams and
Humbert. Their hospitality is genuine and they explain and show

the interesting sherry processes; in short, they tell you about **A sherry bodega in Jerez**
sherry, rather than about themselves.

I would plug Sandeman's because they were especially kind to me, taking considerable care and trouble to check the accuracy of my article on sherry, as well as helping me in other ways. Also, they are next door to both the Riding School and the Palacio de la Atalaya which houses the Clock Museum. Visits are in the morning. Avoid August and September, when holiday, heat or harvest close them to visitors; also the Horse Fair in May when everything gives way to the festivities. Ring them before going.

Do not worry about the language problem: it does not exist in a city where prominent names are Garvey, Harvey, Sandeman, Williams and Humbert (Osborne, Terry, Duff Gordon *et al.* are down the road in Puerto Santa María). As for the Domecqs, they came from France; the great Pedro Domecq lived and worked in London where he married an English girl (and Ruskin tried to marry his daughter); and I doubt whether the current Domecqs would consider any of the three languages as 'foreign'.

Sandeman Coprimar SA, Calle Pizarro, 10. Tel: (956) 30 11 00.
Williams and Humbert Ltd, Calle Nuño de Cañas, 1.
    Tel: 34 59 72.
Pedro Domecq SA, Calle San Ildefonso, 3. Tel: 33 18 00.
González Byass SA, Calle Manuel María González, 12.
    Tel: 34 00 00.
The Tourist Office will give you details on others.

If you can only be in Jerez on a Saturday, all is not lost. By ringing the Clock Museum (Tel: 33 21 00) you can book a visit to the Don Zoilo cellar at the Bodegas Internacionales which is on the corner of Avenida Alvaro Domecq and Calle Paul.

In mid-September the harvest, the *vendimia*, is home, and Jerez celebrates with pomp and ceremony as well as song, dance and bullfights. Each harvest is dedicated to a city such as Copenhagen or Cognac, the grapes are blessed and trod in the presence of mayors and ambassadors, with trumpets, girls in flamenco dresses, doves released and brouhaha. Drinking sherry to the sound of trumpets comes precious close to Sidney Smith's definition of Heaven. There are flamenco *tablaos,* whether at small parties or in the public park before thousands. And, of course, there is eating and drinking. It is a good party at which nobody is a gatecrasher. So if you are around then, go.

Horses in Jerez de la Frontera There is a time and a place. The time is the end of April/early May, immediately after the Seville Feria, when Jerez holds its Horse Fair. In the old days, here as in every Andalusian town, that meant copers and breeders buying and selling. Nowadays it means a colourful festival where horses and riders and sherry and girls in flamenco dresses and singing and dancing and more sherry form an amalgam that is Jerez de la Frontera.

The place, for most of the year, is the palace of the Cadenas. This is a nineteenth-century mansion built for a local banker by Garnier, the architect of the Paris Opéra, and it looks entirely French. The banker went broke and the mansion passed from hand to hand. Then, about twenty years ago, the REAAE (Andalusian School of

Left
Sampling the sherry

Below
Wine harvest festival in Jerez

Sherry vineyards

Equestrian Art) was built in the grounds, and it acquired its Royal warrant in the 1980s. The ensemble of Palace and School is so elegant that you are surprised to learn of the newness of the School.

For four days in the week, between 11 a.m. and 1 p.m., you can watch the daily training session and visit the stables. On Thursday morning at noon you can watch the programme of the horses performing to music. I give more on this in the section on Horses (*see* page 284).

Furthermore, the Real Escuela organizes combined visits that you can book there, or through your travel agent. One of these (for groups only) combines the Thursday performance with a lunch in a sherry Bodega, served in costume of Goya's day, and an evening performance of dancing.

Suggested Walks The Tourist Office in the Alameda Cristina is conveniently at the hub of three differing parts of the town. Most of what I have mentioned so far takes place up in the more elegant and spacious districts; if, from the Tourist Office, you carry on down the Calle Larga, you are in the busy commercial heart of town; if you cut across the Puerta de Sevilla into the Calle Tomería, you enter the older and sleepier districts. You now choose: if architecture is your interest, go straight ahead down Tomería and Plateros; but fork right down to Plaza San Marcos and beyond if you prefer to drift through ancient streets, narrow, dozy, white, and sunbaked, to the gypsy Barrio Santiago, or if you want to take in the Flamenco Foundation and have lunch at the Cocheras.

Whichever you choose, pause first and look around the little square you come to immediately at the start of Tomería. Unostentatious, or sleepily discreet among the others, two of the buildings are elegant town mansions of two or three centuries ago. And sharing the square with them is a hole-in-the-wall dive that foreigners might look at askance. It contains three barrels and a man, and it is what they call a *tabanco*. And it is a mistake to look at it askance: you will see them all over the town; Jerezanos of all sorts drop in for a moment, for a chat, for a *fino* or an *oloroso:* this town not only makes the stuff, it likes it, and still drinks it in a country where beer is utterly dominant.

If you choose architecture, at the bottom of Plateros you come to the church of San Dionisio, an unremarkable Mudéjar building, except for the name. He is Jerez's patron saint, and there could not be a more appropriate one. Just below it in the square is the old Cabildo (literally Chapter House, though we would say Town Hall), which is a Plateresque charmer. From there on down you reach the Cathedral and round to the Alcazaba. The most pertinent critical comment I could make is that they are big... Up from the Alcazaba you come to the Plaza del Arenal, with just behind it the church of *San Miguel*, which is worth a look in a funny sort of way.

It is either a nightmare, or like those women whom the French call *jolies laides:* objectively ugly, but so crammed with personality that they fascinate. It is a fifteenth-century Gothic erection, with the surface of its west portico and tower covered with applied sixteenth-century Plateresque. This central section, then, rises in three storeys of Plateresque, flanked by its Gothic wings, and on top of all that there is a baroque hexagon capped with a stubby spire of *azulejos* (tiles), of yellow, brown and blue. I cannot judge of the interior for the church was closed during my stay.

If quiet old streets and lunch are what you choose, then, using the Tourist Office city plan, get lost in the general direction of Plaza San Lucas. If you happen to be here on a Saturday morning, I would go down Calle Cabezas from the square, and then round the block to the right, for in Calle Liebre is one of the gypsy *peñas*. This is an ordinary down-market bar, but the word means 'club' and it is close to the full sense of the English word 'local'. Sometimes of an evening, more often of a late Saturday morning, somebody playing cards

141

or dominoes may start tapping or humming, and you may with luck and a bit of discretion be in at a complete jam session. And if not in luck, you will have had a cool and refreshing beer or *fino* to break the walk. There are a couple more of these bars in the Calle Cristal Merced. From either, it is not hard to find Calle Oliva, at one end of which is the Palacio Pemartin that houses the Flamenco Foundation. This is a working institution, but you will be welcome to look round, and to see the instructional film, though it will be in Spanish. From just outside the building, the Calle Chancelleria takes you up to the Cocheras restaurant.

A Footnote on Bars I have mentioned the *peñas* and the *tabancos* (which in Seville are called *tascas*), but there is another special sort of bar to be found here, as in any town that has a fraternity organizing the Rocío pilgrimage described in the chapter on Huelva. This is the *rociero* bar. In Jerez it is in the Calle Velázquez, which is in one of the Polígonos or working-class high-rise suburbs. It is actually not so far from the centre as the Jerez Hotel. Go up the Avenida Duque de Abrantes and take the fifth turn on the left past the Cadenas Palace. The locale is nothing – rather dingy concrete and brick like the surroundings. It livens up after 11.30 p.m., and on the stroke of midnight the owner switches out the lights, lights a candle, and leads the customers in singing the Rocío hymn to the Virgin. Every night. And every night, when he has switched on the lights again, he wipes the slate clean and chalks up the number of days remaining until the next pilgrimage – until the day comes to shut the bar and set off on the road to Rocío again.

Museums
Clocks and Walking Sticks, Calle Atalaya. Tel: 33 21 00.
Archaeology, Calle Liebres.

Shopping Buy your sherry during your visit to the Bodegas. Of the usual Andalusian specialities – wicker and esparto wares, and leather goods – it will not surprise you to learn that the speciality here is saddlery. In the unlikely event of you wanting to stock up on tack during your holiday, go to *Guarnicionería Duarte*, Calle Lancería 15.

142

Useful Addresses

Tourist Office: Alameda Cristina, 7. Tel: 33 11 50. Nearly all the Tourist Offices in Andalusia are useful, helpful and usually essential. But this one wins my first prize for enthusiastic helpfulness, closely followed by Seville.

Post Office: Calle Veracruz. Tel: 34 22 95.

Telephone: Plaza Miguel Primo de Rivera.

Police: Plaza de Silos. (Emergency: 091)

Red Cross: Avenida de la Cruz Roja Española. Tel: 34 54 74.

Travel

RENFE Station: Calle Diego Fernández Herrera.

   Office: Calle Tornería, 4. Tel: 34 96 12.

Iberia: Plaza Arenal, 2. Tel: 33 99 08.

Car Rental: Avis, Calle Sevilla, 25. Tel: 34 43 11.

   Hertz, Calle Sevilla, 29. Tel: 34 74 67.

   Europcar, Calle Honda, 18. Tel: 33 48 56.

   Atesa, Hotel Jerez. Tel: 30 60 00.

Bus Station: Calle Cartuja. Tel: 34 52 07.

The Other Sherry Towns These are Sanlúcar de Barrameda, at the mouth of the Guadalquivir a mere 22 kilometres (14ml.) away, and Puerto Santa María (known simply as Puerto) 9 miles down the road to Cádiz. Chiclana, beyond Cádiz on the coast, also produces sherry, though not the best, and I mention it later when dealing with the coastlands.

On the way to Sanlúcar you go through the vineyards. It is a rich experience. The land undulates gently and endlessly beneath a vast sky, the rows of vines stretch to the horizon punctuated only occasionally by a *cortijo* (farmstead) or a *bienteveo* (watchpost), and it ought to be monotonous. But instead, it is somehow elating and luminous, perhaps because of the white soil, whose glare is masked beneath its carpet of green vines; it is as though the vines were floodlit from beneath, and in broad daylight – a strange effect. Perhaps, too, the pleasure you feel comes partly from anticipation, for the Palomino grape has a lovely colour with golden brown tints. I find it worth it to branch off on to side roads and lose myself for a while in all that luminous immensity.

Sanlúcar de Barrameda You go for one reason: *manzanilla*. Jerezanos would never admit any wine in the world could compare with their own, but they will admit without hesitation to the *manzanilla* of Sanlúcar. It is something to be tasted. My own mentor in Sanlúcar reckoned Barbadillo produced good stuff but Argüeso's San León was even better. I would have preferred to make up my own mind, but unfortunately I did not have the leisure – or the wine taster's immediacy of judgement.

The town is two quite distinct places: wine producer and seaside resort. To me it had considerable charm, the slightly sad charm of yesterday's resort – Weymouth say, if you could imagine a Weymouth that lay a short way north of Africa and produced wine. But it must be said that I first went in October when the sun was warm, the air cool and the seafront deserted. So the empty promenade gave it a touch of the autumnal sadness of Lyme Regis in Jane Austen's *Persuasion*. Actually it is not so much sea front as river mouth: just to your right the Guadalquivir, now living up to its name ('great river') meets the cleansing waters of the Atlantic, and on the far bank is the protected, unspoiled brush of the Coto Doñana nature reserve.

The older part of town also has its considerable sleepy charm. The main square, with fountain, palm trees and cafés, is unspoiled. There are one or two mansions that do not want to impose. And the ordinary houses do not try to upstage their neighbours: they are low with a touch of eighteenth-century elegance to their doorways and windows. It is a good-mannered town in an understated way, and seems a friendly one. There were English merchants living here before Queen Elizabeth I came to the throne, and Irish ones at least as long ago and during subsequent periods.

Unless you have friends or business there, I do not think you will want to stay, but if you do, then the *H. Guadalquivir*★★★ (£33) has 150 rooms and is on the main avenue perpendicular to the front, but it can be noisy.

Try eating at the *Bigote* on Calle Bajo de Guía, down near the shore where the fish and seafood pass from sea to your plate with little interval.

If you want to visit a Bodega here, ring Antonio Barbadillo SA on (956) 36 08 94. Address: Calle Luis de Eguilaz, 11.

Puerto de Santa María This is a pleasant, alive, bustling little place. It is a combination of fishing port, resort, sherry port and sherry and brandy producer. The major firms of Terry, Duff

Gordon and Osborne are based here. I know little about Osborne, except that their advertising hoardings, the massive black silhouette of a fighting bull, are the only ones I know of in any country that actually enhance the landscape.

As in Cádiz, the streets are a tight grid, and not to be attempted by car. There is an important bullring, and a Mudéjar castle. I have been recommended the restaurant *La Goleta* on the road to Rota, but it seemed a waste to me to eat anywhere else than the little *cocederos* where you buy your seafood as straight from the Atlantic as in Sanlúcar, and eat it at a nearby bar.

There is a new resort, built from scratch, complete with marina and beaches and all, next door to Puerto and called Puerto Sherry.

The Serrania de Ronda and the White Towns
(i) East–West Together with the three cities (Seville, Córdoba, Granada), the four mountain masses are to my taste the best things in Andalusia. And these mountains of the Serranía have at least as much pull as the others. I do not know why the towns and villages in them are known as the *Pueblos Blancos* since villages throughout Andalusia are white. But these ones are especially attractive. For purposes of describing them, as well as seeing them, it helps if you consider them as forming a rough 'T': the two astonishing towns of Arcos de la Frontera and Ronda stand on their heights at either end of the cross-bar, and the mountain scenery as well as the towns lying between them vary from pretty to spectacular. I do not think it makes much difference whether you tackle them from Arcos in the west or Ronda in the east. The north–south axis, or upright to the 'T', is best explored by coming up from the south.

Arcos de la Frontera Except for the gorge and bridge at Ronda, Arcos is at least as spectacular. Both rise sheer on their eminences, but Arcos sticks up out of a low plain, and stands alone towering above you as you approach, from south or east. (I have to add that approached from north or west, you do not see this – in either place.) Nor is it like Ronda in being divided into the tiny alleyways of the old Moorish town and the more navigable streets of the Christian part: Arcos is all tiny alleyways. Surrounded on three sides by a loop in the River Guadalete, it stands on a narrow wedge of rock, like one of those wedge-heeled sandals, with the square – and the Parador – over the sheer

The 'white town' of Ubrique in the Serrania de Ronda

145

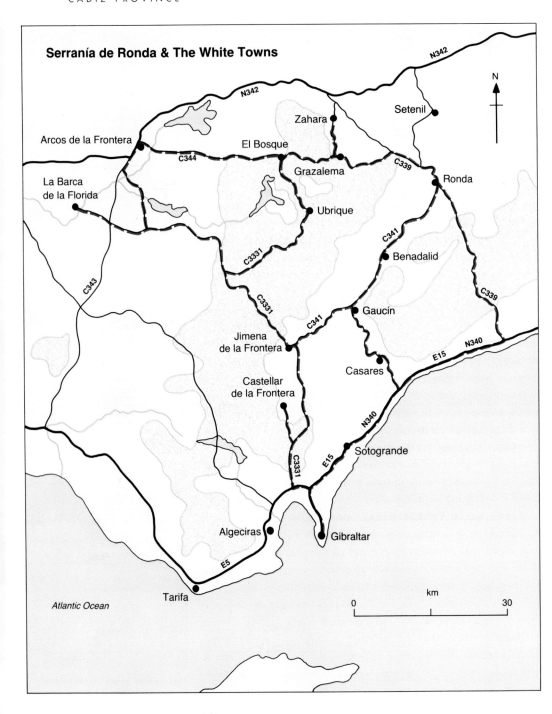

Serranía de Ronda & The White Towns

heel. As you come to it from the toe, it starts as an ordinary mess. Then as you follow the street that runs straight up the centre, the buildings get older and older, and the streets close in on you. It is a splendid place to spend the night.

The only shame is that the square – as attractive as any in Andalusia – is choked with cars, and ruined by them. There is talk of digging a massive underground car park into the rock beneath the town; there is also a strong local legend that there is a lot of water in the rock. They might end up with a car aquarium.

Hotels and Restaurants

Parador N. Casa del Corregidor★★★, Plaza de España. Tel: (956) 70 05 00. (£55) – a fine new hotel, on the edge of the precipice, with many rooms having panoramic balconies.

H. El Convento★, Calle Maldonado, 2. Tel: 70 23 33. (£30) – pay no attention to that single ★. If the Parador were full I would be no less happy to stay here, and in some ways prefer it. There are only 6 rooms; the hotel has the same look-out as the Parador; and the restaurant is the main part of it. I have not eaten there but friends tell me it is one to come back to. You can eat outside on a private, quiet and shaded terrace. This is one of those places one is reluctant to recommend in case too many people get to know of it.

H. Marqués de Torresoto, Calle Marqués de Torresoto, 4. Tel: 70 05 17. (£35 including breakfast) – this one is due to open in 1991. It is a restored seventeenth-century mansion, which therefore has its own fine and private patio, and it looks as though it might be good, though of course I cannot guarantee this. I name it because so far it is in no Tourist Office books, and thus unknown. The owner seems a pleasant man.

Los Murales, Plazuela Boticarios. It is not as good a restaurant as the Convento just round the corner, but not at all bad: I was recommended it by the owners of the Convento because the proprietor, Pepe, is not only an Arcosano but an enthusiast for his town, so that if you can muster a bit of Spanish he is very willing to tell you things about the place.

East from Arcos

El Bosque To see the best of the towns and the mountains you should avoid the main road and head east on the C344 to El Bosque. This is a quiet and attractive village at the foot of the

mountains of the Grazalema Nature Reserve. It has a hotel, the *Truchas*★★, of near-Parador quality and technically known as a provincial Parador (Tel: 72 30 86. £23). There is also an information centre where you can see some of the local flora and fauna on video, which is, alas, the only place I have seen the Cabra Montés, or Spanish Izard. The Golden Eagles, kites and vultures, you may by now be blasé about. If not, you will see them in the Nature Reserve. For botanists, the unique feature is the presence of the Pinsapo, a unique survival from before the last Ice Age.

If by any chance you are doing this holiday on bicycle, cover this Arcos–Ronda stretch from the Ronda direction, for by going eastwards you now have a steady 19-kilometre (12ml.) climb of 760 metres (2,500ft). This takes you through (or rather up) the rainiest area in the whole of Spain, not excepting Atlantic Galicia. This is because you are climbing the west-facing slope of the first mountains the ocean winds hit since... the Andes, I suppose. I did it in rainless October and found the greenery, not just of cork and holm oak but of English-type oak as well, a pleasant change from the tawny colouring of the baked plains. When you get to the top of the Boyar pass 1,030m (3,400ft) a magnificent view opens before you.

But whether coming from west or east, once above Grazalema on the Boyar pass don't leave out the road to Zahara, even if you decide not to go there: it is only a short drive to the top of Palomas pass which at 1,310m (4,300ft), gives you an almost sheer drop of 450m (1,500ft) to the valley, as well as magnificent views all the way up. I would take a picnic, bought in Grazalema, get the car off the road (which you can do just over the top of the pass) and walk a bit. Then watch scenery and, with no more than reasonable luck, eagles will wheel beneath you while you munch. I had been touring mountain roads for two months and had seen umpteen dozen white villages stuck to the slopes, but this road between Grazalema and Palomas took my breath away. The eye's plunge down to the valley below, past the 300m (1,000ft) rock face and away to a misty horizon of hills, is something likely to stay with you long after the holiday is over.

Grazalema was in Richard Ford's day a nest of cut-throats. Things have changed. Seen from the east, by which I mean

**Opposite
Palomas Pass in the Serranía
de Ronda ...**

Grazalema

coming to it from below, I consider it as good a sight as any of the *Pueblos Blancos*. The mountain behind it, a pyramid, almost a pinnacle of rock, rivals the eagle-winged crags behind Tiscar in the Sierra de Cazorla. It gets plenty of visitors, mostly Spanish, and is well geared for them. And yet I find it utterly unspoiled and charming.

You can find the ingredients for your picnic there, or eat there in several places, none of which I would suspect of being tourist rip-offs, but rather of a decent service by villagers to whom modern tourism is bringing prosperity. Grazalema specializes traditionally in making blankets, ponchos and capes in rag-wool. There is even a tourist information girl in the town hall, though I take this on trust: the only other person in the building told me that Amalia had been delayed a moment and was just finishing her breakfast, so if I waited just two minutes...? It was 10 a.m. and I am too familiar with the Spanish desire to keep everyone happy to trust those two minutes, so I went off and explored the village. And, indeed, when I left an hour later Amalia was still at her breakfast. Photographically, the village and mountain are best seen in the morning.

150

Like Bosque, Grazalema has a hotel of near-Parador standard although it is marked in the book as a humble affair. Even more surprising, and rare for hotels that hold you captive for food as well, the cooking is good. They cater mostly for Spaniards wanting a holiday in the hills, so it may be booked up well ahead in the hot months. *HS. Grazalema*★★, Tel: (956) 14 11 62. (£23).

The Romans were here, all around this mountain area, which for some reason surprises me. I mention it here but it applies to most of these perched towns.

Zahara de las Sierras is often and warmly recommended, but I refrain, because you will have seen it from the mountain top at the pass and can judge for yourself.

East of Grazalema the next major place to see is *Ronda*, in the Province of Málaga and which I describe in that chapter (*see* page 161).

Before moving on to the upright of the 'T', in case you do not intend doing that route, it should be said that this east–west run can easily be made to include other pueblos no less deserving of a visit than Grazalema. Not far from the latter village, the C3331 branches south and takes you to *Villaluenga de Rosario, Benaocaz*, and the town of *Ubrique*. I describe the latter on the north–south route.

The Serranía and the White Towns (ii) South–North The journey through the Serranía from south to north, which I have described as the upright of a' T', is in fact more a 'Y'. I enjoy it as much, but for different reasons. The road (the C3331) starts from at or near San Roque, at the centre of the bay, between Gibraltar and Algeciras. Gibraltar never had a Kipling. This is a pity, for generations of British Officers (and, no doubt, Gentlemen) used to ride up to Ronda, to see its marvels and enjoy the cool mountain air.

Time and again in Andalusia I have had occasion to remark on the presence (I am tempted to write 'Presence', with all the capital implies) of the past. One cannot talk of 'ghosts' because the word has the wrong connotations: there is nothing spooky about it. But in Spain, much more strongly than in Britain or France, and in Andalusia more than anywhere else in Spain, the reality of what has happened gives a sheen to the appearance of things. You can stand in the ruins of Italica and feel intensely aware that here, on this pavement, looking at this statue, sitting in this amphitheatre, Hadrian, he who delayed the arrival of Scottish dancing in England, spent his childhood, got keen on his first girlfriend. He was here, but has gone now. You can stand in the Alcazaba at Málaga and feel the same about the Moors; in Córdoba, and feel the Sephardim were here but have gone now; in Víznar, and be intensely aware that Federico Garcia Lorca and others were here. Just the same, the road from Gibraltar to Ronda is enriched, given a sheen, by those great-grandfathers of ours riding up it on furlough, putting up at the inn at Gaucín, laughing with, or swearing at, the innkeeper. All these people, they only left a short while ago – a week, a century, a millenium, what difference does it make? – They are still close. They left behind this suitcase, this doorway, this city, this custom, these features. I am confident that this is no airy-fairy piece of sentimental imagining on my part, since the same phenomenon was remarked and powerfully expressed by Lorca in a ballad about a murderous squabble between gypsies over a card game: The Magistrate comes up the gully with a couple of policemen to inspect the scene and says to them, 'Gentlemen, it's the usual business: five Carthaginians, and four Romans dead.'

From Estación San Roque, the first few miles provide another of those strange contrasts so frequent in Andalusia: It is more like a landscape six or eight hundred miles north. Green verges with grass bramble and convolvulus, gently rounded hills with cattle grazing, it might be the Wiltshire downs during a summer drought. After six miles you come to *Almoraima*, where there is a large and well-wooded hunting estate. Here you can take a left fork and wind up the mountainside to see the picturesque town of Castellar de la Frontera.

If you carry straight on, the valley narrows and there is Jimena de la Frontera, another of those purely Andalusian towns, white and clinging to the hillside with its Castle above. If you want to visit the Romano-Moorish Castle without climbing right up through the town, or attempting to drive up its narrow winding streets, you can quite simply drive on past the town and take the Ubrique road. From there, a turn-off to your left, with a good surface, takes you straight back to the Castle gates. The castle occupies the whole hilltop and must have been important. Clearly the gates and ramparts are Moorish, and so I think is at least one of the three cisterns. Any Roman parts must be either the foundations, or just possibly the round tower at the south end, but I have not been able to ascertain.

For me, the special memory is that a pair of Golden Eagles, nesting in the tower, were circling close over it, a few yards away from me, and then swooping out across the valley that plunges sheer below the west side.

For some reason, Jimena seems in a discreet way to have picked up a British colony. Seven or eight English people have opted to make it their home – a couple of them in the cemetery – and a young Anglo-American couple have turned several of the small steep houses into a hotel, rambling, comfortable and attractive. This is *Hostal El Anon* (props: Garth and Susie Odell). 14 rooms (£20 inc. breakfast), roof-top pool, restaurant. Calle Consuelo 34–40. Tel: (956) 64 01 13. Waymark, who organize walking tours, use them and I can quite see why.

If you are passing through and turn up without booking to find the Inn full, do not despair: at Estación de Jimena, 2km short of town, is the humble and even dubious-looking *Hostal Arcos*★ with a double room at about £10. Inside, once you have gone through the café, it is spanking new, spotless, with private bath and loo for every room.

North from Jimena You have to choose. You fork north–west if you are heading for Seville, or if you want to buy presents of leather-work, which means going to Ubrique; you fork north–east if you are following your ancestors to Ronda.

The north–west road continues to have fine views, always greener in this bit of Andalusia than anywhere else since you are on the rain slopes that pick up the Atlantic southwesters. After 30km (18ml.) you turn right at the Galis pass (a lonely Restaurant on the corner) and continue climbing to a left turn above Ubrique. You are now 490m (1,600ft) up, the woods are thinning, and *Ubrique* is in sight.

Apart from its splendid siting under a massive cliff, Ubrique is a place to buy your presents: anything in leather from coats to wallets. The shops sell cheaper here than elsewhere, but the workshops sell cheaper still. Look around: there is a lot of difference in the type of market the different workshops cater for, and the quality workshops offer some very good things at bargain prices.

Do not plan to spend the night in Ubrique unless you cannot help it. It has a hotel, but the fact that they refused to let me see any rooms was unpromising.

From here you can choose to do the circuit Villaluenga del Rosario–Grazalema–Bosque; or the same clockwise; or make for Arcos or Ronda.

North–east from Jimena, is the old Gibraltar–Ronda road. It is picturesque in itself, and the villages of Gaucín, Benadalid and others are as good as any of the other *Pueblos Blancos*.

The Coastlands:

Cádiz to Gibraltar I would recommend this for those who would like to combine a dose of sun, sea and sand with touring a relatively non-touristy and off-the-track bit of the country. The beaches are very good. The reason they have not gone the way of their inferior counterparts round the corner on the Costa del Sol, is that this is the Atlantic. There are real waves to go with the white sands and cleansing tides and unpolluted water. And to go with the waves, there is the wind that creates them. The further you go north–west, up towards Huelva province and into it, the less the wind is a factor. But as Africa and Spain converge, until at Tarifa they are less than 14km (9ml.) apart, the more they funnel the prevalent westerlies, so that Tarifa has become a mecca for wind-surfers, not for sun-bathers.

Chiclana is for those who want to meet and, above all, hear Spain, rather than just see it. Like the more élitist Jerez, it produces sherry, it is proud of its gypsies, it is one of the high places for flamenco, and it is a keen *rociero* place.

There are two three-star hotels but, more to the point, there are three *rociero* club bars, and you are more likely here than anywhere I know of, to hear spontaneous flamenco sung with no hint of an idea of 'performance'.

Hotels

H. Ideal★★★, Plaza Andalucía, 1. Tel: 40 39 06. (£40).

H. Fuentemar★★★, Carretera de Fuente Amarga (i.e. Fuente Amarga road out of town). Tel: 40 01 11. (£16).

HsR Villa★★, Calle Virgen del Carmen, 14. Tel: 40 05 12. (£12).

Peñas

Mesón Rociero El Camino, Carretera de Medina, opposite the
    Hotel Ideal. Shut Wednesdays. Go as in Jerez for midnight
    singing of the hymn.

La Peña del Caballo. Shut Tuesdays.

El Cerro del Trigo (in the town).

Conil Conil has 2 beaches and at least one Hostal★★. From
Conil you might want to take the small coastal road to El Palmar,
Zahora and los Caños de Merca (where there is a camp ground
and beach) simply to be able to tell yourself you have driven
round Cape Trafalgar. It is a sandstone bluff and its name means
'the Cape of the Cave'.

Vejer de la Frontera This hill town is the most
attractive, as well as picturesque, of any on this stretch. It has all
the features: white walls, browny-red roofs, narrow cobbled
streets, Moorish Castle, panoramic views out over fertile lands
and bull-breeding pastures, and an ability to celebrate feast days,
notable even for Andalusia. They set a bull loose in the streets
on Easter Sunday, and a whole string of them during their April
Fair. They do midsummer proud with their bonfire and
fireworks; and they celebrate the Virgin for nine days (and
mostly nights) in mid-August. That is, apart from all the other
celebrations you would expect of Easter, Corpus Christi, and so
forth.

Hotels

H. Hospedería del Convento de San Francisco★★★, La Plazuela. Tel:
    45 10 01. (£40).

P. La Janda, Cerro Clarinas. Tel: 45 01 42. (£15). Pleasant and
    comfortable.

Zahara de los Atunes The small village bearing this
delightful name (it means 'the Flower where the Tuna Fish
come'), is 10km (6ml.) off the main road, with a gorgeous beach
about 10km long. But do not expect anywhere to be
undiscovered: the whole coast, including this place, is being
adopted by Germans. The massive Hotel Atlanterra ends the
beach. If you do not want to use it, it need not get in your way,
but beyond it is an architected corniche with architected villas
and, yes, architected shrubbery – with another small but lovely
beach beyond. Beyond that you walk and it is rocks.

Zahara de los Atunes

Zahara may not be the backwater I had hoped to discover, but that is a relative matter: four hotels for six miles of fine beach does not make it another Torremolinos yet. And I feel hopeful of the fact that so far it cannot spread inland while it is fenced for cattle-rearing. The owners of large estates are not always willing to sell to the developers; and, with luck, those long, sharp horns on the heads of the cattle should keep people out. I was also curiously comforted by seeing so many vultures wheeling overhead: they seemed, somehow, a sort of guarantee against ice-cream and developers.

Hotels

H. Atlanterrra★★★★, Tel: 43 26 08. (£105).

H. Antonio, down on the beach near the Atlanterra, is really a restaurant (a pleasant one, too) that has eight rooms.
Tel: 43 12 14. (£20) – a good place.

H. Gran Sol, £30 (£23 from 15 October to 31 March).

Bolonia (or Baela, or Bella) Bolonia is the next beach, and still relatively inaccessible. It too, has a superb beach, perhaps a mile long, but the purpose in coming here is the Roman ruins – for the knowledgeable only, I would say. It was clearly much

156

Tarifa

more than a villa. Could it have been a sea-side resort, complete with temple? I am no expert: to me it was just a heap of stones.

Tarifa The town is the southernmost point of Europe, and one of the most African looking of all. For hundreds of years it was a backwater, falling deeper and deeper asleep, until wind-surfing brought it prosperity. The beach is maybe 8km (5ml.) long, and they claim it is one of the three best wind-surfing places in the world, as the Atlantic winds funnel steadily into the straits of Gibraltar.

There is a nice legend about Tarifa, as well known to Spanish schoolchildren as King Charles in his oak to their English counterparts. In 1292, Tarifa was held against the Moors by Alonso Pérez de Guzmán. The king's renegade brother John, to whom Guzmán had entrusted his son as a page, turned up among the besiegers and told Guzmán his boy would be killed if he did not surrender. Guzmán threw him down his own knife. It is not entirely legend: Guzmán was given the name el Bueno, and the family became Dukes of Medina Sidonia, which means it was his descendant who led the Armada against Britain.

If you would like to do some wind-surfing but did not bring the equipment, you can hire it, but better still, in late August, or September, you can often buy it very cheaply: the French surfers come down in droves for their summer holiday, at the end of which many of them sell their boards off cheap to avoid the transport – they intend to buy next year's model anyway. You can achieve the saving in transport, in reverse.

There is a Hydrofoil to Tangier every other day, alternating with Algeciras.

After Tarifa, the hills come to meet the sea, you climb over these foothills with frequent good views of Africa, and a fair number of hotels on the road.

Algeciras is like a southern version of Cardiff: would you recommend that to tourists? Though, even here, you are struck by how much is new – with that Spanish sort of newness that gives you the impression, even ten years later, that the builders forgot to remove the rubble. In fact, the town expanded a lot as the result of Spain blockading Gibraltar in 1969.

There are car ferries to Tangier, Ceuta and Melilla, and one well-known hotel: *H. Reina Cristina*★★★★, Pto de la Conferencia. Tel: 60 26 22. (£60) – it is in some measure a sister-ship to the Reina Victoria in Ronda: both still good, but above all redolent of former days of fame and exclusivity.

Gibraltar As a left-over of Empire, Gibraltar is clearly an anomaly that shares the same endlessly tricky problems with the Falklands and Northern Ireland, to wit that while it is clearly a part of Spain not Britain, 99.6 per cent of its inhabitants want to stay British. As one Gibraltarian put it to me, 'There we are, and we don't know what we are: on the one hand Britain and on the other hand Spain... caught in the middle'. Unlike the other such political problems, Gibraltar's will never be a bloody one. We owe this to the Spanish government's determination to stay friends and allies with Britain, quite apart from the increasing interdependence of the two as members of the Community. As for local opinion, Gibraltar provides the major source of employment, and working people had a hard time during the blockade. They have no jingoist feelings at all.

As you might expect, Gibraltar is a mixture: the climate is Andalusian; the old houses are colonial; the population is a mixture from several sources; and everything else is like a hunk of Portsmouth dropped there. English-style bobbies direct traffic... that drives on the right.

Space is at an absolute premium; nowadays people working in Gib. tend to live in Spain – at Sotogrande for instance. So visit it, but do not go to stay there. Reasons for a visit are the Rock itself; the caves and tunnels that honeycomb it; the barbary apes; a boat trip guaranteeing to take you among dolphins; and a taste of military history.

The Rock is some 335m (1,100ft) high, so the view of both Spain and Africa from the top is good. A cable car runs up every ten minutes. The caves are natural: one at least was inhabited 40,000 years ago. The tunnels (some 30 miles of them) are for the Rock's water supply, and above all for military purposes. They were dug principally during a three-year siege in 1779–83 (when Lieut. Shrapnel had his bright idea), and in the last 50 years, when bomb-proof radar seemed helpful. You cannot visit the tunnels.

But otherwise I found it served mainly to renew my appreciation of Spain. Here is the insularity that imports cotton-wool rolls, puts in plastic cheddar or water-injected ham, and serves it with powdered coffee and long-life milk, all especially imported from good old GB – I tried it for the experience, but stopped at the first bar back in La Linea and had a *cortado* made of real coffee with real milk, and a *tapa* of serrano ham for good measure and half the price.

Málaga and its Province Dividing Andalusia up by its Provinces is one way of parcelling things out. But in the case of Málaga and its neighbour Cádiz, the administrative boundaries make a bit of a nonsense of the natural (and touristic) areas. Besides the Costa del Sol, the two provinces share the series of mountains that constitute their main attraction and which I deal with, under the name Serranía de Ronda, in the Cádiz chapter.

But I shall deal with Ronda itself in this section and, of course, you may choose to see it and ignore the rest. After all, Richard Ford did say of it that 'it alone is worth the voyage out... and back again'. But then he also dismissed nearby Grazalema as a 'cut-throat den', which I can guarantee is no longer true – and a phrase more applicable today to the city of Málaga itself. If you go to Ronda, it would be a pity not to make it part of a visit to at least some of the 'white towns' and their exciting mountain settings.

The commonest access to Ronda, as well as the mountains and white towns beyond, is via the road up from the coast at San Pedro de Alcántara. But they can also be approached from the north-west (Seville or Jerez), or from the east (Antequera), both of which routes are scenic; and from the south, one of the most attractive and less followed routes, by coming up from Gibraltar or Algeciras. Again, I describe these in the Cádiz section, but mention them here because you may well be exploring the area from the Costa del Sol in Málaga province.

A street in Ronda

Opposite
Ronda – a view from the gorge

The Costa del Sol and its resorts are only described in a few words, since the purpose of this book is to help readers explore *Spanish* Andalusia. The difference between the two is growing less as prosperity increases. But it is still radical, even now that thirty years have passed since the pyschiatric ward of Málaga hospital became known as 'waiters' ward' from the number of local lads going down to the coast to find work, and finding the culture shock too great.

There are good things to be found, too, in the northern part of the province: Antequera; the Torcal; and the mountains west of there, including the Chorro and Bobastro.

Málaga itself is not a tourist place, It is a booming, thrusting city of more than half a million inhabitants, with a crime rate comparable to Seville's, but none of Seville's charm or elegance or gaiety or attractions. It has one of the busiest airports in Spain. It services the tourism of the Costal del Sol; and it is a port that trades people and goods with Morocco, the Canary Islands, and beyond. It has the largest, most confusing and ugliest suburban surround in Andalusia, which is saying a lot. It also has the craziest traffic system of any I have ever seen in any country. What it does not have is anything to attract the visitor, other than its Alcazaba.

History The Town Hall bears an inscription reading:

> The most noble, most loyal, ever valiant, first when liberty is endangered, most hospitable and charitable city of Málaga was in its origin an Iberian settlement, then successively Phoenician trading post, Carthaginian merchant centre, city to which Domitian granted its own Laws, and then Visigothic and Byzantine, and an Islamic port under Moslem domination, between the Mediterranean and the Atlantic, between Europe and Africa. The Catholic Monarchs conquered it in August 1487 and, by their decree of 27 May 1489, established its City Council, which celebrated its first Council Meeting on 26 June of the same year.

Together with Algeciras and Almería, it formed a part of the last Moorish kingdom of Granada. With its loss, Granada was cut off from Africa, and fell less than five years later. It shared the decline that followed the end of that rich civilization. There was a genteel revival in the last century that left us the Paseo del Parque,

162

Alcazaba, Málaga

and then, when Spain's economic plight persuaded Franco to let tourists in, came the massive boom of the last thirty years.

Access There is one easy way to visit the city: the railway (from the Airport, Torremolinos, and points west) has a little extension station, beyond the main one. It delivers you to the corner of Calle Comandante Benitez, by the western end of the Alameda. From here, a pleasant stroll down the tree-lined avenue takes you to the Paseo del Parque, from where you can visit the Alcazaba. Thus an hour or so will give you the best of the city.

If, however, you must come by car, here are some tips. Everything is changing so fast that much of what follows may be untrue by the time this appears, but I give it just in case. From the east, access is easy. There is one road in, and you simply join the queue and snarl with the rest. From the west, it is a drivers' Venus' Fly-trap: easy to enter; once in, you are stuck.

From the north, the main thing is to push gamely on and hope to hit Málaga's main east-west axis. This is called at its west end Avenida de Andelucía, then (over the bridge) the Alameda, then at its eastern end, the Paseo del Parque. Of this lot, the Andalucía

163

(known to locals as the Prolongación, which makes sense), is two way. The other two parts are, too, but in a lunatic fashion: the Alameda is west-bound on one lane only, and east-bound in all others; The Paseo is west-bound only, *except for taxis*; almost all other streets are one-way. *And no plan of them exists.* The Town Hall Traffic Office denies this scornfully, and tells you the plan is, naturally, kept at Municipal Police Headquarters, who are equally scornful of such an idea, and refer you, of course, to the Town Hall Traffic Office. The Tourist Office shrugs.

By 1991 they hope to have finished changes to the Plaza de la Marina, right at the centre, and I suspect this will modify the one-way lay-out of Parque. By 1992 they hope to have turned the course of the River Guadalmedina into something more appetizing, and at the same time, widened the riverside roads. And by then, too, the Granada arc of the by-pass should be ready. This could well make it possible for the stranger to find his way in and out of the city.

Until then, my advice is, for all points except Almería, head west out of the city, and then try to work north for Córdoba and Granada. And do not worry if you see a Granada sign too late: they go on occurring for 4 or 5km.

Hotels I do not want to bully you, but go the the Parador: *Parador de Gibralfaro*★★★, (postal address: Apartado de Correos, 274). Tel: (952) 22 19 02 (£45) – it has only about 12 rooms. It is up on the Gibralfaro (an old castle; the name means 'Lightouse Hill') in the clean air above the city; from the terrace, you not only look out over the city and whole coast, you look down into the bullring, which gives new force to the phrase 'grandstand view', if you happen to have binoculars. To get there, take Paseo del Parque eastwards, go straight on past the bull-ring, and at the third traffic light turn left. Thereafter it is clearly signed..

You can also get there up Calle Victoria and turn right at the Plaza Victoria, but... can you find the way into Calle Victoria? Actually, attempting it is quite a good sport, like Russian roulette or driving round the Etoile at rush hour. Otherwise, probably your best bets are:

H. Las Vegas★★★, Paseo de Sancha, 22. Tel: 21 77 12. (£30).

HR California★★, Paseo de Sancha, 19. Tel: 21 51 65 (£22). These are on the eastern side of town, near the beach.

If you are stuck in the area of the Alameda, there is nothing appetizing to be found: Seaports are not the best places for cheap hotels.

HsR Del Sur★★★, Calle Trinidad Grund, 13. Tel: 22 48 03. (£20) – is very central.

HsR Venecia★★★. Alameda Principal, 9. Tel: 21 36 36. (£20) – I hesitate to mention, because the owner is surly and his helper half-witted. But it is on Alameda itself and very easy to find. So it answers the need for a cheap place, quick and easy to find.

Restaurants I have not found anything special, but the Antonio Martin (Paseo Marítimo, Tel: 22 21 13) is as good as any. There are some popular ones near there, along the shoreside road.

Exploring the City The Paseo del Parque, although gobbled up by traffic, is fun. With its palm trees and kiosks and promenades it makes the heart of Málaga look pleasantly *fin de siècle*, like some raddled old lady who lived it up in the social whirl when young, and now lives on memories of former elegance.

The Cathedral I would miss. It was started in the sixteenth century, much was done in the late eighteenth and nineteenth centuries, and I find it as lifeless as a neo-Georgian museum and colourless as its stone.

The Alcazaba The Alcazaba (Moorish Castle) is well worth seeing. It has preserved enough of its fortifications and palace to get a grip on your imagination. Here, as in so many parts of Andalusia, the long-distant past seems to hang about the present and peer over the shoulder of today. The half-ruined Roman Theatre at its base does not bring the past back so vividly as the sight of bits of Roman material incorporated into Arabic brickwork. Neither the invading Arabs nor the Berbers had an architecture of their own when they arrived in 711. (The so-called Moorish or horseshoe arch seems to have come from the Visigoths). But they found a lot of sophisticated Roman stuff and were quick to take both materials and ideas from them.

You climb gently up through the fortified parts, passing now a piece of marble set in the wall or pavement, with its Latin inscription still showing, now a satyr's head used in a fountain. The pleasure at this stage lies in the variety of tiny gardens you come across on your way up. The place was left in ruins after the reconquest and has been heavily restored to its present state, so I

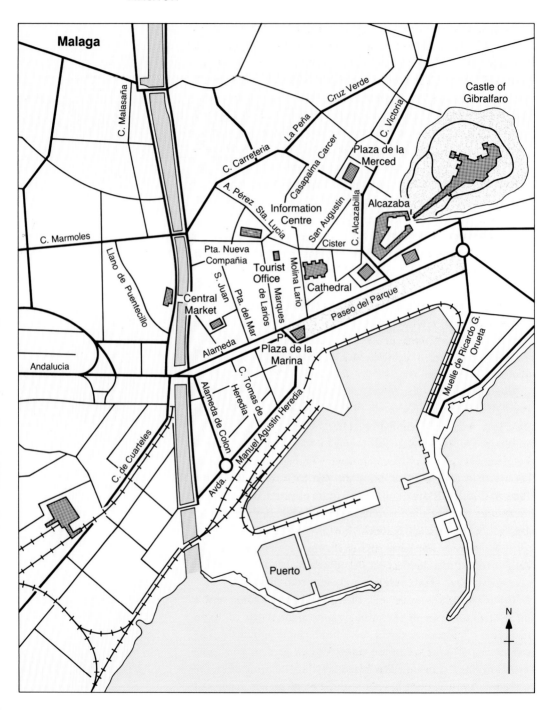

cannot tell to what extent these gardens existed in Moorish times. But it must have been something like this: water, flowers, greenery, all delight to people from a hot dry land. As at the Alhambra, it is brought home strongly to you that the Moorish Potentate, unlike his Christian supplanters, never sought grandeur: he sought pleasure, surprise, delight. At the top you come to the old Alcázar, which now houses the Archaeological Museum. If this is your first Moorish palace you will be duly astonished at how small, how intimate it is. All this is yours for twenty pesetas. It is open at the usual times; mornings only on Sundays; shut Mondays.

The main shopping area lies between the Calle Marqués de Larios, and the Plaza de la Merced.

Museums

Museo de Bellas Artes, Plaza de San Agustín, 6. Tel: 21 83 82. (Cano, Murillo, Ribera; a few very early Picassos — he was born here, left at 14, and never came back.)

Archaeological Museum, in the Alcazaba.

Useful Addresses

UK Consulate: Calle Duquesa de Parcent, 8. Tel: 21 75 71.

Canadian Consulate: Plaza de la Malagueta. Tel: 22 33 46.

Tourist Office: Calle Marqués de Larios, 5. Tel: (952) 21 34 45;
      also at Airport. Tel: 31 20 44.

Post Office: Avenida de Andalucia. Tel: 35 90 08.

Telephone: Calle Molina Larios, and kiosks.

Red Cross: Tel: 25 04 50.

Police: The Comisaria is in the Aduana building (beside the Paseo del Parque), and there is another in the Alameda de Colón.

Emergencies: Tel: 091.

Travel

RENFE: Station: Calle Cuarteles.
             Office: Calle Strachan. Tel: 21 41 27.

Air Iberia: Calle Molina Larios. Tel: 22 78 00.
      Reservations: Tel: 21 37 31.

Buses: Airport buses leave from Iberia, Calle Molina Larios. For other destinations there are various stations and companies. Ask at the Tourist Office.

Car Rental: This is better done at the Airport, but:
      Avis, Calle Cortina del Muelle, Tel: 21 66 27.
      Hertz, Alameda de Colón, 17. Tel: 22 55 97.

Ship: Transmediterranea Office: Calle Juan Diaz, 4. Tel: 22 43 91. There are daily crossings to Melilla, the Spanish enclave in Africa.

Málaga Province The province of Málaga has some splendid mountain scenery, but of its towns only Ronda is a must.

Ronda The road up from the coast is wide, with a good camber, and perfectly engineered gradient. You climb up and up and up until you refuse to believe there could be a town ahead of you. Then you emerge into a vast cup in the hills that looks and feels like a plain, only with crisper air, Shangri-La perhaps, enclosed by a low-looking lip of mountains, and there is Ronda, perched 120m (400ft) up on top of a cliff that is split in two by the **Tajo**, a stupendous gorge.

Ronda should be one of the priorities of any visit to Andalusia, and only partly because of the gorge that cuts through the centre of the town. The coachloads come piling up from the Costa for a quick gawp at the gorge, another at the bullring, and down to the coast again. That is a pity, for Ronda deserves a more leisurely acquaintance. A stroll in the evening, after the coaches have left, can bring back the flavour of this place in a breath-taking way. And the ghosts are friendly, despite the episodes of violence that have spattered such a desirable fortress, from the time when the Romans took it off the Celts through to the more recent violence of the French destroying its Alcazaba and the scarred hatreds of half a century ago.

Like so much in this land, it has a long pedigree: the horse-shoe-shaped southern part of the town, known as the Ciudad, was occupied in turn by the Celts, Romans, Visigoths, and Moors. Then, after the reconquest, the town expanded over the second, slightly gentler part of the hill, called the Mercadillo. In the seventeenth-century it stopped being a refuge and began to show elegance. Indeed, once the British had taken over Gibraltar in the eighteenth century, the reputation of Ronda soon spread and it became the thing for officers then, and throughout the nineteenth century, to ride up here on leave; or bring their families up to the cool of the hills – a Spanish Simla. By the start of this century, when the Reina Victoria hotel was built, Ronda was a place to come to from all over Europe, and the hotel's guest list carries some notable names. Rainer Maria

Malaga Province

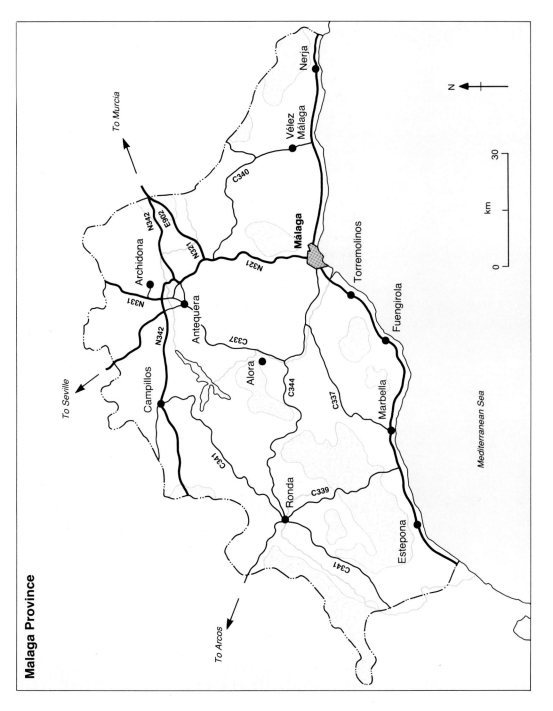

Ronda – the Tajo

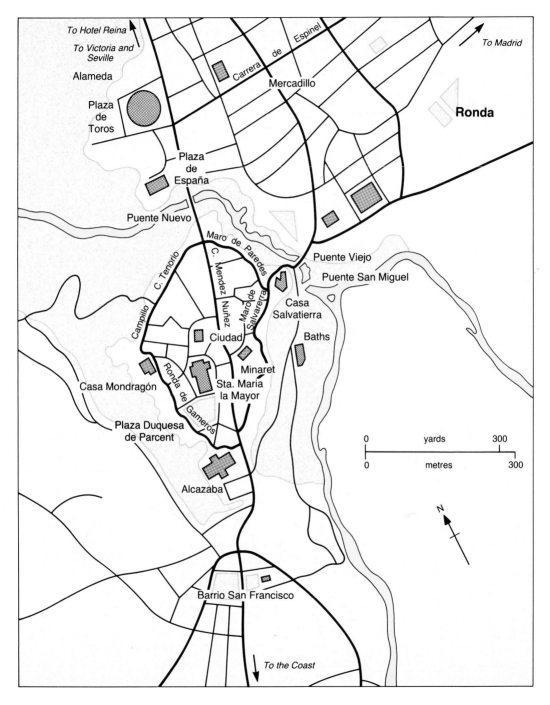

To Hotel Reina

To Victoria and
Seville

Alameda

Plaza
de
Toros

Carrera de Espinel

Mercadillo

Ronda

To Madrid

Plaza
de
España

Puente Nuevo

Maro de Paredes

C. Tenorio

Campillo

C. Mendez Nuñez

Maro de Salvatierra

Puente Viejo

Puente San Miguel

Casa
Salvatierra

Baths

Ciudad

Minaret

Casa Mondragón

Ronda de Gameros

Sta. María
la Mayor

Plaza Duquesa
de Parcent

Alcazaba

0   yards   300
0   metres   300

N

Barrio San Francisco

To the Coast

Rilke was one, which gives strange extra point to the lines

Wer de auch seist, am Abend tritt hinaus
Aus deiner Stube, drin du alles weisst,
Am letzten vor der Ferne liegt dein Haus
Wer du auch seist…

especially of an evening, when the coaches have departed, and you sit on the hotel terrace looking out over the great sweep of valley to the smoky black silhouette of the Sierre de Grazalema, with the evening sky behind it.

The Tajo, the astonishing gorge that splits the town, is hard to see from above. You can walk down to the old Arab mills, from which you can appreciate it fully. The way down is either via a path that starts from immediately beyond the gardens of the Reina Victoria, and takes you along some way west before zigzagging down into the valley, or from the little square called the Campillo in the Ciudad, whence a stepped ramp makes the going relatively easy for most of the way down, with only a short stretch of narrow footpath. Or else you can drive down via the southern suburb of San Francisco at the foot of the Alcazaba.

Whichever way you take, you can walk below the town along the entire sweeping curve of the cliff. My first visit in October gave me no inkling of how rewarding this could be: In May you drown in lush greenery, and the colour of the flowers, wild and cultivated, makes words fall short, so that the gorge itself, the most famous attraction of Ronda, became just another part of the backdrop. During our walk, there were nightingales singing in the walnut groves.

I should add that you can also see the Tajo from another angle, from down by the old bridges in the Ciudad.

Hotels

H. Reina Victoria★★★★, Calle Jerez, 25. Tel: 87 12 40. (£45).
HR El Tajo★★, Calle Doctor Cajal, 7. Tel: 87 62 36. (£17).
Hs Morales★, Calle Sevilla, 51. Tel: 87 15 38 (£10).

Restaurant

Don Miguel, Calle Villa Nueva, 4 – fair food; fine site.

A Suggested Walk Leaving to you all decisions on walking down to the old mills and up again, I suggest you take in the Alameda and the bullring in the Mercadillo, and then do a round of the Ciudad.

The bullring is either the oldest in Spain, or else comes second to Seville's. Either way it is worth seeing: it dates from 1784, and has the elegance you would expect of that period. Bullfighting used, before the eighteenth century, to be done on horseback, and was the prerogative of a gentleman – the Hidalgo or Son of Something. It became what it is now, mainly due to the Romero family who, here in Ronda, gave it its modern form. In September they hold a *corrida* here in the dress of Romero's – and Goya's – time.

Between the Maestranza and the bridge is mostly tat, though it is worth having a drink or a meal at *Don Miguel*, whose terraces are below bridge level, inside the gorge. But once over the bridge in the Ciudad, the atmosphere of the past closes in on you again. Turn right up Calle Tenorio to the Plaza Campillo. Here you have another splendid view and can take the track down into the gorge. But, assuming you prefer something gentler, carry on via the Ronda de Gameros. On your right at the start, the Casa Mondragón is worth a look.

In the Plaza Duquesa de Parcent, the church of Santa María can not quite hide the mosque that it was: the transept tower on the east side was the minaret, and there is a *mihrab* inside. Carrying on towards the end of the bluff, you come to the Alcazaba which the French, with their usual attention to Culture, blew up in 1809. Head back via Calle Mendez Nuñez, until Calle Marqués de Salvatierra forks off right. (This is a general itinerary only: try going down little side streets on your way.) At the junction, a minaret survives from a church now disappeared. At the bottom of Salvatierra, the marquis's house is on your right; ahead of you, through a Renaissance arch, are two older bridges (the left-hand one originally Roman); and, round to the right, the remains of the Moorish baths. Going right down to the bridges will give you a good view of the Tajo from the opposite side to the postcard view, and it is pleasant to carry on up through the quiet untouristy streets. But if you bear left before going through the arch, it will bring you back to the 'new' bridge.

Even if you are not staying in it, it is worth walking north up the main axial street past the Alameda, to the Reina Victoria hotel, to sit on its terrace with a drink. The hotel itself is an attractive piece of Edwardian England with its gabled green roofs, and its attic rooms for your retinue of servants. It is a good-mannered building that manages to fit well into its Spanish surroundings. And the view from its terrace is the best in Ronda. At sunset, the whole turns to silhouette while the disc of the sun disappears behind the Palomas pass. If you look over the edge of the cliff (on which the hotel is built) you can watch the kestrels wheeling below. They are the Lesser Kestrel, which is richly coloured above and the palest fawn beneath. There are also Peregrine Falcons nesting there, which are plentiful enough in Spain to be called the Common Falcon (*Halcón Común*). And if you stay in the hotel, you will hear the Little Owl that nests in the gardens.

If you stay more than the odd day, the town can surprise you: everything I have mentioned so far has concerned either the view or the parts of the city that lie along its main axis. But if you turn off at right-angles into the pedestrian Calle Espinel — almost opposite the bull-ring — you may be surprised at the length of the street and extent of the town, and all of it, up this way, prosperous and seemingly never having heard of a tourist.

Tourist Office: Plaza de España, 1.

The province of Málaga is the only one whose Tourist Offices are less than good. But the one in Ronda is a joke among the inhabitants themselves: if you find it open, please apply to the *Guinness Book of Records*. It only even claims to open weekday mornings after 10 a.m., but even that is a fiction.

Setenil, Aciupo and La Pileta Before you leave Ronda, look out to the mountains in the west. They contain a couple of dozen little towns and villages, all white walled and red roofed, but all different in character, in texture, in site, most of them with their castle overhead, some in narrow ravines, some looking out over sweeping upland valleys, many with vultures or eagles planing overhead, most with a hotel, hostal or simple 'Camas y Comidas'. If you had decided to see Ronda and leave it at that... give it another thought.

Ronda is one of three of the best places to start a tour of these mountains and their white towns (*los pueblos blancos*). The other two are Arcos de la Frontera, in the west, and San Roque in the south, both in the province of Cádiz, and so I have put my description of them in that chapter. But there are three remarkable spots that do not easily fit into any journey within the triangle Ronda–Arcos–San Roque, and are easiest visited as excursions from Ronda.

First, one of the white towns and a remarkable one, is Setenil, on the Ronda–Olvera road, about 19km (12ml.) away. Some of the houses and even streets actually undercut the rock against which the town nestles.

The second, to my shame I have not seen, but report on the witness of friends. If you take the main road (C339) out of Ronda for Algodonales, after 8 or 9 km (5 or 6 ml.) you come to a right turn to Ronda la Vieja (MA449). Another five or six miles and you reach it: the Roman city of Aciupo, 3,000 feet up, with a theatre at the top. The sight is rewarding enough, even though of the town itself only heaps of stones remain, but if you then turn round, you have a breathtaking view down into the valley beneath you. I am told it beats the view from the Palomas pass above Grazalema. I find that hard to believe but, if it is so, then this place is not be missed.

Farm at Ronda

The third is the Cave of La Pileta, signposted from Ronda and about sixteen miles away by the longer and easier of the two routes. It has palaeolithic paintings which, now that Altamira and Lascaux have been closed to the public, have become rarities.

The Costa del Sol From Málaga round to Gibraltar, the coast was in the nineteenth century a stretch of fishing villages, poor and fever-ridden. The Costa today is an international phenomenon that owes its existence to the attraction of its climate; not to the beaches, which are mostly brown or grey and unlovely; and certainly not to the coast road, which has about the worst safety record in Europe. It is a phenomenon created by demand, and is only Spanish in one way – though an important one, too easily forgotten.

In the 1960s, European prosperity meant that people of all sorts, not just the well to do, wanted a holiday in the sun, and could manage it. Places like Torremolinos met that demand with standards of accommodation that were extraordinarily good for the price. The fact that they have gone on giving good value for money is clear from the statistics: upwards of fifty million tourist visits per year in a country of thirty-nine million inhabitants. Horror stories about people arriving to hotels as yet unbuilt, reflect on the foreign tourist agencies, rather than on the Spaniards. So, Torremolinos is a horrible high-rise knees-up, but it is an honest place, catering honestly to the demand.

In the last few years, Spain's astonishing rise to prosperity has meant that the country is no longer a cheap one, and the Costa tourist industry has begun to suffer badly. 1989 saw a decline of something upwards of 30 per cent and the prospects are not looking good.

The high-rise ugliness is a feature of the sixties. As you go further down the coast you get a social history of resort architecture: gradually the developers learn by their mistakes... and replace them with new ones.

Sixteen kilometres (10ml.) on from Torremolinos is Fuengirola. Both for its seaside esplanade and for the main drag you could not believe anything was worse. But sandwiched in between is a real town of sorts, with all the usual things a real town has: shops and people and traffic jams. The beach is brown sand, dirty looking, and with its tideline of jetsam, natural and plastic. It is not a patch on Brighton, but has warmer weather.

Behind Fuengirola, Mijas was probably once a pretty mountain village, 1,500 feet up in the clean air, where you could come to exchange the smell of pine trees for that of sun-tan lotion. But it is now totally overtaken by tourism: souvenir shops, bars, coaches, donkey rides and a gleaming white marble Town Hall five storeys high on the proceeds.

Twenty-four kilometres (15ml.) on, Marbella is the upmarket resort, which means that the hotel and apartment blocks are more spaced out and the golf-courses closer together.

After this, things begin to change. San Pedro de Alcántara is more a real Spanish town than a resort, while Estepona, the last of the towns, is a surprising place. On the outskirts you might be in an Australian suburb, on the set of 'Neighbours', for instance. But the town itself is a strange mixture: most of it is an utterly unspoiled, sleepy southern town, with clean cobbled steets, whitewash, *rejas* (grilles) and flowers, and dogs scratching and children playing and mothers on doorsteps. On to the front of this, a brash facade of Costa touristry is stuck like a phoney film set. Behind it rises the Sierra Bermeja, aptly named: in the evening light it stands a purply red.

From Estepona on down to Gibraltar is depressing desolation: it is all spanking new, and built from scratch by British and other developers, and given names like Paradise Beach, and they have shoved up mock-Moorish villas for ribbon development, exactly as they did mock-Tudor ones for ribbon developments on the Portsmouth road.

All this reaches an apotheosis of sorts at Sotogrande which, to continue the comparison, might be called the St George's Hill of Andalusia. It is an entirely artificial urbanization, a comfortable place for the comfortably off; the roads in are guarded; the place has no nucleus, no centre where you can go to buy a pound of gossip, just houses each safely cocooned in that hushed isolation of gentility that makes me wonder how the wives avoid nervous breakdown. The husbands are mostly away all day in Gibraltar.

Escape From the Costa del Sol there are various ways of visiting Spain. Such are the road improvements that you need never fear the little ones marked in white on the Michelin Map: Casares can be reached as an excursion via a tiny road that turns up into the Sierra Bermeja from about 10km (6ml.) west of Estepona: it is one of the most picturesque and often photographed villages in Andalusia. What is more, the road will take you on to Gaucín, and its memories of British travellers of the past taking the long ride from Gibraltar up to Ronda.

From Fuengirola or Benalmádena you can drive up to Mijas and carry straight on past it, round the mountain to Alhaurín, and from there decide whether to go on to the little Spa village of Tolox for peace, quiet, and walking in the game reserve; or else to see the Chorro and Bobastro, which I describe below.

You can have the same choice by taking the road inland from Marbella, which takes you up to Ojén (One ★★★ Hotel and a ★ Pensión), on over the 2,000 foot pass, and thence inland. You can start a trip through the Serranía from the southern end, via San Roque.

And, of course, you have the options of the main road up to Ronda, or continue round the Straights of Gibraltar (after San

Roque the notorious N340 loses its dangers and becomes good) to Tarifa, Trafalgar and beyond.

East of Málaga Nerja has a certain charm and is not yet too spoilt. There are also some caves to be visited there. Otherwise, I can find nothing to recommend the coast. Inland, for those who prefer scenery and leisure to traffic and haste, I would recommend the old road to Granada. It adds ten miles on to the journey (ninety miles instead of eighty miles) and, of course, it is slower. But the scenery is fine, the roads empty, and you visit Alhama on the way.

From the centre of Málaga (or from the Parador) the Calle Victoria takes you to the (new) Granada road: instead of bearing left to join it, you carry straight ahead and you are on the old Granada road. The pass is 915m (3,000ft.) up and the views good. At Colmenar you turn right to Riogordo, Mondrón, Periana and 6km (4ml.) beyond. Here, you turn left on to the C335. The peaks to your right go up to nearly 7,000 feet, but you are more modest. Less than 30km (20ml.) later you come to Alhama de Granada.

Alhama itself is not much, just a large village sitting on the plateau. But it is perched on the edge of a gorge, with the river beneath falling, falling from mill to mill. The name means 'Bath', and the baths are there, Roman in origin, with the Moorish ones now part of the modern spa. The hotel is 3km (2ml.) out of the village and is closed from October to June.

When Abul Hasan (or Muley Hacen) was beaten here by a Christian army in 1482, it was the beginning of the end of Muslim Spain. The loss of Alhama helped cut the link between Granada and Málaga, and so not only a source of supply but all link with Africa. In less than ten years Granada would fall and a civilization 780 years old be destroyed. The lament for the loss, 'Ay de mi Alhama', was put into English by Byron.

From Alhama you can continue across country, but I would take the GR131 up to join the main road near Loreto. The signpost will probably say Montefrío.

Inland from Málaga There are three good things to visit: Antequera; the Torcal mountain; and Bobastro and the Chorro gorge. Of these I would personally put Antequera relatively low in my priorities and I describe it more in case you happen to be passing that way.

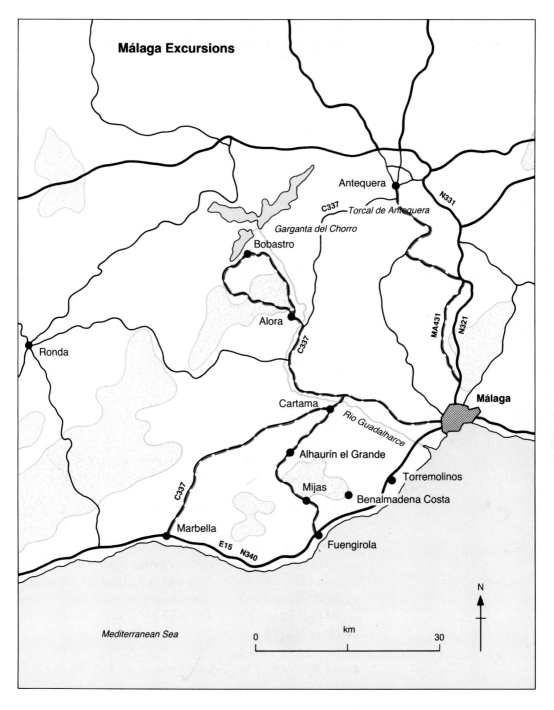

Málaga Excursions

Antequera

C337 *Torcal de Antequera*

N331

Garganta del Chorro

Bobastro

Alora

MA431

N321

Ronda

C337

Cartama

Málaga

Rio Guadalharce

Alhaurín el Grande

Torremolinos

Mijas

Benalmadena Costa

C337

Marbella

Fuengirola

E15 N340

N

Mediterranean Sea

km

0   30

Antequera This is a medium-sized town, important in history, and today busy as an agricultural centre. It stands at the foot (half-way up the ankle, really) of the Sierra de Chimenea. Like many places in Andalusia, it gives you the feeling of its past being still with it, and peering over your shoulder – Roman, Moorish, thirteenth-century Christian, and then stopping at all stations up to the present – all around you and still with you, especially up at the castle.

Once there you see all of Antequera: the more modern part lies hidden under the roofs except for the churches that stand out everywhere, with the Mudéjar brickwork of their towers; all round beneath you, you see very Moorish quarters of the town; and beyond, to the east, the Peña de los Enamorados (Lovers' Rock) rears up 1,000 feet sheer out of the plain, with its inevitable Romeo and Juliet legend.

Just a hundred metres or so after the exit to town (to join the Granada and Málaga roads), on your left is the entrance to the *Menga* and *Viera* caves, which are in fact burial chambers from some 2,500 years ago. Menga seems the most impressive, but I am no judge. There is another called the *Cueva del Romeral* a bit further on, which I have not visited.

There is a comfortable Parador at the edge of town, where they serve a good lunch.

The Torcal is a mountain with at the summit an outcrop of rocks of strange formation. The turn-off is about 11km (7ml.) south of Antequera off the C3310 to Villanueva and Málaga. But it makes a very much more impressive outing if you come up from Málaga (in which case, the turn-off is about 5¹/2km (3¹/2ml.) north of Villanueva). There are various ways to it, but I think the best is to leave Málaga by the main N321 but turn left off it after 5 or 6km (3 or 4 ml.) – it is the only turn. For another mile or two it is all cafés and trippers, and above all, that saddest of features of modern Spain, the perpetual flowering amateur rubbish dump. Then all that stops. The road surface gets a bit ropy, though nothing to worry about, and from that point on you understand why I recommend it.

The road runs first on one, then on the other side of the ridge, so you get double value for money: Now you look down on the main road some 300m (1,000ft) below, and all those travellers drinking in healing lungfuls of carbon monoxide; now you look out over ranges of hills and valleys, with to the north the highest peak, above and behind the Torcal, at 1,370m (4,500ft). The hillsides are covered with almond trees and must be a sight in spring, whether from below on the main road, or from above. You come down *almost* to rejoin the main road at Casabermeja ('Red House' – but they are all white). It is a good village for a pause or snack, as yet unspoiled by tourism. Here you at once turn left again on to the Villanueva road, which is not marked on my Michelin map, but is a good one. Almost immediately you see a broad sweep of valley, Villanueva in the distance and the Torcal sheer above it. Indeed, the valleys of this range are more open and sweeping, more like moorland valleys in northern Britain, and so are the hills, too, in a vague way, so that it is a good area if you like walking.

The Chorro

The top of the Torcal is flat and covered with weird limestone formations. It is an invigorating place and the views of mountains, valley and distant sea make it worth the journey. And it would be a good place to get away from the heat of the coast for a picnic: the air is cooler at 1,070m (3,500ft); there is a surprising amount of greenery; and although there is a state-run reception place (and therefore presumably Sunday trippers) you can find privacy and shade in the maze of rocks, for there is plenty of space on the mountain top. As for the strange rock formations, anyone with offspring should find this an ideal spot to lose them for an hour or two as it is a natural play area.

Málaga to Torcal is about forty miles. You can thereafter decide whether to go on and visit Antequera. The Michelin map makes the return via Almogía look inviting, but the road is a poor one: I sometimes wonder whether to Michelin all roads are scenic as long as they twist.

Bobastro and the Chorro If I had time for only one inland excursion from the Coast – always excepting Ronda – it would be this one. You see some astonishing scenery, natural and man-made. You can get to it from any of the Costa towns between Marbella and Málaga (as long as you remember not to be scared of those little white roads). I went from Málaga and the day took me five hours, including long and leisurely stops for lunch and for walks at Alora, Bobastro, and elsewhere. Find your way to Alora. Thus far it is mostly boring stuff: you are in the

Hoya de Málaga (Málaga Basin), it is low, hot and mostly citrus groves, though Alora is known for its very tasty manzanilla olives.

Alora looks romantic, and in a way it is: it is up on a spur with a castle at its prow. The castle (like so many others) is better from a distance. The little that remains is filled with a cemetery of possibly gruesome interest, since many of the niches have been broken open. But the old part of town near it is the most completely African I have seen in Spain – even more so than Tarifa – with narrow streets of forty-five degree slope off which you can fall into the next: and inhabitants who may perhaps be gypsy but look straight from the Maghreb.

182

Scenery at Bobastro

From there on it gets better and better. Do not fork left for Ardales: Do the circuit anti clockwise for the best views. The gorge of the Chorro itself is phenomenal: only metres wide and upwards of 300m (1,000ft) high. Through this the River Guadalhorce has forced its way. What is more, the energetic can explore it on foot via the Camino Real ('Royal Road') which must be Spanish irony: it is a track through the defile only a few feet wide and not for those who do not like heights.

The excursion goes on being good. You branch left, following the Bobastro sign, and climb a precipitous mountain that had previously puzzled you by seeming to have a chimney atop. On

183

the way up, stop and take a walk where a crude and unobtrusive sign says Iglesia Mozárabe. It is a church carved out of the solid rock in about the year 900, now without a roof. To me it looks unfinished: why, for example, the large circle cut in one wall next to an arch unless it was due to become the second archway of an arcade? But the history books imply that it was completed and then destroyed together with the whole hillside fortress and township (of which nothing now remains) when the Caliph Abd el-Rahman III at last managed to get the better of Omar Ibn Hafsun. You do not *have* to know the story to enjoy the place, but I think it helps. If you do not want it, skip the next two paragraphs.

Omar Ibn Hafsun was a native of Ronda and a *muwallad*, that is to say a Christian convert to Islam, or else one of a family that had converted. He bore an Arab name because you could only convert to Islam by being adopted by a tribe (clan would be a more accurate word) and exchanging your name for an Arabic name. These people were often the source of unrest because they did not have all the rights and privileges of Arab Moslems. Added to this, the people of Ronda have always had a reputation for cocking a snook at authority, and for being the meanest knife-fighters in Spain.

Ibn Hafsun was a true Rondeño: in his youth he murdered a man, took to the mountains, and set up as a bandit. Before long he had made Bobastro his headquarters and was gaining a big following; some out for loot, others political or social malcontents. The site was pretty well impregnable, as you can well imagine if you have seen it, and I suppose the mountain-top reservoir implies a water source big enough to supply thousands. Ibn Hafsun seems to have been splendidly gifted as a leader: he was cunning and brave; clever at persuading others to join him, and with a gift for inspiring and keeping loyalty once they had. And he had a genius (and zest) for persuading his enemies to accept a truce or a deal on which he would promptly renege. Time and again he got out of tight corners in this way, and one wonders how he managed to make them go on falling for it. In fact, he was a sort of Pancho Villa of the Dark Ages, part brigand, part revolutionary and rallier of the oppressed. There is a note of admiration in the accounts of early Arab historians that even makes him seem a Robin Hood: 'He was so respectful of women that any one of them might travel from city to city unmolested', writes one. In 899 Ibn Hafsun converted to Christianity – hence this church. By then he held power over large tracts of Andalusia. Bobastro was only taken after his death. The victorious Caliph destroyed it, dug up the Hafsun bodies and displayed them crucified in Córdoba.

The place is so remote, so excitingly wild, that the realization that some three thousand people or more once lived here adds an element of shock to one's exhilaration.

A short drive takes you to the preposterous top of this mountain – the entire summit covered by a reservoir. Where did the water come from? If the history is true and the Caliphs found it impregnable, Ibn Hafsun must have had a massive water supply. But a spring *that* big, *this* high up? Today the water feeds the turbines of a hydroelectric station.

Back down at the bottom, turn left and continue the circuit. At Ardales, there is a cave with both prehistoric paintings and stalagmites and stalactites, but I have not seen it. The mountain scenery over the pass back to Alora would be impressive, if anything could be after what went before.

At Cartama you can cut across to Coín or to Alhaurín el Grande whose claim to fame is recent, and rather moving: Gerald Brenan lived his declining years in a farmhouse just outside town. When he began to get too old to look after himself, it was decided to take him back to England. The Mayor and Corporation protested, saying in effect, 'He chose to live with us: he is ours'. And they voted him a pension for life and all necessary nursing care and facilities. He died here two or three years ago. That says something good to know about Spanish people and about Gerald Brenan, both.

Alhaurín also has a good restaurant, the *Casa Paco;* try the fish baked in rock salt. The fact seems to have got known, for the diners when I went were an incongruous mix of ordinary local folk and up-market Costa-mongers, British and German, (Alhaurín is only a few miles around the mountain from Mijas).

Right
The Alhambra

Below
Granada seen from the Veleta (11,200ft)

Granada means first and foremost the Alhambra and the gardens of the Generalife, and quite rightly so. All too often, places famous for their beauty raise such expectations that the reality cannot live up to them, but I have yet to meet anyone who has been disappointed by the Alhambra.

However, there are many other good reasons for visiting both the city and the province of Granada. Astonishingly, you can drive right over the top of the Sierra Nevada and view Andalusia from 11,000 feet; you could easily spend a week and more exploring the beautiful upland valleys of the Alpujarra on the other side of the range; there is a lot of fine upland country, empty and relatively unvisited, to be explored to the east and north, including the cave-houses of Guadix and the Renaissance palace of Lacalahorra in its remote and exotic site; and the city of Granada itself offers a lot else besides the Alhambra. And all this omits the possibility of you wanting to ski here, especially in spring when you can combine a morning's skiing with an afternoon's bathing down on the coast.

Although the heat of summer here can be as burning as anywhere, the city stands at 2,200 feet so the air is not oppressive. But take note of this fact if you are susceptible to sunburn.

Do not let your first impressions on entering Granada sour you: virtually wherever you come from, you hit the Paseo de Ronda which is a never-ending line of soulless blocks with a canyon of traffic thundering through it day and night. It will not feel much better if you have to come into the centre via the Avenida Constitucion and Gran Via de Colon: the nineteenth century was as careless of Granada's heritage as the 1960s. The pleasant heart of Granada is between the Cathedral and the Puerta Real (also known as Batallas, and as José-Antonio); its soul is up on the Alhambra; and its life is down at the University end of Calle Alarcón (after 11 p.m.).

History The Iberians, the Phoenicians, the Carthaginians, the Romans and the Visigoths were all here. The Albaicín quarter was the Roman city of Illiberis. The name Granada comes, not from the pomegranate (which is what it means in Spanish), but from a Carthaginian suburb called Nata which became Gar Nata al-Yahud under the Arabs and thence Granada. There is some evidence to suggest that the al-Yahud ('the Jew') part comes from the times of the great Ibn Nagella family who may have built an earlier castle up on the hill. Certainly, Samuel Ibn Nagrella, known as ha-Nagid (the Prince), was in a position to as he was pre-eminent as statesman and soldier as well as rabbi and poet:

I billeted a strong force that night
In an old fort, ruined long ago by other troops.
We slept there in it and around it,
And its owners slept beneath us…

Even in translation, the lines can send a shiver down your spine, over a distance of a thousand years.

With the Christian reconquest of Seville and Córdoba, Granada grew in importance: craftsmen, artists, thinkers and doctors flooded in to this last Moslem enclave, which in those days extended from Almería to Algeciras. And the next 250 years, under the rule of the Nasrid family, saw a final flourishing of Moorish civilization before it was destroyed under Ferdinand and Isabella in 1492.

The last act of the drama has become overlaid with a varnish of stories that grew in the last century through Washington Irving and others. They are good stories. How King Abul Hassan (or Muley Hassan, or Muley Hacen, or Mulhacen) fell for Zoraya (aka Isabel de Solís, a muwallad girl); how his wife Ayesha got peeved about this and feared for the inheritance of her son Ibn Abdallah, now known as Boabdil or Bobadil; how this turned into clan warfare, with the Abencerrajes siding with Ayesha against the Zegris and Zoraya; how Boabdil eventually handed over the keys of the city in exchange for a mini-kingdom in the Alpujarras; how he reached the pass still known as the Moor's Sigh (el Suspiro del Moro) on the N323, turned back for a last look at his lost kingdom, and wept; how his mum said: 'You weep like a woman for what you could not defend like a man.' (It is a twentieth-century codicil that nowadays he would look south to the Costa and weep.)

It is all good stuff, and some of it may even be historical; it takes us up to 1 January 1492. What followed is certainly historical but much less pretty. At the impulsion of Cardinal Cisneros, the promises made to the Moors were broken, and they were hounded, even those who had agreed to convert to Christianity. They were driven to rebel and then crushed, while the Inquisition got to work on anybody accused of any divergence in dress, race or habit. One of the most mindlessly mean of the Cardinal's ploys was to destroy the Moslem Baths (Alhamas): the Christians had no use for such practices; to the Moors, personal cleanliness was a deeply imprinted social trait. The hounding went on into the seventeenth century.

Meanwhille, the northern carpet-baggers who took over Moorish land did not understand irrigation, and the fertile Vega began to revert to wilderness. Granada declined and its population dwindled. Even in the 1920s, when the Alhambra had become a traveller's Mecca, Gerald Brenan could think it 'shoddy and bedraggled like a gypsy girl sitting under a damp hedge'. Only with the economic boom of the 1960s did the population climb back up to its present 280,000, and the city acquire its prosperity and its hideous high-rise periphery.

Today's Granaínos are a paradox. They seem to have inherited much of their Christian ancestors' intolerance – some five thousand intellectuals and Republican sympathizers (including Spain's most famous poet and dramatist, García Lorca) were taken up to Viznar and shot in 1936–7; such things happened in those traumatic days, and I would not have mentioned it but that, in spite of Ian Gibson's diplomatic conclusion to his book on the subject, the Town Council's recent gesture of a 'memorial park', in the wording of its inscription, and the manner of its lay-out, more resembles spitting on his grave than making amends. Meanwhile, the name of the founder of Spanish Fascism still stands clean and clear, decorating the façade of the Cathedral in letters two feet high. And then the paradox: although the present day Granaínos are not in fact descended from the Moors, they seem also to have inherited from them their fierce, almost obsessive love for their city: for the Moors had made Granada and the whole Vega into an image of their Djanet, their Garden of Paradise; their grief at the loss of it echoes down the centuries.

What to See The Alhambra, including the gardens of the Generalife, of course, and at all costs. But also the Albaicín, which is the ancient Moorish quarter, and for many people the Sacromonte, too, where the gypsies live, many in cave dwellings,

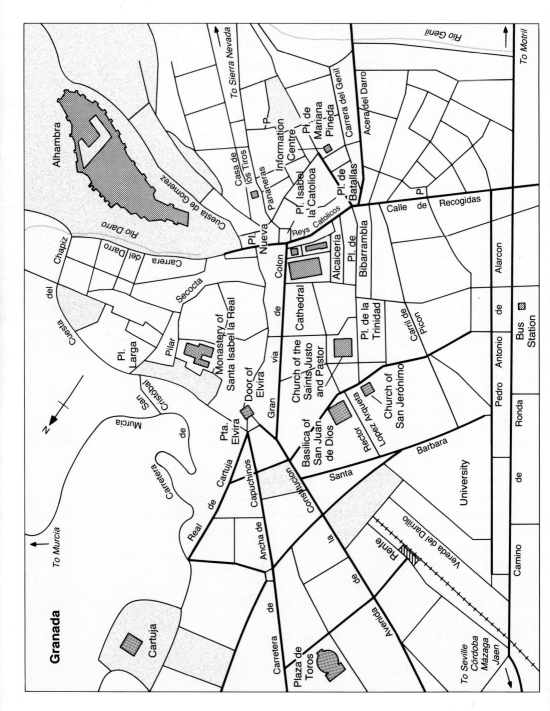

and go about their ancient skills of singing, dancing, and extracting money from tourists. The Cathedral, because of its Royal Pantheon (la Capilla Real), and one particular statue. And one other thing that may have more specialized appeal: the Charterhouse (la Cartucha).

Hotels Hotel accommodation can be difficult because its high season is March, April, May, September, October – and in October there are a lot of congresses to clutter the hotels up, too. The soulless, thundering districts I mentioned seem to penetrate further into Granada, and more unavoidably, than many other cities. So you have this choice: either go for one of the seven hotels that are up on the Alhambra and so out of the city itself (and incidentally, therefore, in cooler air); or decide between those that are quiet but hard to find and those that are easy to find but in noisy streets.

The Albaicín

Your transport is another factor, unless you arrive earlyish in the day with plenty of time to explore. Whether you come by car or train may well dictate your choice of hotel. So instead of making personal recommendations, I shall simply give some choices with these various factors in mind. My own preference would be for a lodging up on the Alhambra, with excursions down into the town; or, for cheaper lodging, one of the five Hostales I list on the Cuesta de Gomérez, though not if you have a car, when a lock-up garage becomes imperative.

First, those up on the Alhambra: I list all seven, whether I know them or not. The existence of a garage, I am assured, is not necessary here.

Parador Nacional San Francisco ★★★★, Alhambra. Tel: (958) 22 14 40 (also 41 and 42). (£70) – this must be one of the finest places to stay in the world: A late fifteenth-century Franciscan monastery actually inside the gardens of the Alhambra, which therefore enables you to drift around by moonlight when the general public is excluded. But you will have to plan your holiday around it as you need to book about a year ahead.

H. Alhambra Palace ★★★★, Peña Partida, 2. Tel: 22 14 68 (£60) – this large palace is perched on the hillside half-way down, so you would need a taxi or a trudge to get to either palace or town. Not my idea of a good position.

H. los Alixares ★★★, Avenida Alixares del Generalife. Tel: 22 55 06. (£35).

191

H. Guadalupe ★★★, Avenida de los Alixares. Tel: 22 34 23. (Price varies £28–£38) – I do not know it, but have heard pleasant things said.

H. Washington Irving ★★★, Paseo del Generalife. Tel: 22 75 50. (£35) – this one is a little way down the hill among the trees; a bit old fashioned, and tatty but good service.

Hostal América ★★★, Calle Real de la Alhambra, 53. Tel: 22 74 71. (£32) A tiny and charming place with beds for 22 only, right up beside the palace. They open between 1 March and 8 November. They do not accept Credit Cards, but otherwise I am amazed they say they only need about two months advance booking (except for Holy Week). Rafael Garzón seems a pleasant chap and speaks English. I have not tried beds or food, but unless they are nasty (which I do not think for one moment) this place would come a close second to the Parador for me: It is set back with its own tiny garden, in the only street up in the Alhambra complex – an old and more or less unspoiled one, next door to the famous Polinario's where Manuel de Falla and García Lorca met weekly.

Pensión Residencia Doña Lupe ★, Alhambra. Tel: 22 14 73. (£25) – I did not know about or look for this one: A ★ Boarding House suggests it is fairly basic, and Residencia means they serve no food.

Hotels down in the town: (a) Easy to find but noisy streets:

H. Luz Granada ★★★★, Avenida Constiitución, 18. Tel: 20 40 61. Garage. (£60).

HR. Condor ★★★, Avenida Constitución, 6. Tel: 28 37 11. (£35). (Constitución is near the Railway station).

HR Ana María ★★★, Camino de Ronda, 101. Garage. Tel: 28 92 15. (£35).

H. Rallye ★★★, Camino de Ronda, 107. Tel: 27 28 00. (£28). If you come by train and are low on cash there are a couple of Pensiones in the Avenida del Doctor Olóriz, which is straight ahead of you as you leave the station, and which are about £5–£10. I have not looked closer.

Hotels down in the town: (b) Quiet but harder to find:

H. Kenia ★★★. Calle Molinos, 65. Tel: 22 75 07. (£35). – no garage mentioned, but a quiet and pleasant old house converted.

Hostal Residencia Los Arrayanes ★★, Calle San Diego, 9. Tel: 25 97 71. Garage. (£14). – this is the one I would go for in this price range – if you can find it. If you can get your car to the Acera de Darro (aka Avenida José Antonio) drive south down it and take the fourth right (Calle Veronica de la Virgen); San Diego is the second crossroad and the Arrayanes is by the corner. Quiet and all mod cons. If there is no room, there is a 24-hour lock-up garage within two hundred yards, on the corner of Calle San Antón and Calle Pino, and close to it the small, clean…

HsR. Salvador ★★, Calle Duende, 6. Tel: 25 87 08. (£19). For budget travellers without the problem of a car, the Cuesta de Gomérez is half-way between Cathedral and Alhambra:

HsR California ★★, at no. 37. Tel: 22 40 56. (£13).

Hs. Landazurri ★★, at no. 24. Tel: 22 14 06 (£16).

HsR Britz ★, at no.1. Tel: 22 36 52. (£14).

HsR Gomérez ★ at no. 10. Tel: 22 44 37. (£7).

Hs. Navarro Ramos ★, no. 21. Tel: 22 18 76. (£7).

The Alhambra (Open 9 a.m.–6 p.m. daily; Saturdays 9 a.m.–6 p.m. and 8–10 p.m. Sundays free.)

Alcalá al-Hamra, 'the Red Fortress': This is what you mainly see from below, on its spur of the foothills of the Sierra Nevada. But within the red walls is a whole complex of castle, pavilions, palaces, gardens, a street, a friary, a church, a Renaissance palace. And next to it, on the slope of hill just above, are the gardens of the Generalife, which contain the rulers' summer palace, and are not to be missed. The fact that the walls of the citadel *are* red has not prevented brochures, and even some guidebooks repeating the romantic clap-trap, whereby the Alhambra was named after a beautiful red-headed favourite. I suspect this belongs in the same category of pseudo-etymology that wrecked our Welsh Rabbit, by turning it into an ever-so-genteel Rarebit.

The five or six different palaces, extant or disappeared, were built at different periods, by different kings, unlikely each one to have a red-headed popsy. Which leaves only the castle. And to name a fortress after your girlfriend, seems dangerously like comparing her to a battle-tank…

I shall concentrate on the Nasrid Palaces and gardens, because they are unique in the world. And I shall skimp on the rest, because unless you have a week to spend up here, or have an

The Myrtle Court

amazing cultural digestive system, I do not believe it possible to take in the whole lot without protest from head or feet.

It may help if I start with some general pointers. Christian potentates in their building always aim to show their grandeur; the pleasure of living is secondary, if it is considered at all. Would you enjoy, would you find delight in actually living in Versailles? Sitting down to meals in a room the size of a concert hall, with the food tepid after a journey of several hundred yards from the kitchen and eaten off dishes of quickly cooling gold on which fat would congeal and your knife would scrape like fingernails on slate? Before you enter the Mexuar, take a last look behind you at Charles V's idea of a desirable residence.

Moorish potentates built for pleasure, not for grandeur. Wealth and power enabled them to create delight rather than pomp. And surprise is an ingredient of delight: Here are no vistas, nothing to herald what is coming; entrances and exits are small and tucked

194

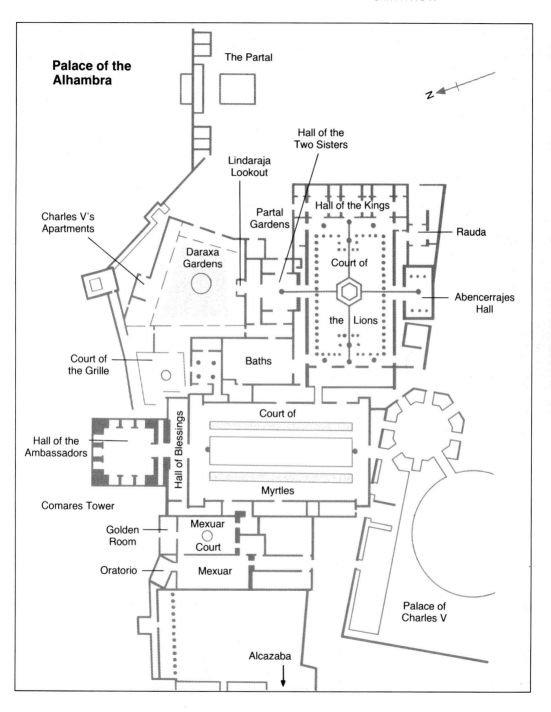

Palace of the Alhambra

The Partal

Hall of the Two Sisters

Lindaraja Lookout

Hall of the Kings

Charles V's Apartments

Partal Gardens

Rauda

Daraxa Gardens

Court of

Abencerrajes Hall

the Lions

Court of the Grille

Baths

Court of

Hall of the Ambassadors

Hall of Blessings

Myrtles

Comares Tower

Golden Room

Mexuar Court

Oratorio

Mexuar

Palace of Charles V

Alcazaba

away in corners; when you come in you have to turn your head before you see.

Descending from tent-dwellers, it was the richness and luxury of textures, rather than structure, that appealed. It is often pointed out that this luxury is here achieved with humble materials: brick, wood, tile and plaster. But that omits the chief ingredient: light. As Burkhardt phrased it: 'The ultimate secret of this art is the alchemy of light.' These builders also aimed to take the pleasantest things in the natural world and involve them, rather than to shut them out, or view them only through insulating windows. So flowers, shrubs and breezes join sunlight and shade as an integral part of their architecture.

And above all else, coming from dry lands, they appreciated, better than any before or since, the gift of water. In this place it is everywhere present, tinkling, limpid, crystalline; refreshing to the eye and ear. It is usual to recommend people to come here in the spring when the flowers are out, the air is cool, and the snow is on the Sierra Nevada. I count myself lucky to have paid my first visit in August during an exceptional heatwave. With the temperature well into the 40°s every day, the palace and its gardens were paradise. Moslems are lucky in this respect that their religion implies no taint of sin or guilt in sensory pleasure.

Visit As you enter the compound by the *Torre de la Justicia* and then the *Puerta del Vino*, you have before you the large *Plaza de los Aljibes* (Cisterns); to your left is the *Alcazaba* or castle, to your right, the Renaissance Palace of Charles V and, ahead and to the right, your access to the Nasrid Palace. You first visit the *Mexuar*. This was originally an administration area and has been so adapted in the century following the reconquest, that it is interesting rather than a revelation.

It leads to the *Mexuar Courtyard*. Here on your left is the *Cuarto Dorado*, and very nice, but turn right: Everything before you suggests a prelude. The Patio is almost bare, and the two doors facing you, unpretentious; but the decorated wall, the enormous cedarwood eaves, and the three steps up to the doors seem a presage. And they are. The right hand door led to the Sultan's private appartments (not open to the public); the other, via an easily defensible zigzag, brings you, whether ambassador or potentate, to one of the two great areas, the so-called *Comares*

The Lions' Court

Palace: the *Patio de los Arrayanes* (Myrtle Court) and the *Ambassadors' Hall*, or Sala de los Comares.

Here, the combination of richness and elegant serenity need no guide. But though the overall impression and atmosphere are what count most, never forget, after that first impression, to take a look at ceilings, as well as at the tile-work, and the detail of surface carving. Here in the Ambassadors' Hall the ceiling is built up of a three-dimensional composition of wood and ivory tiles and is elaborately symbolic: seven clusters representing the seven heavens revolve round the still centre that is Allah's dwelling place. It is likely that the symbolism was given point by placing the Sultan's throne beneath Allah's Firmament, under His protection. Originally both the ceiling and the carved plaster walls would have been richly painted.

The portico or antechamber is called the *Sala de la Barca*, i.e. Barakha or Blessings. The view back from the south end of the court is piquant in its contrast between the delicate arcade of the Blessings Hall and the massive solidity of the Comares tower. The first-floor chambers round the court were winter quarters, with a hall over the south portico, with lattice windows to hide the faces of the ladies of the harem, and a gallery above. None of this can be visited. Part of the building beyond the south portal was destroyed to make way for Charles v's palace, and the portal now leads to the crypt of the Palace.

The Partal

So here you take another unobtrusive doorway through to the *Lions' Court*. This is really a separate palace – or rather, that part of the complex which was reserved for the Sultan's family and private life. Once again, in this, one of the most famous and photographed buildings in the world, it is the intimate scale that strikes. That is, once you have had time to get over the impact of it.

The fountain was placed here relatively recently, and it would seem that the triangles on the heads of two of the lions, which, if superimposed would make the star of David, are considered proof of their Jewish origin. But the argument that they could not have been Moorish since they figure a living creature seems unconvincing when, some thirty feet away, a Moorish ceiling depicts both men and animals. Whether the lions represent the twelve tribes of Israel or the signs of the Zodiac, is for scholars to argue out, and makes no difference at all to the pleasure they afford the eye. In the Middle Ages everything in Nature, let alone in Art, was symbolic to Muslim, Jew and Christian alike.

The chambers to north and south of the court have names that are not significant, in that they were invented later, but you need them to find your way on the plan. To the north is the *Sala de las Dos Hermanas* (Two Sisters Hall), and through it, the *Sala de los Ajimeces* (*ajimez* is the architectural term for window with two lights divided by a column) and the Lindaraja Balcony (*Mirador de la Lindaraja*). These were the quarters of the royal women. It has been called decadent art; most people would prefer to call it breath-taking. The word *Lindaraja* applies to the balcony window and means the 'Eye of the House of Ayesha', so that the other name you will see applied to the court outside, Daraxa, also makes sense: *Dar*, the 'house'; *Axa*, 'Ayesha'.

To the south is the Sala de los Abencerrajes, perhaps less pretty, perhaps more beautiful: certainly its dome must count as one of the finest.

The Lions' Court is closed on the east by the *Sala de los Reyes* (Hall of the Kings) made up of three alcoved chambers, as fine as any in decoration, but unique for the leather ceiling panels, painted with story-telling scenes, probably by a fourteenth-century Christian artist working under commission; if not, then by a Moor who had learnt from a Christian artist. In the gardens, well away from the palace, for reasons clear to anyone who has smelt a tannery, is a small tannery in which these leather panels were shaped by moulding.

You leave the Lions' Court by another corner doorway, but this one is out of key with the rest. It is a tower gateway that seems to belong to an older, grimmer age. Its name, *La Rauda*, tends to confirm this: It means 'The Cemetery'. This takes you out to the *Partal Gardens*, from which in turn you can visit the last three surviving parts of the palace complex.

Down and round to your left is the *Daraxa* garden and beyond it the *Patio de la Reja* ('Iron Grill') both of which are Christian modifications of the sixteenth-century, although they used elements taken from the Moorish palace. The bowl of the fountain, for example, came from the Mexuar court. The Patio de la Reja has its own charm with its Tudor-seeming galleries. And it is worth visiting the apartments that were used by Washington Irving when he wrote his tales in 1829, but were intended for Charles V three centuries earlier.

But the chief thing to see here are the *Baths*. You enter them from the Daraxa; they are what we now call Turkish baths with steam-room, hypocaust, rest-room, changing room and all. But since they date from the fourteenth-century Nasrids, their builders show as intense an appreciation of light as anywhere in the Comares palace. Small, star-shaped holes in the celing send hard-edged rays down to pierce the steamy dimness.

Back in the gardens of the *Partal* is the last surviving building of another Moorish palace complex: the pavilion or portico (*partal*) that gives it its name. It blends with the Tower of the Ladies-in-Waiting, which is part of the wall fortifications, in an elegant whole. Such airy grace, standing to the main palace as some sort of Petit Trianon, might be thought to be of later date. Surprisingly, it is now considered to be the earliest of the palace buildings extant. There was much more to it, now vanished. On either side are Moorish houses (with frescos) and a small Mosque, but neither are open to the public.

You can visit the towers all round the walled hill-top; you can climb all over the castle – the view from the roof of the western watch-tower, or *Torre de Vela*, is panoramic; you can walk round outside the walls in the Adarve (i.e. Battlement) gardens; you can eat in the restaurant of the Parador. All that depends on your powers of absorption, which may be much greater than mine. But I suggest you should not leave without just taking a look into Charles V's palace: it is a very successful Renaissance building, and in the inner court you can no longer see the visual damage it has done to the Nasrid architecture. If you are still game for more, it is also a museum and picture gallery. Personally, I have always preferred to stay ignorant, and carry away uncluttered my impressions of the Nasrid palaces.

But whatever you elect to do on leaving the Partal, please do not forget the Generalife.

The Generalife To see the Alhambra without including the Generalife would be a pity, particularly as walking round it is as restful as wandering round any beautiful garden, and gives fine views over the Alhambra into the bargain. It was made as a summer retreat for the rulers, and is less a building with gardens, than gardens with pavilions in them. You can visit them via the gateway into the Alhambra (called the Puerta del Agua because

**Opposite
The Generalife**

201

The Albaicín

this is where the water was brought in from the Generalife and ultimately from far up the valley). I prefer this as you come straight in among the groves, the roses and stocks and lilies, and can wander from there the short distance to the Acequia (Watercourse), where water and pavilions and flowers and light take over from flowers and trees and water and light.

The Albaicín and Sacromonte The Albaicín is Granada's answer to Córdoba's *judería* and Seville's Barrio Santa Cruz. But it is not the same as either: it does not have that preserved feel, that hint of history pickled in formalin that the *judería* can sometimes give; nor the bursting vitality that the Barrio Santa Cruz gets from its nightly invasion by students; it seems more naturally inhabited by ordinary people, as well as being more open to the sky and air, and fresher (you are over 2,000 feet up). And it has the double advantage of being picturesque and worth seeing in itself, and giving you magnificent views of the Alhambra, glimpsed at first, then seen in full from the Mirador San Nicolás or various other places.

These views are not only of the whole Alhambra from the Torres Bermejas to the Generalife with the Sierra Nevada beyond. You also see up the Darro valley with its closer steeper mountains; and down over Granada and out beyond to the whole vast fertile plain that the Moors brought to fruition. In front of you are a palace and gardens whose peculiar delight, in the blazing heat, is largely created by Moorish skill with water; to your left, the source of that water, tapped and canalized from eight miles away; to your right is the plain made fruitful by the same skills, and which must to the Moors, coming from arid lands, have seemed like paradise. It is, I think, no accident that people here to this day appreciate water as a drink, and will sip and savour an untried water as a Frenchman would wine. Certainly I find that as a thirst quencher I often prefer the Lanjarón water off the slopes of the Sierra Nevada to beer.

It must have been near heaven to the Moors – the hedonistic heaven of the *Rubaiyat* – and this I believe to be the first source of the fierce love for their city you find in so many present day Granadinos, and at the origin, too, of the much-quoted lines of Icaza, on seeing a blind beggar:

Dale limosna mujer
que no hay en la vida nada
como la pena de ser
ciego y en Granada

(Give him alms, woman, for there is nothing in life
so sad as being blind and in Granada.)

The Albaicín is the old Moorish part of Granada. Originally, it was a separate city: Boabdil surrendered 'Granada and Albaicín' to the Catholic Monarchs in 1492. The old palace, from before the building of the Alhambra, stood where Santa Isabel is now; some of the surviving stretches of wall probably date back to the eighth-century; and churches such as San José, that replaced the mosques, still have their minarets as bell-towers. For the first few years it remained Moorish. Thereafter, because they were systematically impoverished, it was less subject to renewal and modernization than the rest of the city.

So today you have what is still visibly an old Moorish city, with some of its houses dating from then, and the others on the same pattern. And, more than its equivalent quarters of Seville and Córdoba, it is still a living entity. What is more to the point is that it is a charming place to wander in, giving sudden spectacular views of the Alhambra and the mountains beyond, and glimpses of the little gardens that the Moors kept hidden within the walls of their homes.

The Sacromonte lies beyond it, the gypsy quarter where many of them live in caves that can be visited, and where at the sight of a tourist, they will pick up their guitars and skirts and perform – for a time and at a price. The gypsies of Granada are *marginados*, outliers who are not part of the social contract: they make me feel I am demeaning them, having them perform for casual cash like fairground monkeys. I am too conscious that in western Andalusia, in places like Chiclana and Jerez, they are integrated, accepted members of society. But that is merely an opinion; in writing this book, I, too, can be said to be 'performing for casual cash' yet I do not feel demeaned. I discuss this further in the section on Flamenco (*see* page 300).

If you want to visit Sacromonte, go the whole length of the Carrera del Darro, turn left up the Cuesta del Chapiz and then right at the Casa de Chapiz. After that it will not be long before junior predators take you in hand.

Visit to the Albaicín What follows is a suggested itinerary with variations. But a variation you might consider if you do not like too much uphill walking, is to take a no. 7 bus from Calle Reyes Católicos up to Calle Pagues (which is a couple of streets north of the Plaza Larga) and do all your walking back downhill.

Key areas are the Plaza Larga (at the end of the stretch of inner wall that runs up from near the Elvira Gate) and the Mirador San Nicolás, a short way south of it. Other notable bits are round the Santa Isabel monastery, along the Carrera del Darro and, if you are game for more (and especially for more panoramic views), north of the Plaza Larga, up between the Mirador San Cristobal and up at the Plaza Cruz de Piedra. But none of these is important: there is a lot of pleasure in getting lost among the alleys and lanes and tiny squares (*callejones, carriles, plazoletas*) in the area around the Plaza Larga and Saint Nicholas. The streets are such a maze that I am assuming you carry with you the town plan handed out by the Tourist Office. Do not worry about getting lost: even in spots where you cannot see the Alhambra or the Cathedral to steer by, downwards is the way home.

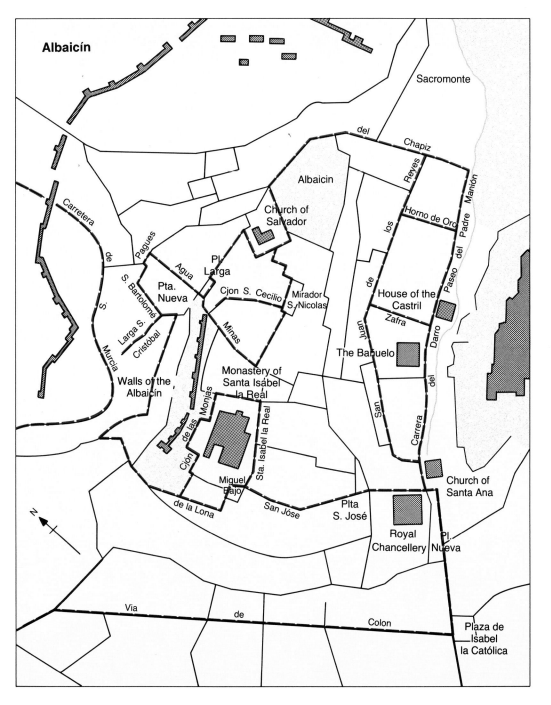

Albaicín

Sacromonte

Carretera
de

S. Bartolomé
S.
Murcia

Pagues

Albaicín

Church of
Salvador

del
Chapiz

Reyes

Horno de Oro

los

Padre Manjón

Agua
Pl.
Larga

Pta.
Nueva

Cjon S. Cecilio

Mirador
S. Nicolas

de

Paseo del

House of the
Castril

Darro

Larga S.
Cristóbal

Minas

Zafra

The Bañuelo

Juan

Walls of the
Albaicín

Monastery of
Santa Isabel
la Real

Cjón de las Monjas

San

Carrera

del

Church of
Santa Ana

Miguel
Bajo

Sta. Isabel la Real

N

de la Lona

San Jóse

Plta
S. José

Royal
Chancellery

Pl.
Nueva

Via
de

Colon

Plaza de
Isabel
la Católica

The route you take depends on where you prefer to start from. If the Plaza Nueva is convenient, I suggest you walk up by the river bank, the *Carrera del Darro*. At No. 31 you come to the *Arab Baths*, one of the very few that survived, and open to the public, admission free, during the normal hours. At no. 41 is the Castril, a Renaissance house that now holds the Archaeological Museum. Its front is an oddity: it is carved with emblems and inscriptions that suggest the first owner had some fairly loopy ideas.

Between these two buildings, the Calle Zafra is as good a place as any to begin your climb. The church of *San Juan de los Reyes* replaced a mosque and kept the minaret as a bell-tower. By its unadorned simplicity it shows it was one of those built soon after the reconquest, when images would have been offensive to recently converted, or 'converted', Moslems. From here drift upwards, keeping left rather than right when in doubt, and you will come to the *Mirador San Nicolas*, a tiny esplanade with a splendid view. From here you will see over, and partly down into, the Moorish houses, and up and across to the whole Alhambra. The drinking fountain and trough is typical of ones to be seen all over Moorish Andalusia. I took what I thought a good photograph of a child and a dog both drinking, but only realized on developing it that I had focused on graffiti unsuited to this gentle volume.

If a taste is all you want or have time for, you can make your way back to the Plaza Nueva by dropping down to Calle Nuevo San Nicolas and zigzagging south and west down to it by the Chancelry and old Gaol.

Otherwise, you will find it worth it to leave the Mirador San Nicolas at its north-west corner, and go via the Cementerio and Callejón San Cecilio to the old city gateway, the *Puerta Nueva*, so called because it was indeed new once – when the Moors built the wall. Through it is the *Plaza Larga*, a pleasant spot to take stock, or a snack, or even a meal, but in this case go just a little further up to the *Calle Pagues* where *El Ladrillo* is fun and plentiful.

Here again, the energetic can continue up the Calle Agua and either left and up onto the Murcia road to the *Mirador San Cristobal*, from which the view is also good, or else left and right and so up to the Puerta Cruz de Piedra, up by the outer walls, and which gives an even higher lookout point. If you opt for this latter, then I suggest returning by taking the Calle San Luis, turning off to the right down any of the first four or five side streets.

My own less energetic preference from the Plaza Larga would be to go back through the Puerta Nueva, through the little Minas square and then keep right to *Santa Isabel le Real*. Round the north side of this, between it and the wall, runs the Callejón de las Monjas, which gives access to the *Daralhorra* (House of the Honourable Woman, a sort of Dower House) now restored. (Open: 10 a.m.–1 p.m. and 3–6 p.m. Ring the doorbell.) From here, you can get back to the Plaza Nueva by the Callejón del Gallo, past San Miguel Bajo, down Calle San José to the church of *San José* (another that has kept its minaret), and so to your starting point. Or else you can drop down to the Carril de la Lona, right to the Cuesta de Alhacaba, and so down to the Puerta de Elvira. The arch of the gate stands as it was in the eleventh-century; it was the main entry to the city, where Ferdinand and Isabella marched in; and it was a place of execution where (for Lorca buffs) Mariana Pineda was put to death.

In fact, the Elvira Gate is the other most likely convenient point of access to the Albaicín. If that is your case, I am afraid you will have to read my itinerary backwards, or else throw the book away and do your own exploring – which might be just as much fun.

The Cathedral and Surroundings (Open for visits: 10.30 a.m.–1 p.m. and 4–7 p.m.; the Capilla Real opens: 10.30 a.m.–1 p.m. and 3.30–6 p.m.) To the historian of architecture the Cathedral may be interesting, especially for its west front and chancel – interesting, but ugly. So, unless that is your line, the Cathedral itself has nothing to attract you (though the organ is one of those triumphant Spanish affairs with flaring trumpet pipes. It dates from 1745, and the organist is good). But the Cathedral Sacristy and the Capilla Real (Royal Chapel and Pantheon) are worth seeing.

Sacristy In the Sacristy, on a stand under a large and unexciting canvas is a statuette by Alonso Cano called the Inmaculada (the Immaculate Conception). I know of no work of the seventeenth or eighteenth centuries so compelling. It is like umpteen other religious figures of the period, and yet utterly unlike. The simplicity of the Virgin's posture conveys the simplicity of the person, and her serene absorption makes the

207

Capilla Real

figure fade as statue and come alive, gently, quietly, under your gaze. Words are poor substitutes: if you can do so, see it.

Beware: It was intended for a lectern; a copy was made by an imitator, which is now in the Sacristy-museum adjoining the Capilla Real. Do not be fobbed off with it: the two are identical, except for everything that matters.

Capilla Real The Capilla Real is best approached from outside by the south-east entrance, rather than coming to it through the length of the Cathedral. As you see it, it is a fine example of Plateresque and pleasing to the eye whether architecture interests you or not, though most of the building is late Gothic, or Isabelline. The famous Madrasa (the Moorish school) on your left as you approach the chapel, has nothing to show since it was rebuilt in the eighteenth century. The Capilla Real, inside, is an anthology of early-sixteenth-century sculptors and builders. Beyond a fine Plateresque grille are the tombs of the Catholic Monarchs, together with their daughter Mad Joan and her husband Handsome Philip. The Spanish habit, throughout history, of giving their rulers nicknames can be more fun when you translate them, though I doubt whether Fat Sancho would have agreed. It somehow goes hand in hand with their outspoken independence, which is just as long-standing: There exists the text of a declaration (from the fifteenth century, I think) that goes, 'We, who are as good as you, take you, who are no better than us, as our sovereign lord.'

In the crypt, beneath the tombs, plain and grim, are the actual lead coffins. But incipient necrophiliacs need not apply: I am informed that Napoleon's soldiers were here and the coffins are empty. I can understand them wanting to rob the graves, but what on earth did they want with the remains?

In the Chapel itself is a fine Dierick Bouts Triptych, and in the adjoining chapel museum several Memlings, two Roger van der Weydens, one Botticelli, and two or three more Bouts.

Corral del Carbon The Corral del Carbon nearby is one of the most interesting buildings in the city. It is just on the other side of the Calle Reyes Católicos, as you cut across from the cathedral via Calle Lopez Rubio. It dates from the fourteenth century (though, as you see it, mainly sixteenth century) and is the only surviving *fondak* or *khan* (Inn or Caravanserai) in Spain. Although restored, it gives a good idea of what it was once like. You can go in — today it is an Arts and Crafts centre – but you miss nothing by just standing in its courtyard and looking round at the galleried rooms above, and at what were the storage and stabling below.

Alcaicería The Alcaicería, the old silk market, is in the area immediately south and west of the Cathedral. The Souk once occupied a host of alleyways. After a fire in 1843, a simplified evocation was built. It still has enough colour to be worth wandering through, and maybe buying a souvenir. And at the bottom or western end of the Zacatin, *Bib-Rambla* Square is a pleasant place to sit out with an ice-cream, horchata, beer or whatever. You will soon, if not already, be getting familiar with these Arabic names: Here *Bab* is 'Gate'; *Rambla* is 'sand', or a sandy, dry river-bed, though the gate itself has been transported to the Alhambra where it stands in the Alamedas, the avenues of trees below the walls, that were a gift of the Duke of Wellington. The word *alcaicería* means 'covered market', and by implication the place where precious things were sold. In this area and in those days, silk was the important product, and the Alpujarras rich in mulberry groves.

La Cartuja (Open: 10 a.m.–1 p.m. and 4–7 p.m.) The Charterhouse of Granada is on the northern outskirts of the city, up the Calle Real de la Cartuja and Paseo de la Cartuja. But, in case you have the time, the following will, I hope, help you decide whether you want to see it or not.

It runs pretty well the whole gamut of Spanish Baroque, from the balanced, through the elegantly delicate, to the wildest excesses of the Churrigueresque. The nave I think successful of its style, though it is so rich in ornament as to constitute a dictionary of Baroque elements. It was built through most the seventeenth century, up to about 1660.

The Sacristy (1727–46) is something of an apotheosis of rococo, with not a straight line in sight and immensely rich surfaces. But the overall effect is light, delicate and harmonious. Too richly sweet for my palate, perhaps: an architectural zabaglione.

But the Sanctuary is a Churrigueresque fantasmagoria. It is such a mind-boggling, submarine riot of the carvers' and plasterers' crafts that you would not be too surprised to see marble robes waver gently like seaweed in the tide, and a shark drift slowly past your eyes. One wonders what debaucheries of the imagination those austere, self-denying Carthusians suffered – or enjoyed – in this place. Filling most of it is a baldachino, a sort of monstrance. It is a twenty foot high pile-up of marble and jasper, black, white and pink, whose rockery (as it were) is overgrown with heavy hunks of gilding. Encrusted on to it like clams on a reef are four sentimental ladies showing a bit of arm and leg, one of whom seems completely overcome. Well, and so would you be if you found yourself sitting holding a trout – and what's more, staring straight at a St John Baptist who is a dead ringer for Vanessa Redgrave, and who appears to be modelling a smart little sheepskin number, unveiled by two cherubic Christian Diors. They certainly upstage the Founder of the Order, St Bruno, standing in the other corner, who merely looks like Yul Brynner's kid sister.

If you are interested in Baroque, do not miss it; if you are not, I would not miss it either.

There is a certain ghoulish interest, too, in the gigantic canvases to be seen in the Refectory. Badly painted in drab, flat tones are scenes of revolting torture. The fortitude of the victims may have been edifying to the monks at supper, but it can hardly have helped their digestion. I would not have mentioned these paintings but that the events depicted did happen, and uncomfortably close to home. In 1534, a dozen or so gentle and courageous old men were dragged out of the London Charterhouse, behind Smithfield, to be butchered for refusing to deny the Pope. And the executioners may have included your or my grandad.

Museums and Galleries

Archaelogical Museum, Casa de Castril, Carrera del Darro, 41. Open: 10 a.m.–2 p.m. Shut Mondays.

Hispano-Muslim Art, Palace of Charles v, Alhambra. Open: 10 a.m.–2 p.m. Shut Sundays.

Provincial Fine Arts, Palace of Charles v, Alhambra. Open: 10 a.m.–2 p.m. Shut Mondays.

Casa de los Tiros (House of the Muskets – Local History and Popular Arts). Plaza del Padre Suarez. No opening times known: it is under restoration at the time of writing.

Gómez Moreno Museum, Calle del Aire, (by the Alhambra Palace Hotel. Admission free. Ring at the door during normal hours. Shut Saturdays, Sundays and Mondays.

Manuel de Falla House and Museum, Callejón de Falla (next door to the Manuel de Falla Auditorium and near the Gómez Moreno Museum). Free entry. Open: 10 a.m.–2 p.m. and 4–7 p.m. Shut Mondays.

Casa de los Pisas (Mementos of St John of God). Callejón de los Pisas. Open: 9 a.m.–1 p.m. Shut Mondays.

Song and Dance Some books suggest that Granada is the only Andalusian city that goes to bed early. Not so, but it does tend to confine its evening entertainment to certain areas. If you are mentally or really under thirty, and do not want to spend your evenings tucked up with a good Washington Irving, you might try going down to the northern end of the Calle Pedro Antonio de Alarcón. Here life begins after eleven, warms up towards midnight and by one thirty is roaring. The street is long so go to the north, or University, end. Parents should not get worried if their offspring have not come back by three or four in the morning.

At this point, a reminder that for the Spaniard alcohol has no macho associations, and that the slightest sign of drunkenness is privately despised, viewed with pity, and left alone at the earliest polite opportunity. As for enjoyment, I think it has been well expressed by the English footballer Gary Lineker, who until recently was working in Spain (I quote from an interview with Simon Barnes):

> 'They like to spend their money on living, not on houses. Spaniards like to sit down, get a good meal, and argue. You say something, they'll disagree – and that's a good evening.'

He is referring, from the height of his twenty-something years, to married couples; but, with minor variations, the same applies to the younger and unmarried. A crowded pub or bar and loud music is all that is needed: the laughter and entertainment are provided by the customers. With the coming of freedom in 1975, the music was pretty much wall-to-wall rock. And since the Spaniards seem to love noise (in 1988 Madrid officially overtook Rome as the most noise-polluted city – to the delight of the Romans), rock at high volume.

The pendulum has recently begun to swing, in an interesting way: wherever you are, in bar or street party, if Sevillanas are played it won't be long before somebody starts to dance them – and the odds are there will soon be several pairs dancing and many of the rest of the clientele marking the rhythm with that peculiar Spanish clapping that sounds like pistol shots. At the far end of Calle P.A. de Alarcón you will see that the rock bars are no more crowded than the *Machaco* across the street, where the loudspeakers belt out Sevillanas and other more or less pop flamenco. Inside, married women and girls, students, typists and lawyers, in jeans or the latest gear, will be all twirling hands and arms and bodies, and then, in the interludes, picking up their beer and conversation where they left it.

Flamenco, or at least good flamenco, is never easily found by the tourist, simply because the best singers and dancers may earn their living performing in *Peñas*, or clubs, but are unlikely to be found churning it out several times nightly in public locales. Of the commercial *tablaos*, I am told that the *Peña Platerías*, Calle

Patio de los Aljibes, 13, or the *Reina Mora* up on the Carretera de Murcia, by the Mirador San Cristobal, are as good as any.

Shopping Pottery and textiles are the most characteristic products you can buy here. If you are going to visit the Alpujarra, my own view is that you can get the best of both there, especially at Trevélez. But if you want the Fajalauza ware (blue and green designs on a white background), or if your visit does not go beyond the city, then you should buy it in the Albaicín, for example at:

Cerámica Al Yarra, Calle Bañuelo, 5.

Cerámica Aliatar, Plaza de Aliatar, 18.

Cerámica Fajalauza, Carretera de Murcia.

Cerámica Miguel de Yedra, Carretera de Murcia.

Or, for modern design:

Carmen Vila, Calle Bocanegra, 14.

For textiles, again, if you can, go to the Alpujarras. On the Murcia road, at Ugíjar, is the Alpujarran Weavers' Co-operative; the village of Bérchules is noted for its weavers; and the already mentioned shop in Trevélez. In the Albaicín, there are shops in the Cuesta Alhacaba, the Cuesta de Chapiz, the Puente Mariano, the Calle Guatimosín, and the Plaza San Nicolas. There is a good workshop, the *Tejidos Artísticos Fortuny*, down in town in the tiny Plaza de Fortuny. It is a short walk from the central Plaza Isabel la Católica, via Pavaneras and Escolástica.

For Antiques, try the Calle Elvira.

For sweet pastries, as always in Andalusia, you should try the Nunneries:

Convento de San Bernardo del Cister, Carrera del Darro.

Convento de Santa Catalina de Zafra, Carrera del Darro, 43.

Convento de las Comendadoras de Santiago, Calle Santiago, 20.

Or try the shops:

Flor y Nata, Avenida de la Constitución, 13.

Flor y Nata, Calle Mesones.

Lopez Mezquita, Calle Reyes Católicos, 29.

Useful Addresses

Tourist Office: Plaza Mariana Pineda, 10. Tel: 22 66 88. Open: 10 a.m.–1.30 p.m. and 4–7 p.m., Saturday 10 a.m.–1 p.m. No one seems sure yet whether this is the new permanent site, or whether the Office will return to the Casa de Tiros when restoration is complete.

Post Office (Correos): Puerta Real, 1. Tel: 22 48 35.

Telephone (Telefónica): Calle Reyes Católicos, 55.

First Aid: Tel: 22 12 63.

Red Cross (Crus Roja): Calle Escoriaza, 8. Tel: 22 20 24.

Ambulancias Alhambra Granada, c/A. Mora, 2. Tel: 28 44 61, has an international service.

Police: Comisaria (National Police, to whom theft or other crime must be reported, not least for your insurance). Plaza de los Campos.

Emergency Tel: 091.

Travel

RENFE (Railways): Office (for ticket sales), Calle Reyes Católicos, 63. Tel: 22 31 19.

Station, Avenida Andaluces.

Air Travel: Iberia, Plaza Isabel la Católica, 2. Tel: 22 14 52 and 22 59 51.

Buses: As usual, various places according to the Bus Company. But buses from the city up to the Alhambra (no. 2), and up to the Albaicín (no. 12), leave from the Batallas Fountain, at the junction of Acera del Darro and Carrera del Genil. The no. 7 for Albaicín leaves from just nearby. And the no. 11 does a circular route that takes you between Reyes Católicos, the station and the Paseo de Ronda bus station. The daily service up to the Sol y Nieve area near the top of the Sierra Nevada leaves from the Puerta Real. Most long-distance coaches leave from the Camino de Ronda, 97 (Alsina Graells Sur Co.) or from the Station on Andaluces, 10 (Bacoma Co.).

Car Rental: Atesa, Tel: 22 40 04.

Avis, Tel: 25 53 58.

Europcar, Tel: 29 50 65.

Hertz, Tel: 25 16 82.

Granada Province The possibilities that may interest you are the Alpujarras; the peaks of the Sierra Nevada; Alhama; and Guadix and Lacalahorra.

I shall only cover the first two here. Alhama seems to me best taken in as part of a journey between Málaga and Granada, and as the odds are you would be doing it after flying in to Málaga, I include it in that chapter.

Mulhacén, Granada

Guadix alone is a bit disappointing though the drive up out of Granada, on the Carretera de Murcia (N342), and the Mora pass, gives spectacular views – behind you. But if you include Lacalahorra, and the badlands around Tabernas and 'Mini Hollywood' in Almería province, then you have a good tour: I discuss it in the Almería chapter (*see* page 240).

The Sierra Nevada The highest peaks of the Sierra Nevada, the snowy mountains, are about 40 km (25 ml.) from the city by a road, the highest in Europe, that goes up to within a few metres of the second highest peak, La Veleta 3,400m (11,200ft). However hot you are, however still the air, however blue the sky or blazing the sun, take a jersey and, if you can, some sort of wind-cheater, too. It seems crazy; but not when you get to the top.

You can tell just be looking, from almost anywhere in the Alhambra or on the Albaicín, whether there is snow on top or the road is clear. But it does no harm to check, by ringing 48 01 53 and getting a report in Spanish or English on the state of the road. The road surface is excellent right to the top. Down the other

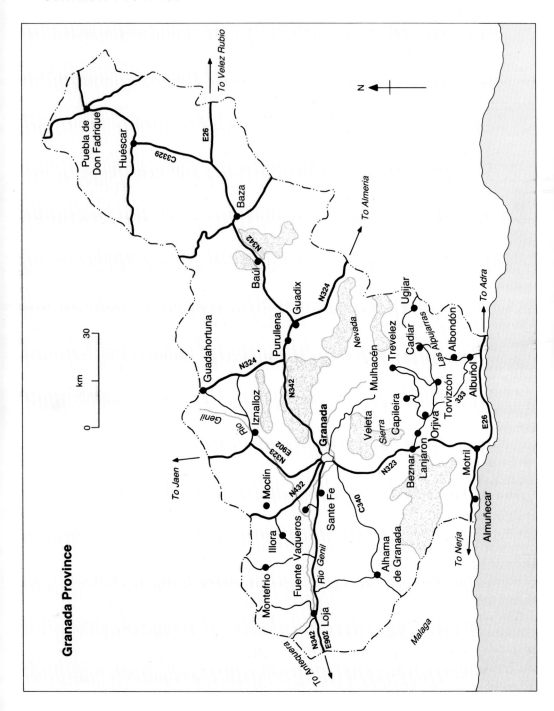

Granada Province

side to Capileira in the Alpujarras the road has not been surfaced, at least at the time of writing. But it is perfectly practicable both for cars and cyclists.

At about 30km (18ml.) and 2,440m (8,000ft) you come to Sol y Nieve, the winter resort. The whole mountain round here is accessible for walking, but I would not recommend that as your reason for coming – there are plenty of places just over the other side of the mountain that would make a walker's paradise. Here it is rather bare and shaly. When you reach Sol y Nieve, if you get out of the car for a stroll or the view or to say hello to the cattle with ominous horns that browse this high, it may look hardly worth it just going on the few hundred yards to the summit. Furthermore, it will still be warm and you will wonder why the jersey and the wind-cheater. That is the illusion created by mountain air: As the crow flies, that nearby ridge is more than 5km (3ml.) off and 900m (3,000ft) higher. When you get there, the illusion will work the other way round: Sol y Nieve looks half-way down the mountain. But there is no illusion at all about the change in temperature.

At the top you are within a few yards of the summit of the Veleta. To the east, the highest mountain in Spain, Mulhacén (3,480m/11,400ft), is just another part of the ridge, only 61m(200ft) higher, and seemingly half a mile away (though, in fact, three miles). It feels like the roof of the world. Your view is limited only by the haze. Ideally, on a clear day you would see Africa, and the whole coast round to Gibraltar in between. I suspect that in practice this does not often happen or, if it does, then the air will be too clear for comfort and the weather will not be long in driving you away.

What is the pleasure of driving up to the top of a hill and then down again? And why this particular hill? If mountains are what you like, you can go higher in Switzerland, more often and on more different mountains. Certainly the attraction here does not lie in the foreground: you are standing on a whopping great heap of what geologists, with happy phrase, call decomposing mica schist.

I think it is because of the loneliness of Mulhacén. This mountain seems higher because from 11,000 feet you look right down to sea level – indeed, to the sea. Then, again, there is the pleasure in the sheer contrast, the unlikeliness, of passing from the

heat of Andalusia straight up to the cleansing bite of this air in
your lungs. To the north and west of you, other mountains reach
6,000 feet, but that is still more than Ben Nevis' worth beneath
you, and this peaks feels alone.

Yet perhaps the reasons that I perceive are not the true or the
only ones. In the chapter on Jaén I quote the enthusiasm aroused
by the Cazorla range in the British botanist Oleg Polunin. Listen
to a Spanish geographer on the subject of the northern and
southern slopes of the Sierra Nevada:

'The northern valleys are petrified by snow and ice; the
southern ones roasted by the heat of the sun. In the farm houses
around Granada people crouch beside an open fire, and keep the
doors and windows well shut; in those of the Alpujarra they sleep
in the moonlight, on piles of straw, in the open air. The farmers
of Guejar or Monacil store away acorns and cherries; those of the
Contraviesa put by almonds and oranges. The former keep
potatoes under the snow; the latter dry figs in the sun. In the
south there are wide rolling hills, light blue in colour; in the north
menacing peaks rise up, shadowed and black.'

These are different perceptions from mine, but the geographer
is clearly as aroused to enthusiasm as the botanist, and his
colourful oppositions, do not forget, are occasioned by simply
turning to face south and north.

Landscapes always look more spectacular when viewed from on
high: the slopes steeper; the plains flatter. To the north-west, the
Pandera range of 6,000 feet sticks up like a pimple out of the plains,
hiding Jaén. To the south-west, and close to, the Sierra de Almijarra
mercifully screens Málaga and Torremolinos from sight. Beyond it,
in the distance, you can see the jumble of the Serranía de Ronda,
and you may possibly be able to distinguish the Sierra Bermeja
rising up from the sea behind Estepona. Sixty miles north-east of
you are the highest of the other ranges in the area: The Sierras of
Sagra, Segura and Cazorla, which reach over 7,500 feet, still short
of you by some 3,500 feet. And tucked in down at your feet is
Granada, peeping round the spur of the Alhambra.

There is a daily bus, leaving from the Batallas Fountain at
9 a.m. and starting back at 5 p.m. It will take you as far as the
University Hostel, leaving you about 13km (8ml.) of trudge to the
summit.

If you come in the winter or early spring, then you need a completely different set of data. The ski slopes are from 3,350m (11,000ft) down to about 2,070m (6,800ft), and the snow is usually good from December through to late in April. 18 lifts (10 T-bars), 25 marked runs; 13 hotels, of which four are ★★★★, four are ★★★ and five are ★★; twenty-odd restaurants and a few discos; sixty miles from Málaga Airport, twenty miles from Granada.

The Alpujarra In all Andalusia, this is the place I am most likely to return to for a holiday. It is a series of upland valleys created by the fold between the Sierra Nevada on its northern flank and the Sierra de Contraviesa, which is the last ripple between it and the sea. For centuries it lay forgotten and more or less isolated from the world, except for the little spa town of Lanjarón at its western end. In the 1920s Gerald Brenan came to live here: His description of it in *South from Granada* put the place on the map. Gerald Brenan was one of those British writers (Richard Ford is the other most notable of several examples) who are better known and loved in Spain than in their own country. But the map he put it on is remote, and the impact of his book gradual; this is still a friendly mountain community, where you can eat and sleep well for a few pounds, and walk or ride for hours

The Alpujarra

without seeing a soul. The villages mostly cling to the hillsides, with plentiful water for their crops. At either end, around Orgiva and Ugíjar, the valleys open out a bit, and it was here, I imagine, that the mulberry groves grew in the Middle Ages when silk made the Alpujarra prosperous. Today, with water never short, it is a fruit garden; apples, pears, almonds, cherries, oranges, lemons, peaches, quinces, pomegranates and the inevitable olive groves. But, of the hill slopes, the memory that dominates is the herby smells brought out by the sun beating down, and the rock-reflecting heat, on thyme, rosemary and lavender, juniper, broom, cistus and heather and the pungent pines.

The Alpujarrans are a mountain people, perhaps rather ugly compared to most Andalusians, but who share with all Spaniards the easy smiling helpfulness that makes me like to be in Spain. It is not certain where they stem from: the Moors were given this place by treaty as a kingdom in 1492. But when the Christians reneged and started to persecute them they rose under Aben Humeya and were finally crushed in the late sixteenth century, driven out of here, and the Alpujarra repopulated by Spaniards from the north. And yet today there are many Moorish-looking faces.

After the fleshpots of the Costa del Sol, or the cultural heat of the inland cities, I would strongly recommend you try a few days here. The western end is the best, but rather than stay in one of the two towns, Lanjarón or Orgiva, take your courage in your hands and choose one of the many villages, and put up at a humble inn. Sometimes they do not even announce themselves as a hotel or boarding house (*hostal*, or CH *Casa de Huéspedes*). The sign merely says *Comidas y Camas* which is 'Food and Beds'. You will sleep comfortably in clean rooms (the nights are distinctly cool up here), you will eat some of the best food in Spain, peasant cooking with delicious soups and stews, drink some distinctive wine (not even recognizably the same drink as the acid stuff that peasant wine so often is in France or Italy, but smooth and strong and refreshing) and, if I can persuade you to put your prejudices where they deserve to go, drink the tap water in complete confidence. Do not forget that it is purer than anything out of a tap in England: the local water is put in bottles and sold all over Spain; while we have yet to bring ours up to acceptable Common Market standards.

The fact that bed and board will amount to a few pounds only (and the wine, pennies) is not my reason for trying to persuade you: you will get a taste of a real Spain and, I hope, a feeling of contact with its people. The one drawback is that you cannot expect a private bathroom. Some villages have 'proper' hotels – there is a particularly horrible-looking one in Pórtugos (it desecrates this unspoiled landscape) call the *Malagueño Nuevo*, where you can enjoy all the sanitary impersonality of the Developer's trade. Well, it is your choice after all. The places friends took me to were the *Casa Moreno* in Torvizcón, the *Fonda Sierra Nevada* in Pitres, the *Hostal Alvarez* in Trevélez, and others even more unpretentious. I do not think it matters: they were all clean and pleasant.

On the Michelin map no. 446 most of the roads seem to be marked with a green line, signifying scenic route, but strangely they omit what I think the best one: a little way out of Cádiar, a minor road GR433 branches south, and joins the GR443 near the Venta del Tarugo. Here you can turn left and carry on down to Albuñol, Albondón (where the local wine is made) and the coast. But I prefer to keep right on the GR443, which runs along the crest, and so has less hairpins and gear changes, but splendid views on both sides. Pay no attention to the road's low status on the map: it is well surfaced and good.

But, clearly, you are going to get much more out of the area if you walk or ride: from the inside of a car you cannot watch a Golden Eagle at work, or smell the herbs... which brings me to horses.

Most of the best things were shown me by three people who organize riding treks, so I surely owe them a puff. Such treks are growing more popular in Spain and can be done in various parts of the country, notably in the Serranía de Ronda. My lot are called Aventura Ltd. and I give the details in the section on Horses (*see* page 284). It is a commercial venture, of course, but it does not seem like it. Three people who live there and like horses, really work to give you value. And what, above all, it brought home to me was how much you miss by sticking to the roads. These mountains look wild but they are in fact covered in a network of old mule tracks. In a week's riding, I doubt if we covered a quarter of a mile by road.

The Alpujarras has some exciting riding country

The three villages of Pampaneira, Bubión and Capileira that sit one on top of the other on the road up to the Veleta (*see* Sierra Nevada, above) are more touristy than most. Bubión boasts an ★★★ *Apart Hotel*, which somehow disqualifies it for me. But I like the sign outside Pampaneira that says 'Pampaneira: Viajero Quedate a Vivir con Nosotros' (Traveller, stop and live with us.) It is the word 'Live' when they could have said 'Stay' that does it, I think. From them eastwards a whole string of pleasant villages cling up on the hillsides, culminating in Trevélez which claims to be the highest in Europe. The name means 'Three Parishes' and it straggles a long way up on the slope to Mulhacén, so it may even be true. More to the point is that it is a good base for a walk up to Mulhacén; one of its tourist shops has a good selection of woven ware, and of pottery, especially some with an off-white (tin glaze?) base and pale blue-grey patterning; and Trevélez hams rival Jabugo, which is saying a lot. You may like a mini-lexicon for the honey sold here: *Azahar* = citrus blossom; *Romero* = Rosemary; *Encina* = Holm-oak, ilex; *Milflores* = thousand flowers.

222

Eastwards from here, after Bombarón, the valley opens out again, you pass Gerald Brenan's village Yegen, the mountains start to dwindle and you reach the eastern 'capital', Ugíjar. With 3,000 inhabitants — the same population it had 150 years ago — it is as unspoiled as anywhere, though a regional centre of pilgrimage, which affects one bit of the town. Here there is a *Hostal Pedro*, clean and modern, if you want a private bathroom. Cheap, too, at £12 double, though if you happen on a disco night, you may pay in other ways. There is also an old *posada* or muleteers' inn, where cobbles and cribs have given way to marble and tables, but otherwise nothing is changed. The old lady has not tried to go up-market, and acts as hostel to itinerant workers, so I would not put up there, but shall not forget her sardines grilled over embers with a touch of fresh oregano. When I told her so, she looked surprised, muttered *cocino a lo pobre* ('poor man's cooking', though it also means the customer gets no choice). But then a look of pleasure touched her grim old face with a curiously girlish air.

Bedmar

Jaén and its Province The province of Jaén has some of the best things in all Andalusia to offer the holiday visitor. The towns of Ubeda and Baeza show that not only the Moors but the Christians, too, could create elegance and charm. They are still backwaters enough, and tucked far enough away from the main arteries of modern Spain, as well as from the main tourist routes, to please the ear as well as the eye: they are golden to both. And the forests and mountains of the province are an attraction that could well hold you for longer than the townships.

Jaén itself, the capital city, is nothing. It is like those hideous suburbs you have to fight your way through to get to the delight at the heart of Seville, Córdoba or Cádiz. But here there is nothing else: this place has as its heart seven-storey brick and concrete, carbon monoxide, noise and heat. I exaggerate: there is a Baroque Cathedral at its centre, like a stag at bay, surrounded by yelping.

And, high above all that, a fourteenth-century castle perches on a crag and offers the one reason that might bring you here: After all, if you are going to see a building, why not sleep in it? The castle has been extended as a Parador, modern, but added so

224

cleverly that on the north side at least you would hardly tell the difference. On the south side you would, because there the bedrooms have large windows looking away from Jaén, over a chasm, and up to the spectacular crags above. So the only reason for going to Jaén is to stay at the Parador, and look up at the mountains looking down on you, and down on the plains looking up at you. The latter provide an endless perspective of olive groves closed only by the haze of distance.

Parador Nacional Castillo de Santa Catalina ★★★★, 23001-Jaén. Tel: (953) 26 44 11. (£45).

If your main purpose in coming to the province is the Nature Reserve, you may well want to stay right in it:

Parador Nacional El Adelantado ★★★, Sierra de Cazorla, (Jaén). Tel: (953) 72 10 75. (£43) – this is a sort of luxurious hunting lodge, perched on the forested slopes of the range, 8km (5ml.) up its own little road, and not much more from the source of the Guadalquivir.

Otherwise, I assume your base will be Ubeda or Baeza, both of which are lovely places – they are only 8km (5ml.) apart. If you want to stay at a Parador, then Ubeda; if not, then Baeza. I discuss the possibilities under the two towns.

Access If you are coming from the south, I recommend you turn off the N323 at Iznalloz (it sounds like somewhere over the rainbow but is a sleepy hollow with an Arab fort, where the children will stare at you as at a Martian). After 8km (5ml.), turn left (watch for it: the sign is sudden) on to the C325. From here to Ubeda the scenery is beautiful, the road is good, and you will have it almost to yourself, though here, as everywhere, they are working to build a fine new highway, so the traffic may be there by the time you read this. After driving through some splendid mountains you emerge to a serene landscape ahead of you and see two villages on two humps about three or four miles ahead. At least, that is the impression. But it is an illusion created by the clear upland light, for they are Baeza and Ubeda and they are more than twelve miles away. You then come gliding down out of the hills, straight down through the long village of Jodiar and down to the Guadalquivir.

Ubeda is a remarkable little town of some 30,000 people that has split so clearly into old and new that the old has stayed pretty

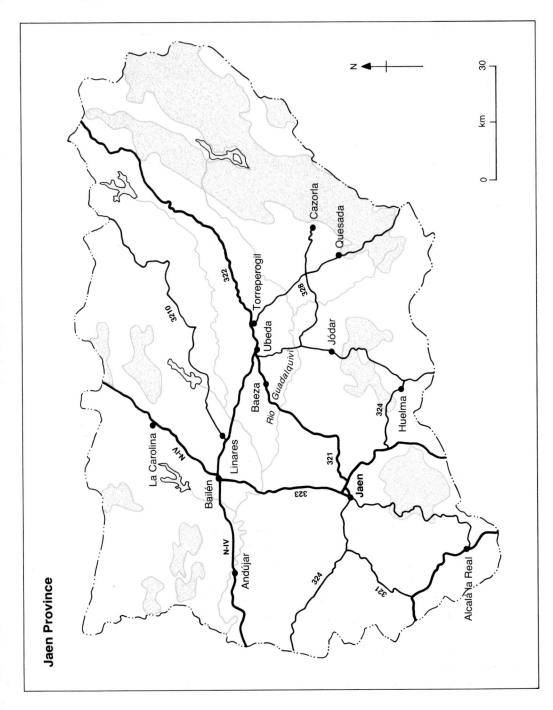

Jaen Province

La Carolina
N-IV
Bailén
Linares
322
3210
N-IV
Andújar
323
324
Baeza
Ubeda
Torreperogil
Río Guadalquivir
328
Jódar
321
Jaen
324
Huelma
321
Alcalà la Real
Cazorla
Quesada

N

30
km
0

Ubeda

well untouched. It is an almost complete Renaissance city, warm and golden in its elegant quarters; and with narrow, cobbled alleyways, giving on to ancient walls, sudden tiny squares, Moorish remnants and noble houses hidden away. If you confine yourself to the 'kulture' guides, there is perhaps a slightly museum atmosphere, as of the past enshrined and lifeless. But wander around, including the back alleys with the noble monuments, and the impression gains on you that at any time (after the siesta perhaps?) the streets may be a-bustle with Montagues and Capulets.

But from the Plaza de Andalucía northwards, the town is as noisy and busy and neutral as any other, with Calle Ramón y Cajal a main thoroughfare for commercial transport between Andalusia and Albacete.

Hotels

Parador Condestable Dávalos ★★★, Plaza de Vázquez Molina, 1. Tel: 75 03 45. (£50) – this is one of the palaces of what must be the most perfect Renaissance square in Spain. The building is austere from the outside, with a delicately arcaded and balconied patio inside. There are only 25 rooms. To stay here, you should have a taste for peace, quiet and the utmost elegance.

Otherwise, hotels in Ubeda are all up on the main artery, Calle Ramón y Cajal:

HR Consuelo ★★, at no. 12. Tel: 75 08 40. (£16).

The Parador, Ubeda

Hs.R La Paz ★★, Plaza de Andalucia, 1. Tel: 75 08 48. (£20 to £11) – eccentric: the rooms on the top floor are vast and good value; descending to slums on first floor.

Pension Sevilla ★★, at no. 9. Tel: 75 06 12. (£10) – clean and value for money.

But, if you are not a determined Paradorian, why not stay in Baeza at Señor Adriano's (*see* Baeza, page 000).

Restaurants The Parador is the best bet. The *Gallo Rojo* in Calle Torrenueva looks inviting but seemed to me to try too hard. I ordered game mountain style and got hare that I could not manage. It reminded me of the Kipling character who roars at his cook, 'Worcester Sauce is a condiment not a fluid': I wanted to roar, 'Rosemary is a herb not a vegetable'. But a French couple told me they had dined well at an unpromising looking place on the ground floor of the *Hostal Castillo* in Calle Ramón y Cajal. I was just getting my coffee after an ordinary meal at the popular *Paz*, under the Hotel, when a liqueur was put in front of me, casually ordered together with theirs by a party at another table,

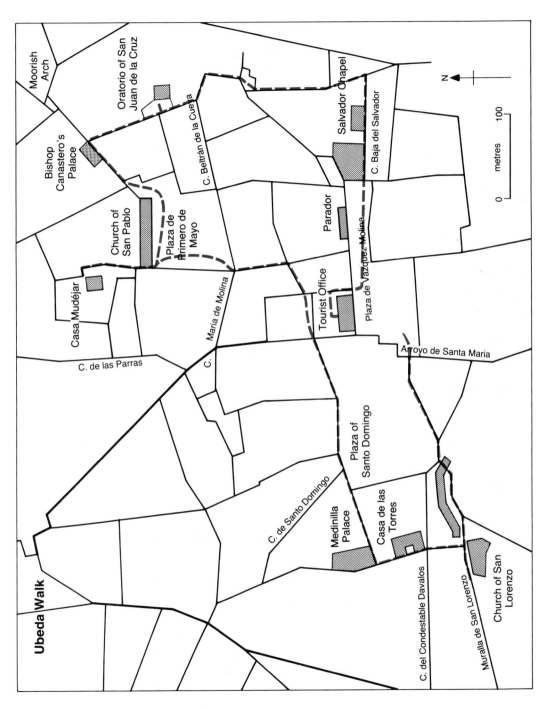

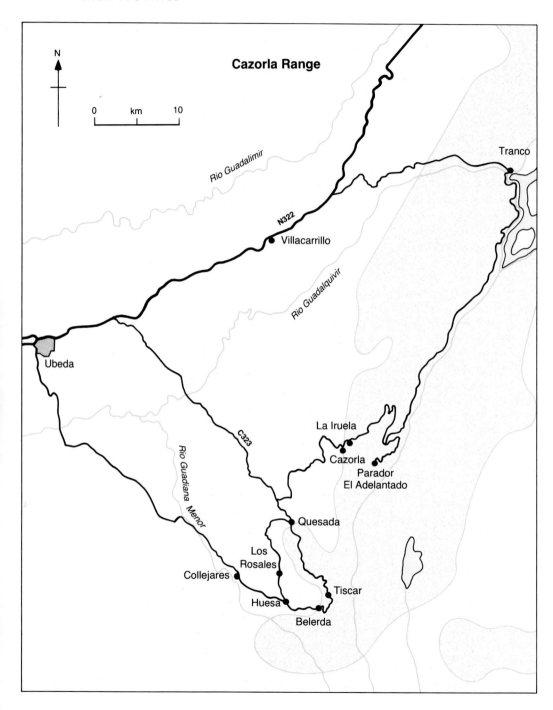

N

Cazorla Range

0   km   10

Rio Guadalimir

Tranco

N322

Villacarrillo

Rio Guadalquivir

Ubeda

La Iruela

Cazorla

Parador
El Adelantado

C323

Rio Guadiana Menor

Quesada

Los
Rosales

Collejares

Tiscar

Huesa

Belerda

'for the foreigner sitting on his own' no doubt. Such courteous gestures are not too rare in Spain, and well able to turn a forgettable meal into a pleasant memory.

A Suggested Walk The Tourist Office is in the Cadenas Palace (sixteenth century by Vandelvira, who together with Diego de Siloé, seems to have built most of Andalusia's Renaissance mansions).

Round to the south side of it, the Plaza de Vázquez Molina begins to illustrate the most extraordinary feature of this town, which is that buildings of varying styles and period seem to harmonize into a single style, united by the golden sandstone, and perhaps, too, by the good manners of the architects. On the north side, the Renaissance in its most strictly classical phase; to the east, the Salvador chapel, of the same century, but richly Plateresque; to the south, the church, both earlier and later, still seems to blend and belong, together with the prison, mansion and grainstore, older looking, though still of the sixteenth century.

If you walk east, down the Calle Baja del Salvador, you quickly come to the edge of town, just as it would have been in the sixteenth century: a bit seedy, a bit shoddy, but cleansed by the upland light and the view out over the olive groves to the Cazorla mountains.

Turn left and up the humble and ancient Callejón de Navarra until you come to an oratory on your right. Here Saint John of the Cross died on 14 December 1591. On the basis of two or three of his poems alone, he must be counted one of the finest poets in history: not even Dante comes nearer to expressing the ineffable, and yet he seems to do so with the quiet simplicity of a sleeping child's breathing. Not much remains from his day, though his followers (the Discalced Carmelites) have tried to reconstruct his cell, and there is one remarkable drawing of his, that Dali used for the composition of his Crucifixion. The 400th centenary will gather litterati and religious alike: as the *Penguin Dictionary of Saints* has it, 'His writings... have made no little appeal even to some who make no profession of Christianity.'

At the end of this street, to your right, you see one of the old Moorish gates to the city. Turning left brings you into the Plaza del 1° de Mayo (aka Plaza del Mercado) which is much more lively than Plaza de Vázquez Molina: it has birds in the acacias, schoolchildren chatting between lessons, and old folk taking the air. It also has the old Town Hall and St Paul's church, once again illustrating Ubeda's ability to blend styles: the church alone covers four centuries, but you have to look hard to see this.

Up past the church's west door, at Calle Cervantes, 6, is a fourteenth-century Mudéjar house. It is the Archaeological Museum, but to my mind much more worth seeing in itself than for its exhibits. (Open: 10 a.m.–2 p.m. and 4–7 p.m.; Sundays 10 a.m.–12.30 p.m. Shut Mondays). From here back to the Tourist Office is simple: straight back down through the Plaza del Mercado and past it. But there is another loop to this walk that I would not miss.

If you turn left out of the Tourist Office, a narrow street faces you that starts as the Calle Corazón de Jesús, takes other names, and ends with the much older and pagan name of Calle Sol y Luna. It drifts you along, past sleepy and seemingly forgotten houses, palaces. (the Contadero, just up in the first right-hand turn, eighteenth century yet still managing to stay in harmony with the rest) and churches. But carry on until the end, then turn left, and on your left is a mansion not to be missed.

The Casa de las Torres is pleasantly Spanish with its Plateresque façade, but in its courtyard it almost rivals Seville's Casa de Pilatos. Here, too, is a fine marriage of last Gothic, Moorish and Renaissance. There is a filigree elegance to it. At the bottom of the street take a few steps to the right, for the view, then to your left the old city wall, with its fountain and drinking trough, and so through it by the Granada gate and a short step back to where you started from.

This walk follows my own interests. It may well be worth your reading it and rejecting whole stretches of it in favour of other things. For example, to turn right instead of left at the end of Calle Baja del Salvador at the start, and so take in the old ramparts and more view, rather than St John's oratory. Or else make it include the charming little square and tumbledown church of San Pedro.

Shopping In this small town, the only suggestion I might make is that Ubeda specializes in patterned esparto mats and carpets. If this interests you, then pick up the walk just after the St John's oratory, but at the end of the street turn right down through the Moorish gate. Opposite you now is the Cuesta de la Merced. Climb up it and it will lead you to the Calle Valencia, which is where you will find the right sort of shops.

Useful Addresses

Tourist Office: Plaza del Ayuntamiento. Tel: 75 08 97. Open: 10 a.m.–1.30 p.m. and 6–8 p.m. Saturday and Sunday 10 a.m.–1.30 p.m.

Post Office: Calle Trinidad, 1. Tel: 75 00 31. Open 9 a.m.–2 p.m. Saturday 9 a.m.–1 p.m.

Bus: Calle San José. Tel: 75 21 57.

Medical Help: Residencia Sanitaria. Tel: 75 11 03.

Police: Plaza de Andalucia. Tel: 75 03 35.

Baeza is charming. It has been important. It has been the capital of a kingdom. It has had a government, a University, a place in the world. But now what it has, above all, is charm.

Its cathedral was shut when I was there, but I do not care: I do not even care to know what the various buildings are, or when they were built; and I certainly refuse to outline a walk for you through the town. When you go there you will see why: you find yourself being drawn to drift down this street or saunter up that one – and it does not matter; the place is just a pleasure to be in, and your pleasure in no way depends on your not missing this or that building.

Baeza

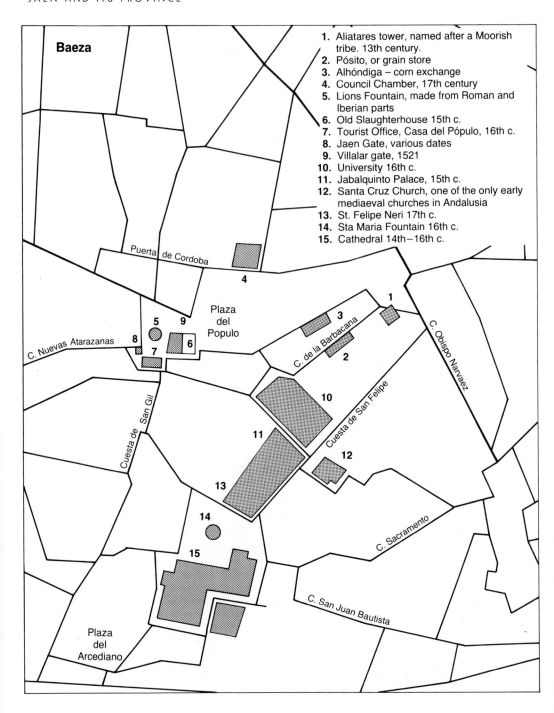

Baeza

1. Aliatares tower, named after a Moorish tribe. 13th century.
2. Pósito, or grain store
3. Alhóndiga – corn exchange
4. Council Chamber, 17th century
5. Lions Fountain, made from Roman and Iberian parts
6. Old Slaughterhouse 15th c.
7. Tourist Office, Casa del Pópulo, 16th c.
8. Jaen Gate, various dates
9. Villalar gate, 1521
10. University 16th c.
11. Jabalquinto Palace, 15th c.
12. Santa Cruz Church, one of the only early mediaeval churches in Andalusia
13. St. Felipe Neri 17th c.
14. Sta Maria Fountain 16th c.
15. Cathedral 14th–16th c.

Puerta de Cordoba

Plaza del Populo

C. Nuevas Atarazanas

C. de la Barbacana

C. Obispo Narvaez

Cuesta de San Gil

Cuesta de San Felipe

C. Sacramento

C. San Juan Bautista

Plaza del Arcediano

Hotels If you are being economical, or if there is no room at the Parador in Ubeda, take rooms in Baeza: there are three Hostales listed for the town, and they may be very nice and all that, but I would go to none of them. For in the street just behind the Tourist Office, is a Hostal with no name posted, and no stars. Yet if you are a foreign visitor to Spain and wanting to taste things Spanish, rather than the international anonymity of efficient hotels, then it is doubtful whether you would have more vivid memories from staying in the sixteenth-century Parador at Ubeda, than at the Hostal of Señor Adriano in Baeza, for £11 per night for a double room with all mod cons and spotlessly clean. Actually, I would choose Señor Adriano's place: there are good Paradors in many places; inns like this are harder to find. The house may well be as old as the Parador; it is built round a patio that he has roofed over with perspex and in which the *azulejos* and the potted plants mingle with the chairs and customers in a way that is slightly Victorian and entirely Spanish, a way that no hotel could emulate. The Hostal belongs to Baeza and they deserve each other.

Hostal Adriano, Calle Conde Romanones, 13, 23440-Baeza, (Jaén). Tel: (953) 74 02 00 – the one drawback that I can see to this Hostal is that it figures in an American guidebook of enormous sales, so you would be wise to check in advance that there is room.

Exploring the Town The town is as Renaissance as Ubeda, though somehow the main square, the Paseo, has an air more Regency than Tudor. Leave your car in it; the Tourist Office is in the delightful little Plaza de los Leones off the bottom (or western) end. One of the buildings here is a sixteenth-century slaughterhouse. At lease the cattle met a graceful end. The fountain is reconstituted from relics of Roman days (the local myth is that the lady above the lions is Hannibal's wife). One of the arches is from the old city walls, but the other was put here by Charles V as a reminder, a sort of slap in the face to the town, which in those days was an important city, but which had sided with Castilian rebels against this Germanic ruler. If only Franco had dealt thus with towns on the losing side.

Many of the old buildings and streets, as well as views, are to be discovered by going up the steps on the south side of this

View from Baeza

square, and then getting lost. The University and Cathedral loom massive, and need no identification; the palace of Jabalquinto is easily identified by its Isabelline front dotted all over with cones, rather reminiscent of the House of Shells in Salamanca.

If I had had to write this book in Spain, I would have chosen Baeza to do it in. Ultimately, for me, Andalusia would mean: Seville for living; the Alpujarra for refreshment; the Serrania de Ronda for exploration; Baeza for tranquillity.

Sierra de Cazorla The Sierra de Cazorla and Segura is largely a National Game Park and Nature Reserve. It is a gorgeous area for the variety of its scenery, from spectacular crags and defiles to open valleys sweeping across and up to the crests beyond, from badlands to lush mountain gorges where the sun shines through the poplar leaves and sparkles off the water of the streams, from bare hot rock to the heavily scented dark green of pine forest. I shall recommend two drives in these mountains, with a variant, and they will go in increasing order of preference as far as I am concerned. But first I feel the need to point out that no car drive can get the pleasure of the mountains that you get by walking – whether to fish, shoot, bird watch, botanize or simply walk. If you stay at the *Parador El Adelentado* up in the Reserve, and get up early, you have a good chance of seeing the Spanish version of the Ibex, the Cabra Montés – or at least so I am told. From the road, your chances are slim.

For fishing (brown and rainbow trout) and shooting (boar, deer and various game birds), you will need a permit from Icona (Institute for the Conservation of Nature): find out via the Tourist Office, locally, in Madrid, or in London.

Bird-watching here, as in the Alpujarra, will involve extremes from Golden Eagles to Warblers: I am no twitcher but I have seen both – as well as many other raptors and small brown birds unidentified (by me). For botanizing, Oleg Polunin's book (*see* Further Reading, page 319) devotes a chapter to this Sierra, and his enthusiasm for the beauty of the place helps show why it is worth visiting:

> As one drives up into the mountains from the town of Cazorla, one leaves behind wide horizons, and undulating brown plains covered with neatly planted rows of olive trees, and enters over

the rim an entirely different landscape of jagged mountains and forests. Ahead lies a wild and untamed region, for long inaccessible; the haunt of eagles, game and trout... It is a country of deep ravines, sparkling streams, magnificent gnarled trees, enormous bare weather-worn cliffs and bluffs, and fantastic views.

Drive 1 From Ubeda, take the N322 Albacete road and turn off 9km (6ml.) beyond Villacarrillo. This will take you up the young Guadalquivir to the Tranco Reservoir, and much of it is as beautiful a river gorge as you could see, with the sunlight glowing through the poplars and sparkling off the water. At Tranco, turn right and drive along the lake's edge and beyond – almost the whole length of the Reserve and almost to the headwaters of the river. Finally, the road turns left for the Parador, but unless you are staying there you turn right and climb over the range by the Puerto de las Palomas ('Doves' Pass'), with immense views both behind and before. You come down (from 4,000 feet to 2,500 feet) to La Iruela and Cazorla: each is stuck onto the mountain-side and each has not one but two castles above it, but Cazorla is unpicturesque and touristy, while La Iruela is what Cazorla ought to be – *and* it is overhung by a sheer rock face of several hundred feet. From Cazorla, return to Ubeda via Peal de Becerro. The first and last sections of this drive are magical; the middle bit, beside the lake and to the start of the Paolomas pass, is pretty.

As a variant, I suggest you turn right a couple of miles before Tranco and take the high road south-west parallel to the lake-side one, but on the other side of the ridge. It eventually takes you back to Villacarrillo, is good as a road, and a bit wilder and less touristy.

My second suggestion, for the sheer variety of its scenery and its sudden, breath-taking views, is one of my favourites in all Andalusia. It can be added on to Drive 1, or reached from Ubeda by turning off the N322 at Torreperogil and heading for Quesada.

Drive 2 – Quesada to Tiscar The Michelin map no. 446 marks it as a complete circuit of scenic route, but the few miles between Quesada and Tiscar are so spectacular that the rest, while good, cannot quite match up to it. It is not the size: the Tiscar pass is less than 1,130m (3,700ft) up, and the highest peaks nearby not above 6,000 feet, which hardly compares with the

Sierra de Cazorla

Sierra Nevada less than a hundred miles south. But the changes, the rock formations, the meadows, the side ravines... Try exploring them: an unsurfaced road does not mean a dangerous one; you will come to unexpected pastures, gullies and cliffs. And then, when you come over the pass and down to Tíscar itself, you see the jagged peaks and the vistas that I had not thought existed outside of Leonardo's canvases.

Actually, Tíscar does not exist other than as the name of a cave where the Virgin appeared to somebody. (Our Lady must have a notable predilection for caves: she has appeared in them all over Europe.) This puzzled me, as I went there mainly because of Penelope Chetwode's account of staying there in 1961. But a few minutes' chat with some old folk solved the puzzle: there is a hamlet below the Tíscar Sanctuary which the locals call Don Pedro but which has no signposted identity. Penelope Chetwode made so many friends among the villagers of Andalusia that one forgets she had only a smattering of Spanish, and might well have assumed the village was also called Tíscar. One old man remembered the English lady who rode through these parts and stayed at his father-in-law's Posada, 'but that was a long time ago, maybe twenty-five years or even more'. I went down to Don Pedro, in first gear, and there a child told me she had never heard of any Inn. But she took me to her grandmother, and the old lady showed me the house that had been the Posada of Don Alberto and Doña Francisca.

The rest of the circuit is fine, but nothing can quite match up to this first few miles (and note well that to get the best of the drive you must do it from north to south). So I suggest you turn down at Tíscar to Belerda, a mile down the gorge, which is bigger than Don Pedro but just as unaware of tourists, and much as it would have been fifty years ago.

Do not forget to look back up to Tiscar before it is out of sight, at the rocks and the watchtower above: You will see why the poet Antonio Machado calls it an eagle. The road from Belerda to Huesa is easy, and was made a pleasure for me because there was a village Romería going on. This can occasionally involve thousands of people, with colour and music and display. But for a forgotten village like Belerda, it is a cross between a holiday, a pilgrimage, a picnic, and a country walk. There were a priest, a couple of nuns and upwards of a hundred villagers, nearly all young, the small boys lagging behind to throw stones or fight, the girls in giggling gaggles, or singing arm-in-arm and, somewhere in the middle, a group of them taking turns to carry the statue of the Virgin. When they got to whichever little country shrine they were heading for, they would have their picnic, say a few Aves and Novenas, laugh a bit, play a bit, sing a few hymns to the Virgin, and as many other songs as they could drum up. I expect folk songs would be interspersed with Paul McCartney, Paul Simon, or even something more recent; but all, whether hymns or pop, would be sung in those slightly shrill voices harmonized at a major third throughout and, in these parts, with an added touch of Andalusian quarter-tones in the cadences. I once heard Melanesians sing the Old Hundredth in a way that made me ask the missionary what the exotic music was: I think Paul McCartney would enjoy, and perhaps not recognize, one of his songs buried under such a deep veneer of local tradition. There are still places in Spain where pop culture has not yet taken over…

In Huesa you must decide whether to head straight for home, in which case ask for Collejares; or else complete the circuit to Quesada, and so home via Peal de Becerro and Torreperogil, in which case ask for Los Rosales. The advantage of the latter is that as you come over the hill to go down into Quesada, you get a panoramic view of Cazorla in the distance with the mountain range above it and stretching to the horizon.

Almería and its Province Of all the eight provinces of Andalusia, Almería is probably the one with least to attract the tourist. The city has a massive castle – the largest in Andalusia, though not the most interesting; there is a cathedral fortified against piratical incursions; and there is an ancient suburb of partly cave dwellings, called the Chanca. Otherwise, perhaps its best feature is its name: *al-Mariyya,* Mirror of the Sea. The province has some considerable interest inland, with enough things to see to make a worthwhile tour. On the coast there is one good bit, and the rest I would avoid.

Next after its neighbour Murcia, Almería is the driest, hottest, most African corner of Spain. Two cloudy days is the average in the summer, with less than seventeen rainy days in the year.

The rugged landscape of Almería

Its most interesting history ended about 5,000 years ago with a cave drawing near Vélez Blanco, the *Indalo,* a stick man with a bow over his head. The symbol has been adopted by every other bar, restaurant, hotel and souvenir shop in the province, heedless of whether its meaning was frightening (*Indra?*) or simply rude. Seeing it kept bringing back into my head the jingle:

'…while round the maypole dances Miss Prism,

plainly not knowing its symbolism…'

Almería Like Huelva, the city was almost totally destroyed by an earthquake, this one in 1522. The old town had stood between the Castle, the Chanca district and the sea. That area still looks in many places as though it is crumbling. It was largely rebuilt around the Paseo de Almería, which is its heart today;

while the twentieth-century boom is all eastward. But the decay was long: at its most prosperous, under the Moors in the fourteenth century, it had about 300,000 inhabitants – twice today's figure; at one stage in the seventeenth century, the number dropped to less than 500.

Today's boom – and it has about the highest growth rate in Spain – is largely because of such new technology as drip irrigation and growing under plastic. This has two consequences for the tourist. It means an overcrowded city; and in the surrounding countryside it means tens of thousands of acres under plastic sheeting. Wherever you come over the mountains, both here and in neighbouring Granada, your first impression is likely to be that the Mediterranean is all glistening silver. One blink of the eyelids, and you realize that miles of plastic sheeting somehow does not have the same magic.

Almería itself is a workaday city, hot, crowded and rather dusty, going about its own affairs and giving the impression that it would wonder what a tourist was doing there. So would I. The centre of the town's life in the evening is the top half of the Paseo de Almería, as pleasant a place for a *tapa* as any town in Andalusia.

Hotels

Gran Hotel Almería★★★★, Avenida Reina Regente, 8. Tel: 23 80 11. (£50) – is on the N340 Málaga–Murcia road, at the centre of town, thus easy to find.

H. Playaluz★★★★, Bahia el Palmer. Tel: 34 05 04. (£50) – is about 5 miles west, on the road in.

H. Indalico★★★, Calle Dolores Sopeña, 4. Tel: 23 11 11. (£31–£38 + Garage £4) – is in centre if you can brave the crowded narrow streets.

Hs. Guerry★★ Paseo de Almería, 47. Tel: 23 11 77 (£20) – is excellent value, particularly as its restaurant, while not pretentious, is appreciated by locals. They have an arrangement with a private garage 100 yards down the road.

H. Torreluz★★, *Torreluz II*★★★, and *Torreluz IV*★★★★, all with garage and all on Plaza de Flores. Tel: 23 47 99 – would seem a good way of deciding on the spot, though I have not tried them. Prices: £25, £30 and £50 respectively.

A Suggested Walk Starting at the Puerta Purchena, at the top of the Paseo de Almería, oblique down the Calle de las Tiendas

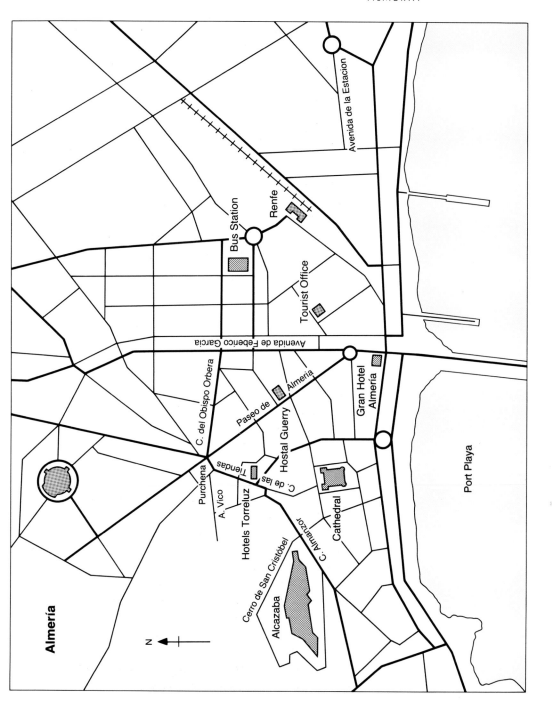

Almería

N ←

Avenida de la Estacion

Bus Station

Renfe

Tourist Office

Avenida de Federico Garcia

C. del Obispo Orbera

Paseo de Almería

Gran Hotel Almería

Hostal Guerry

C. de las Tiendas

Purchena

A. Vico

Hotels Torreluz

Cerro de San Cristóbel

C. Almanzor

Cathedral

Alcazaba

Port Playa

Almería castle walls

(the old Drapers' street). Second right brings you into the Plaza de la Constitución, a pleasant enclosed square, a sort of mini Plaza Mayor, a century or so old. Keep right out of the far end of the square, into Calle Almanzor, whence the first right leads up on to the Cerro de San Cristóbal (St Christopher's Hill). From it you look over both Alcazaba and town, and can carry on round to the Alcazaba entrance. Beneath you as you do so is a Centre for preserving endangered species from the Sahara. The creatures do not feel out of place here. If you do not want too much of a walk, the second right in Calle Almanzor slopes directly up to the *Alcazaba*.

This is the biggest castle built by the Moors (in the tenth century, by Abd er-Rahman III, who built Córdoba's Medinat az-Zahara). Over the centuries, all sign of the palace within the fortress walls has vanished, and there has been much addition and restoration. What remains of it is enough to be impressive, though it would not be easy to put your hand on any one stone and say 'This has been here since AD 1,000'. Today it makes a pleasant public garden, with shade under the jacarandas. From the top, what remains of the vast enclosure makes it look a bit like a section of the Great Wall of China. Open: 10 a.m.–2 p.m. and 4–8 p.m. (summer); 9 a.m.–1 p.m. and 3–7 p.m. (winter).

Back at Constitution Square, if you go a short way downhill, to the south, you come to the *Cathedral*. It was built in the sixteenth and seventeenth centuries with massive solid walls, this time to keep out the descendants of the Moors long since banished to Africa, but returning to beat up the city as Barbary pirates. (When the Moors were still here, they had a fine reputation as pirates, too.) Interesting, possibly, but not beautiful as architecture.

Barrio de la Chanca The Barrio de la Chanca is at the western edge of town and is considered an attraction because its houses are half built into the hill. Personally, I would be content to glimpse them from the Alcazaba, since there are so many cave houses in Andalusia, and you can see inside them (and better ones at that) at Guadix or the Sacromonte (Granada), or many a village northwards from Guadix.

Museums Museo de Almería, Carretera de la Ronda, 91. Tel: 22 50 58. Open: 10 a.m.–2 p.m. Shut Sundays and Mondays.

Shopping Again, the Paseo de Almería is the hub, with perhaps the best shops running east and west from the Puerta Purchena at the top, with others in Calle Tiendas which slants back down from Purchena. Specialities of the area are, as with the Alpujarra, pottery, *jarapa* (rag wool rugs and capes), and objects woven from esparto grass.

Useful Addresses

Tourist Office: Calle Hermanos Machado, 4. Tel: 23 47 05.
Post Office: Calle Dr Gómez Ulla. Tel: 23 72 07.
Telefónica: Calle Navarro Rodriguez, 9.
Police: Calle Alcalde Muñoz, 34. Tel: 23 82 66
   (Emergencies: 091).

First Aid (Cruz Roja): Carretera de Ronda, 20. Tel: 22 50 00
(Emergencies: 25 71 98).

Travel

RENFE: Office, Calle Alcalde Muñoz, 1. Tel: 23 12 07.
Station, Plaza de la Estación. Tel: 25 11 35.

Air Iberia: Paseo de Almería, 42. Tel: Bookings 23 09 33;
Information and ticket sales 23 00 34.

Buses: Avenida de la Estación, 27. Tel: 22 05 38.

Ferry: (to Melilla), Trasmediterranea Co., Parque
Nicolás Salmerón, 28. Tel: 23 61 55.

Almería Province
Inland – A drive from Tabernas to Granada
In this most African corner of Spain, I can remember driving from here to Murcia and, where the land juts out to the city of Cartagena (i.e. Carthage – it was built as an outlying city, and a base from which Hasdrubal attacked the Romans), the road was Sahara dry, an impression reinforced not only by the occasional cactus, but also by the occasional skeleton of a cow. Now, thirty years later, the roads are good, the cattle are not left to die, but the scenery is still of an exotic desolation.

Between Almería and Velez Rubio up in the north-east, over the Filabres and Estancias mountains, you would see fine scenery, few human beings, and no tourists at all. The rivers on the map here are not called river but *barranco* or *rambla*, gully or dry bed, some of them only ever filled by the occasional flash flood. Just up beyond Velez Rubio is Velez Blanco with its theatrical castle. Beyond it are the Cueva de los Letreros and other caves that sheltered the early Iberians, migrating here from the Sahara, five or six thousand years ago. If you want to get away from things, there can be few, if any, areas in Europe where you could do so more thoroughly.

But supposing a less expedition-like holiday, or the need for mod cons, you can still get a taste of the area by travelling between Tabernas and Lacalahorra. And this you can do from a base in this province or from Granada.

It is not surprising that the area near Tabernas became 'Mini Hollywood' and was used for the Spaghetti Westerns of Clint Eastwood, amongst many others. Today the ghost towns of the

Left
Mini-Hollywood near Tabernas

Below
The Moorish castle of
Tabernas

wild west have become ghost film sets. And if there are enough tourists around, the nostalgic local ex-extras will, I am told, happily lay on a gun-fight. I came across a couple of them playing cards in the Tombstone Gulch Saloon. They were drinking cola, not whisky.

The place is fun, with its Wild West town back to back with a Mexican village, and the Red Injun tepees thirty yards to the east. The whole is rendered slightly daft by the fact that, among the handful of horses and longhorns that linger on here, are a couple of sad-looking camels, left behind by Lawrence of Arabia. They drift, sneering and disconsolate, among a group of futuristic baddy-chariots, peeling relics of what must have been a wholly daft cowboy sci-fi. The arid landscape is perhaps more fitting than we at first realize, since in the background (given a slight error in camera angle) stands on its hill the Moorish castle of Tabernas, built for an earlier shoot-out between goodies and baddies, in days that had no cameras, but were just as technicoloured.

Indeed, the whole road from Tabernas to Granada is a worthwhile experience. The first stretch to Gergal is a vision of what can happen to a land without water. Then, as you climb, the badlands, the dead gulches and jumbled rocks open out on to a vega, an upland plain, smooth and fertile, sweeping away to a line of purple hills. You are out of dry Almería and in the province of Granada.

In October, when I passed through, the crops were all in, the vast stretches of almond trees lace-like, and the whole expanse was a blending of delicate browns, yellows and creams hazily tinged with purple, pink and blue. Given the amazing transformation of Andalusia by the wild flowers and blossom of spring, I can imagine this vega might be breath-taking.

The closer hills to the south are the Sierra Nevada. On a hill at their feet, about a mile from the main road, red and prominent and alone in this great landscape, stands the *Palace of Lacalahorra*. With its domed towers, it looks quite unlike any other Andalusian castle, except in being spectacularly sited. In fact it is a Renaissance palace, built in the early fifteen hundreds, and closer in feeling to the French châteaux than any Alcázar. Most of the decoration has been stripped, but the central court and staircase are still elegant. Even so, the same is true of it as of most castles, that it gives more pleasure viewed from afar than examined from inside. In this instance, the combination of its strange shape, allied to the fact that it is here at all in this remote and empty place, make it worth seeing. Here you are no longer on the mountains of the moon, but it is still a far cry from Surbiton or Huish Episcopi.

As so often in Andalusia, the journey itself makes much of the pleasure and to come to Lacalahorra from the Alpujarras is a different experience. There is a road that cuts north over the Sierra Nevada via the Puerto (pass) de la Ragua 1,975m (6,477ft). To climb up that way, and then to see suddenly swing into view the whole landscape I have described, with Lacalahorra on its red pimple some three thousand feet beneath you – that is a *coup de théâtre*.

Fourteen kilometres (9ml.) west is *Guadix*, best known for its cave-dwellings. Clearly this is a tourist attraction, and I wish I could get enthusiastic. Perhaps my interest is so tepid because no self-respecting modern troglodyte would be without his telly. Picture a host of ant-heaps covering a slope, each one whitewashed over some part of it, many of them with a patch of fenced-in garden, complete with washing line, plastic bucket and dusty hen. And then picture the whole scene festooned in television aerials and wiring, above you, beside you, below you. Telly aerials at eye-level take the romance out of life. I could not bring myself to ask to see one of the houses. A young man standing beside the road, on his roof, did offer to show me his – for a thousand pesetas. I told him that for a thousand pesetas I would buy my own, and left.

Guadix also has a Moorish castle, and attractive enclosed square. It has a Cathedral of about the same date as Granada's – and, like Granada's, its walls display to the world in letters clean, clear and well tended, the name of the founder of the Spanish Fascist party.

Six kilometres (4 ml.) west of Guadix is the village of *Purullena*. It appears to consist only of cave-dwellings and road-side shops, with the latter more prominent. Do not spurn it: a lot of the pottery – there is a vast quantity of it – is reasonably priced, and you can get hold of goat- and ox-hide rugs.

After this, there is a short respite for the driver trying to enjoy all this scenic documentary stuff, and then you climb up through fresh

The Cabo de Gata

pine woods and mountain air to the 1,220m (4,000ft) of the Puerto de la Mora (the Moorish Girl's Pass), and then again another fine 915m (3,000ft) pass before you emerge, as though on to a balcony, to look down over the Alhambra, the city of Granada, and the whole rich Vega spread out before and beneath you.

The Coast In the western part, from Adra to Almería, the hills hang back from the coast, giving room for vast areas of

250

plastic. Recently, resorts have been sprouting, too.

Almerimar, for example, is perfectly horrible. You turn off the N340 (Malaga–Almería), drive across a few miles of flat, amateur rubbish-tip, down a dip, and behold: they have changed the plastic detritus for oleanders and palms and lawn; one expensive hotel; one golf-course (Gary Player designed); two hotels looking rather like those high-rise developments you see coming into

251

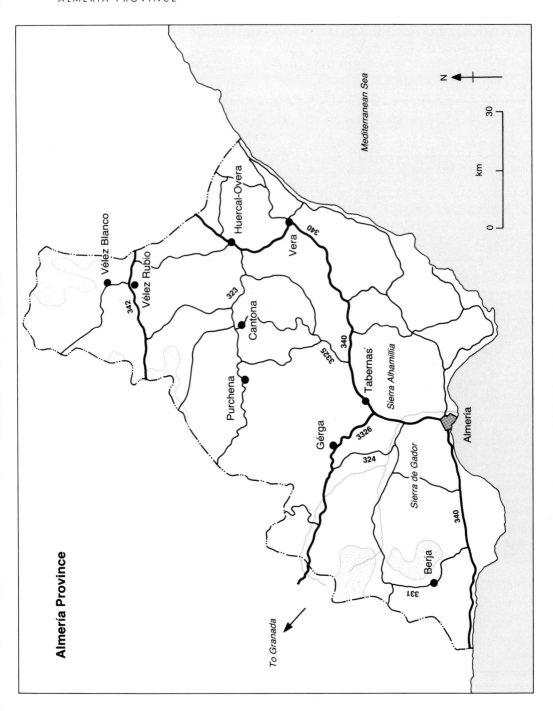

Almería Province

Mediterranean Sea

N

30

km

0

Huercal-Overa

Vélez Blanco

Vélez Rubio

342

323

Cantona

Purchena

Vera

340

340

3325

Tabernas

Sierra Alhamilla

Almería

Gérga

3326

324

Sierra de Gador

340

Berja

331

To Granada

Waterloo, and occupied by rather sad-looking package-tourists; and an incipient and hopeful yacht harbour (doesn't Marina sound grand?). There are seven other such developments and I would pay not to go to any of them.

To the east of Almería is flat dusty beach and saltings for the 24 kilometres (15 ml.) or so to the Cabo de Gata (Agate Cape). From here on round the cape, is a slightly hairy drive that may amuse: steep, twisty, narrow, arid with the bright blue sea beneath you. It leads to isolated sandy coves: I would have said 'lonely' but that they seem never without one German camper-car, its occupants earnestly tanning up for the winter.

Eastwards beyond this the new developments begin, just tolerable perhaps, and partly the work of small-time English entrepreneurs at San José. And then from Carboneras onwards mile on mile of beach-side development, no high-rise hotels, thank God, and many of the villas and apartments imaginatively designed as African cubes with curving variations. But they are still beach-side developments: tawdry café, road, dusty verge, beach, gritty towel, sea, heat, glare, salt.

Most guidebooks seem to think that Mojácar is different and better. It was so once, quite recently. Only a few years back, the women wore their kerchiefs like yashmaks, and drew the *indalo* on their doorways to avert bad luck. But today, there is only the framework left of this once Moorish hill-top town, the rest is simulation, one package-tour hotel, a grotty restaurant, and only hidden pockets of genuine residents survive. If sun, sea and sand is what you want, then give thanks for the *Parador de los Reyes Católicos,* down on the beach. But I would go elsewhere.

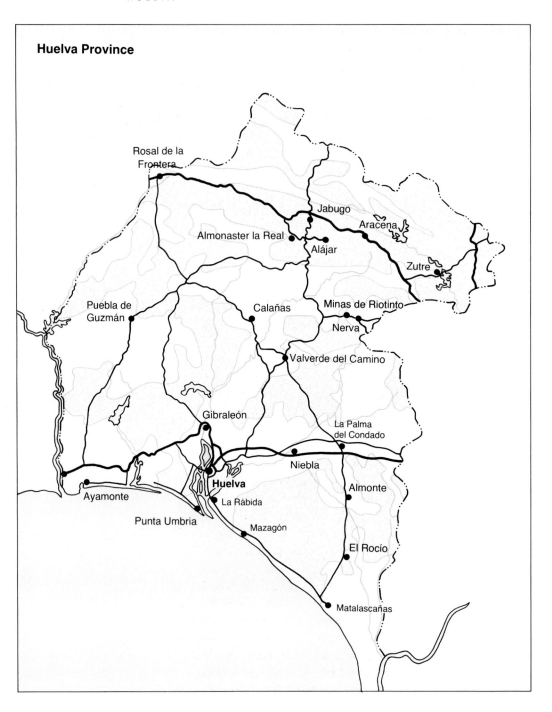

Huelva Province

Rosal de la
Frontera

Jabugo

Aracena

Almonaster la Real

Alájar

Zutre

Puebla de
Guzmán

Calañas

Minas de Riotinto

Nerva

Valverde del Camino

Gibraleón

La Palma
del Condado

Niebla

Huelva

Almonte

Ayamonte

La Rábida

Punta Umbria

Mazagón

El Rocío

Matalascañas

Huelva and its Province Huelva is a whole province with its capital city, but it would not make sense to treat it in the same way as most others, by a visit to the city and excursions out of it, for Huelva is simply not a city to visit, and indeed some parts of the province are dreary, too. But there are four or five things that I consider very well worth visiting, of which two bring people from all over the world. These are the Coto Doñana, the largest nature reserve in Europe; and the Pilgrimage of the Rocío, perhaps the most spectacular, colourful and festive, at least in the western world. Apart from these, you may be attracted to Huelva Province by the monastery of La Rábida, which was virtually the source of Columbus's journey of discovery; the Sierra de Aracena, a beautiful mountain area, more gentle than the others, and including limestone caverns; the best beaches in Spain; the fortified town of Niebla; the mines of Rio Tinto.

Huelva The city of Huelva, poor thing, could attract no one. It has a history as rich as that of most Andalusian cities, but thanks to the events of 1 November 1755, little or no trace of it remains. The date is famous in history for the Lisbon earthquake, the disaster that shocked the world and jolted Voltaire into changing his ideas (and writing *Candide*). Meanwhile, unnoticed, it also destroyed Huelva.

The province's period of greatness came somewhere about the sixth century BC, when this was part of the kingdom of Tartessos, about which nobody knows much. The Bronze Age had come, and the copper deposits of the Rio Tinto, still big business today, made peoples from all round the Mediterranean come here to trade. When Jonah had his disagreement with Jehovah and tried to escape, it was to Tartessos (probably Cádiz or Huelva) that he booked his passage, though he got no closer than the whale's belly.

Minerals were still making the place important under the Moors. And Columbus's expedition of 1492, sailing from Palos de la Frontera, just down the road, gave it renewed activity. But shortly after that, Seville won the monopoly of the Americas' trade, and from then on Huelva went into a long decline, accelerated by the 1755 earthquake. It bottomed out in the last century with the arrival of the British and the exploitation of the mines by the Rio Tinto Co. (later RTZ), which gave employment to thousands. Unless you are pushed by the spirit of pilgrimage, however, I doubt whether you will want to visit the Rio Tinto Company's 1917 Housing Estate in the city, despite its being under a preservation order as of 'Histórico-Artistic interest'.

The economic boom that started in the 1960s brought back Huelva's prosperity, but this, to the visitor, means concrete dreariness, rubble and dust; massive factories belching smoke and stink for miles downwind over the railway lines, pylons and cables, the mud flats and rubbish dumps.

Despite this return to prosperity, I get the impression that Huelva is twenty years behind the others. Its shops have the same goods; construction is in full swing; yet I sensed − or imagined − an atmosphere in cafés and streets that took me back to Franco's days and made me glad to leave.

Hotels If you are stuck in Huelva, I recommend
H. Luz Huelva ★★★★, Alameda Sundheim, 26. Tel: 25 00 11 (£48).
H. Tartessos ★★★, Calle Martín Alonso Pinzón, 13 and 15. Tel: 24 56 11. (£29) − it has a recommended restaurant (the *Doñana*) in the same bleakly concrete block.
If you want to go downmarket, just remember that this is a sea port: the cheap ones I looked at were slummy without being quaint.

But if you are not stuck here, then according to which of the sights in the province you want to see, I recommend you stay at the *Parador* near Mazagón, or at the *H. Cortijo* in Matalascañas; and for the mountains, at the *H. Sierra de Aracena* in Aracena. I give the details in the relevant place. The Coto Doñana and Aracena can be visited from Seville, but it seems an unnecessary trek, unless you have good reason.

La Rábida La Rábida is an attractive little fifteenth-century Franciscan monastery, 10km (6ml.) out of Huelva. Curiously, the name comes from the Arabic for 'monastery', but I have not been able to discover that there was such a thing here before the reconquest. Its guest cloister and part of its brothers' cloister were destroyed in 1755, but they were rebuilt harmoniously, and the rest of the monastery is as it was in 1492. Then it had ten inmates; today it has eight: it is like that.

The significance of all this is that Columbus could not get backing for his projected voyage − until he stayed here. The Prior,

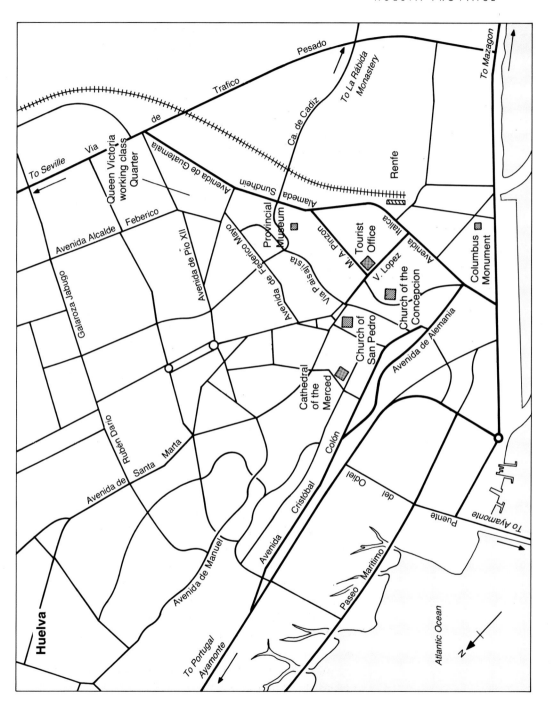

Huelva

Sierra de Aracena

Juan Perez, was not only a scholar and no bigot; he was also Queen Isabel's confessor. Both facts were crucial. Without Church backing, Columbus did not stand a chance; the Church tended to think the earth was flat; and the queen was a blinkered woman: whatever a churchman said was all right, must be all right. So the discovery of America is owed in some part to this place. The Queen gave her support, and Columbus and the Pinzón brothers sailed from just up the road at Palos de la Frontera, from which the sea has now receded.

I went to La Rábida out of duty to this guidebook, but I am glad I did. The little monastery is a delight. Its two tiny cloisters are filled with flowers, sunlight and inviting shade; and its rooms, with low ceilings and furniture of the period, are filled with Columbiana, and evocative. Visits are every half-hour, guided by a friar. The one who showed me round was much more keen on the modern improvements to the chapel and some not very interesting twentieth-century murals. But this was his life and home, and they were his enthusiasms, rather than standard dope such as would be pumped out by a professional guide, and I preferred it. There is no charge, but a contribution is expected – and deserved.

Aracena and its Sierra It is part of the Sierra Morena, whose mountains are not nearly as high (just under 3,000 feet at most), and pleasantly varied. At Alajar, for instance (a village apparently forgotten by time), the only difference from other mountain ranges, is that forest covers the ridges. But on the northern slopes things change: within a few miles you have more gentle slopes, flatter upland bits and above all a preponderance of deciduous trees. It would make fine walking country and is fruitful – literally: apples, pears, peaches and then mile upon mile of old chestnut plantations. The trees are large and old but all in lines, with occasional plantations of poplars, yellow in autumn. The people are recognizably the same mountain people as the Alpujarrans, straightforward and friendly without fuss.

It is a good place, and the fact seems to have been recognized by a number of English people. Not the ones who go to the Costa for sun or tax haven, but younger people who have decided to make a life here. I was first told of this by a pleasant old village shopkeeper – the shop, in the tiny village of Galaroza, was so attractive that I had to pull up and look round inside. She talked of the families who had settled, with properties bought cheap, done up, and now being farmed – fruit and chestnuts almost all of it. A fourteen-year-old lad on a bicycle, seeing my English number-plate stopped to say hello, and said dad had farmed in Kent – I presume driven out by the invasion of French government-subsidized Golden Delicious.

Aracena itself is a pleasant little town of about 6,000 inhabitants, though at weekends in summer it gets its share of Sevillans coming up to escape the heat. It offers the inevitable castle, a church, a cave, a hotel and a couple of restaurants. The hotel is the *Sierra de Aracena* ★★, Gran Via, 21. Tel: 11 07 75. (£20). The restaurants are the *Meson de Pedro* next door, and the *Casas* on the Plaza San Pedro. The church is the Priory (or possibly Templar), one up beside the castle. Its tower shows by its decoration that it was, like the Giralda in Seville, an Almohad minaret.

And then the cave, the *Gruta de las Maravillas* – limestone caverns that seem to occupy a large chunk of the hill on which the castle stands. I am no fan of caves, but this one is said to be not only the biggest in Spain but also even better than the one at Nerja (which I had found an excuse not to see). So I did my duty. You walk just over 1km (3/4ml.), past lakes of limpid water, through chambers of stalactites and -mites and other such growths, some of them in technicolour: they made the other visitors say 'Ooh' and 'Ah' but made me feel I was exploring a giant's gut. If you have never seen such caverns, or if you have keen offspring, I should think it is much to be recommended. In fact, the offspring may find it the more so because I was told (but cannot guarantee) it was used for one of the Harrison Ford films. No cameras or videos allowed; do not wrap up warm, it stays at a constant temperature between 16 °C and 18 °C; it is best to visit during the week; if you go at weekends you may have to wait an hour or so for a place in the next batch.

Almonaster la Real Less than 30km (20ml.) west of Aracena there is a little mountain village called Almonaster la Real. The name itself is promising, since '*al*' is an Arabic, and '*monaster*' a Romance word. Above the village, perched on a rock, is (what else?) a castle, and beside that the church that gave the village its name. To see the church I would be willing to go through the cavern twice.

The books say it is fifteenth century and that might even be partly true: the walls and vaults were put up by Mudéjares, and therefore date from after the reconquest. But the bits it is composed of are partly Roman, partly Visigothic, and it does not stop there: one of the bits of Roman marble bears the remains of an inscription in Hebrew; the capitals come from at least three different civilizations; the font from goodness knows when. And as if all this were not enough, the building is to this day more clearly a mosque than a church.

There is a *Mihrab* in the east wall... or what ought to be the east (Mecca-facing) wall, but is in fact the south wall. I suppose this might be following the example of the great Mosque at Córdoba.

At a later period, others have converted it to a church by turning the building sideways (as it were) and putting an altar on the east side. Since the building is square, this might not seem to matter, except that the arcading is all wrong for it. But the effect is to preserve the Mosque more completely than any other that I know of in Spain. Was it poverty or tolerance that made the Christian builders do so little to disturb the Mosque? Clearly, the restorers have been at work here, and I expect they cleared away a lot of florid Christian iconography, but that was all surface decoration, and not structural.

What matters more is that restoration does not seem to have killed the spirit of the place, as it so often does, by stuffing ghosts and putting them in glass cases. It has an atmosphere strong enough to hush you; a feeling that (in Eliot's phrase) 'here prayer has been valid'. And this is just as strongly overlaid with a feeling of the presence of the ages – Roman, Visigoth, Jew, Moor and Christian – not so much ghostly as calm and happy, up here in cool and simple shade, with the sun blazing down outside and over the unending hills.

Beside the church, a coffin has been cut into the solid rock on which church and castle are built – something not done, so far as I know, after the sixth century, and suggesting therefore that this was a Visigothic church before it became mosque. And there is a largish flat area, presumably once occupied by monastery buildings, but now making a pleasant, grassy look-out point.

Balzac thought of all human beings as stories on two legs. This building makes me feel the same way. It is such a pile-up of intriguing puzzles, that together make a story waiting to be read, or at least teased out. And the story looks tantalizingly good. A Hebrew inscription on a Roman column in a Christian church with a Moslem *mihrab*... all in the back of beyond, up in these hills. Whatever happened here, happened more or less all over Andalusia. But nowhere else that I know of, have the episodes of its story survived so legibly.

And, just to put the cherry on the cake, if you go out by the west door (splendid views) and turn right, you come to two more doors. The one into the tower is kept locked (echoes of Bluebeard) but go though the other: you will emerge inside the keep area of the castle to find... a bullring. It is so small that a full-sized bull could hardly be got into it, let alone charge around goring people. And that is even supposing you could get up on to this hill-top what Tom Lehrer described as half a ton of angry pot-roast – you cannot get a tame car up here.

If this interests you, you must go to the first floor of the Town Hall (Ayuntamiento) in the village square and ask for the key (*la llave del castillo* = LA YAHVAY DEL CASTILYO). Get this password roughly right, and you will be rewarded with a stage prop from Bluebeard, armed with which you can not only clunk and creak your way in but also, with luck, have the place to yourself. Turn left out of the Ayuntamiento, left again at the corner of the square, and climb.

Jabugo Eight kilometres (5ml.) or so north-west of there is one of the most prosperous villages in Spain: Jabugo. Spanish mountain ham (*jamón serrano*) has a possible rival in Parma ham, otherwise there is none to touch it. But the ham from this village fetches higher prices than any other. One of the reasons given for the quality of *jamón serrano* is the diet of acorns (the acorns of the cork oak are large and presumably succulent). But Jabugo is surrounded mainly by chestnut trees. It may explain something.

Aracena and the various mountain villages of the area are on or near the main road N631 from Seville to Portugal.

The Coast and its Beaches The difference between the Atlantic and the Mediterranean is the only reason why the grey and grotty beaches of the Costa del Sol have been overdeveloped, while those between Gibraltar and Portugal, with their great stretches of clean, pale golden sands, are still largely empty. On

261

the Atlantic coast, the sunshine and heat are the same, but wind and tide exist. Between the Portuguese frontier and Cádiz, this means no more than it does on the Algarve. Only east of Huelva Province, as Africa and Europe funnel closer together, does the wind become a factor until, at Tarifa, it is so strong and constant as to make a wind-surfers' paradise.

Punta Umbria Punta Umbria is an unpretentious resort 24km (15ml.) out of Huelva, and used by folk from Huelva, Seville and Jerez. But the beach is 19km (12ml.) long as well as being broad, and the sand is pale. It has nothing particularly Spanish about it – it could be a seaside resort anywhere. And this applies more or less to any beach between Huelva and Portugal.

One difference, apart from the latitude, is that the Spaniards have been active for a long time in the way of afforestation, and here this means mile upon mile of parasol pines, not only scenting the air and making pleasant scenery, but also fixing the dunes and bringing prosperity: Spain has a lot of timber.

Eastwards from Huelva, between Mazagon and Matalascañas, is one twenty mile long beach of fine sand-coloured sand, most of it with little access except for a few camp grounds. In the middle of it is a Parador which is set back a bit for privacy, but with its gardens giving directly on to the beach. There is a picnic ground in the woods nearby, with access to the same part of the beach, but it is only open at weekends. It is *Parador Nacional Cristóbal Colón*, Carretera Mazagón–Matalascañas. Tel: 37 60 00. (£40–£50).

Matalascañas Matalascañas (or Torre la Higuera) is the only resort in this area. It is brash and booming and new and I would not bother to mention it but for its ease of access to the Coto Doñana, and its beach. If you go down on to the beach and face right you see eighteen miles of sand to the next township, with only a couple of camp grounds and the Parador between; if you then face left, you see a further sixteen miles of sand, all part of the Nature Reserve, though with a few permitted shellfishers and (for some weird reason) an occasional motorcyclist. Any other human is there illegally, so the beach is mainly frequented by seabirds: during my November visit I saw mainly terns, sanderlings, and oystercatchers, perhaps newly arrived from Norfolk.

In summer you would have to book some months in advance and the prices are about double; from November to March or

April, the prices are about half and these are the best months to see the Coto Doñana.

Hotels My choice would be the *Cortijo*, with the reservation that they are currently doubling its size and I do not know whether they will keep the character I describe.

Cortijo ★★, Tel: 43 02 58 or 59. Its official address is Sector E, Parcela 149, which tells you something about Matalascañas. You find it by crossing straight over the Almonte–Metalascañas road and then taking the third on your right. At present the rooms are all ground floor and open on to patios, like the Andalusian farmstead that gives it its name. Each bedroom has an antichamber large enough for a sofa, table and stools, so no claustrophobia. I do not think either receptionist speaks English, but you can ring and book by asking for René (the barman, an educated Chilean refugee). Out of season, a double costs about £19, breakfast included; in season £37.

On the other hand, out of season and at the same time as me, a family took a vast flat/room with beds for all four of them at the *Aparthotel Gaviota* for a total cost of £20. An Aparthotel is a place that caters mainly for weekly boarders with a room resembling a studio flat including kitchenette but no service other than the cleaning.

The Coto Doñana This is the largest nature reserve in Europe and the best reason for going to the province of Huelva.

It is a vast area of marshland, thicket and dunes, that was originally a small inland sea or large lagoon near the mouth of the Great River (which is what Guadalquivir means). The river meandered and silted up the lagoon, the fine sands in the silt were first carried to sea, then washed back to form the beaches of this coast, and then here, where the prevailing south-westerlies meet the shore head on, driven back inland in an impressive series of shifting dunes. And because the marshes are salt and the land floods, the area remained blessedly free of human occupation. The blessing was for the birds: even today, when water pollution and private interest still threaten much of the country, some 125 different species of bird live and breed here, while 150 more species use it, in their tens or even hundreds of thousands, as a staging post in their migration between Northern Europe and Africa. So geese from the polar regions share it with

263

Coto Doñana at dawn

flamingos up from Africa; egrets and azure-winged wagtails and all sorts. There are other creatures, too, but in lesser numbers: boar, deer (Red and Fallow), mongoose, otter, and lynx, as well as horses and cattle that have reverted to the wild. In the opinion of the wardens working here, the lynx and the Imperial Eagle may be fighting a losing battle to survive, though it is not hard to see the Imperial Eagle.

As for the flora, my ignorance is painful, but even I was excited to be shown the Mandragora. Not because of its beauty, as the plant looks, to my ignorant eye, like a cross between a baby spinach and an African violet. But because of the enduring legend: if you pull it up, it screams...

The Coto is made up of three sorts of area – I believe the term is 'ecosystems'. First come the shifting dunes that gradually

264

swallow the pines and scrub ahead of them, and spew them out, dead or alive, behind. Even here, the troughs are often moist, and hold things of interest to the botanist or ornithologist. But their slopes and crests mostly show the tracks of fox, snake and insect.

Then come the stabilized sands, areas containing cork oak and pine as well as a flora that varies according to the dampness of the soil. Here boar and deer forage and graze below, and the buzzards and Imperial Eagles nest above. Here, too, there are small villages of charcoal burners' huts, and one forlorn-looking mansion.

Then, wide and flat, come the salt marshes, Here the change with the seasons is most striking. Summer in this Province sees virtually no rain at all; by August, the marshes are a dry cracked plain. Winter is fairly rainy; by January, and often earlier, the marshes are one big shallow lake. The spring rains keep the level up until March or April, when it is turning green; May sees the flowering; then the evaporation starts.

When to Go December through to May are best. I was unlucky to go in the November of an exceptionally dry autumn, and the marshes had not yet filled. January to March are the very best months since the marshes are likely to have plenty of water in them for the aquatic migrants, and they are to my mind the best months for escape from English weather. It will not be hot here in winter, but you can expect day-time temperatures of about 17° C on the (many) good days, though less in wind or rain. The Coto is still at its best in April and even May, but who wants to leave England then?

If, however, you are planning a spring tour, you might consider timing it to take in the Coto Doñano together with the April Fair in Seville, taking into account that the date of Seville's Feria depends on the date of Easter. The juxtaposition of the colour and bustle and music and festivity in Seville, with the peace, freshness and wide skies of Europe's largest Nature Reserve, could make a sensational holiday – in the exact meaning of the word.

How to Go Except for specially authorized scientific visits, you may only go on a conducted visit, taken by a warden. Unless you plan a party of twenty strong, this will mean going by Land Rover with a few others. Your driver is a naturalist before he is a tour guide, so if you can find some means of communicating, it will not feel like a package deal: he will stop to look at anything you want, and is genuinely keen to explain. Binoculars are a help. And I would suggest it is thoroughly worth while to buy the Spanish edition of Peterson (*see* Further Reading, page 000): it gives the name of every bird in both English and Spanish, as well as the other Romance languages.

Parties leave from the *Acebuche*, which is a reception centre a mile or so out of Matalascañas on the Almonte road and clearly marked on your Michelin 446. The half-day (4-hour) tours leave at 8.30 a.m. and 3 p.m., though they ask you to be there a quarter of an hour early, and cost 1,750 ptas. The full-day tour goes no further but is for birdwatchers who want to spend hours at it. Time of departure is by arrangement, and it costs 2,650 ptas. You need to book: (955) 43 04 32. This is the Acebuche number, and the girl at the desk speaks English.

School study visits are available at slightly reduced prices. For such visits it is possible to find lodging at much reduced prices at a hostel in Rocío, via the *Cooperativa de Marismas del Rocío*, Playa Acebuchal, 16, El Rocio, 21750 Huelva. Personally I would not trust letters – the two organizers, Agustín and Sebastián, do not speak English. But you can get them at 43 04 32 where the Information girl does speak English. The hostel can sleep up to 60 in rooms for 3 or 4; and the price per person including breakfast is 1,375 ptas. Do not forget that, as with all prices in this book, that obtains up to 31 March 1990. Thereafter add about 7 per cent per year.

There are a couple of other information and exhibition centres in the Coto. *La Rocina* (Tel: 40 61 40) will also help you book in, if you can not get the Acebuche. It is open mornings. There is also the *Palacio Acebrón* (also open mornings) which is a turn of the century mansion, now an exhibition hall. Both these places are on the fringe of the Coto, and have marked walks to offer.

Hotels It is about 110km (70ml.) from Seville. I would find that tedious, even for the 3 p.m. visit. The *Parador Cristóbal Colón* (*see* page 262) is some 25km (15ml.) away. Frankly, I did not regret using the Cortijo (*see* page 263) just down the road. If stuck, try one of the Hostales at the crossroads in La Palma del Condado, rather than Almonte. Try for the:

HsR La Viña ★★, Carretera Huelva–Sevillea, km601. Tel: (955) 40 02 73. (Price varies £12–£18).

One last point before leaving the subject. It is possible to pay the Coto a four-day visit direct from England as a package deal through your Travel Agent. On a bleak February day in England, it could be a serious thought.

The Rocio The Romería, or pilgrimage, to the shrine of the Virgin of the Dew is unparalleled in the western world. You can not describe its adherents as fanatics or fervent, although they are both, without giving the wrong impression. The fact is, the journey, as well as the Whit Sunday procession on arrival, is also a gigantic and prolonged picnic and festival. Brotherhoods from all over Andalusia, indeed from all over Spain nowadays, organize the journey, that involves days and nights on foot, on horseback, and in covered wagons. The wagons have white tarpaulins, and are richly decorated with flowers: the riders wear the *traje corto,* the short jacket, black or grey trousers and flat hat, of the Andalusian horseman; the women wear the bright flamenco dresses; guitars, fifes, drums abound; and flamenco music mingles with the *rociero* hymn.

At Rocío itself the Virgin is carried out and processes round in a crowd that today tops a million. Then they all go home, and in the Peñas Rocieras, the *rociero* bars all over Andalusia, they chalk up the number of days till the next one – and follow it a lot more closely than we do our shopping days to Christmas. And the village of Rocío remains, empty and vast, like a Hollywood set for some gigantic ghost town in the wild west.

The groups coming from Madrid and Barcelona thunder across Spain in coaches. But if you are fortunate enough to be invited to join the *rocieros* from the south, then you progress slowly across country, ferry across the mouth of the Guadalquivir, and so up the Via Pecuaria, a trail running through the heart of the Coto Doñana. Or if you happen to be near Sanlucar de Barrameda in the days preceding Whitsun, the *rociero* wagons make quite a sight.

Coming dates for the Rocío are: 1991, 19 May; 1992 7 June; 1993, 30 May; 1994, 22 May; 1995, 4 June.

Niebla On the Seville–Huelva road where it crosses the Rio Tinto (the Red River) some 27km (17ml.) out of Huelva, stands Niebla. If you are passing that way you may think it worth turning in. It is entirely surrounded by massive Arab walls and is all red: walls, soil, and river – though the redness of the latter looks suspiciously frothy and chemical.

The chief asset of the town is that it is forgotten. It is a sleepy byway, where nobody, no guidebook, will order you to look at this or that. There are still some Arab houses; the interior of Santa María de Granada is a Mozarabic survival. If you have come to Spain to get lost in the past, stop here a moment.

Rio Tinto Mines Upstream from Niebla, half-way between Huelva and Aracena, you come to the Rio Tinto mines, like something out of Jules Verne or Dante's Hell, according to your vision. Entire hills have been cut and terraced away into chasms, grandiose and horrible. They are perhaps summarized by the beautiful sapphire-blue lake just to the north, where a sign by the waterside reads 'Danger, Do not bathe: Acid Water'.

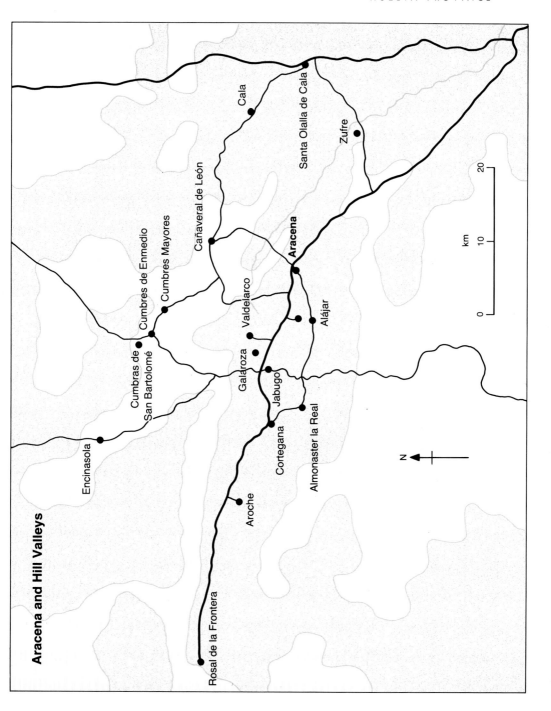

Aracena and Hill Valleys

Cala

Santa Olalla de Cala

Zufre

Cañaveral de León

Cumbres de Enmedio

Cumbres Mayores

Aracena

Valdelarco

Alájar

Cumbras de
San Bartolomé

Galaroza

Jabugo

Almonaster la Real

Cortegana

Encinasola

Aroche

Rosal de la Frontera

N

km
20   10   0

Part Three: **Further Information**

Granada

History The following account makes no attempt to list events and dates. It is highly selective and heavily slanted in an attempt to achieve two aims only. The first is to explain who the Andalusian Spaniards are. For this purpose I pay rather more attention to the Moorish period than to others, and it should perhaps be read in conjunction with the following section on the Jews in Spain. My second aim is to explain what has happened more recently, and where they are heading now.

The Racial Mix Let nobody pigeon-hole the Andalusians as 'A Mediterranean race'. Like the other Spaniards, though in different proportions, they are an amalgam as rich and varied, as mongrel, in fact, as we are. The Iberians, whoever they were, may have come from the Sahara when the Sahara was fertile. The Celts came here, as they did to Galicia, Brittany, Cornwall and so forth. The Phoenicians colonized Cádiz, among other places, and it is thanks to them that the citizens of Cádiz can boast the longest continual history of a city of any in the West.

By the tenth century there was no clear distinction between Arab and *muwallad* (i.e. Christian converts to Islam). To be converted you had to be adopted by one of the Arab clans, so the Converts had assumed Arab names, and even genealogy; meanwhile Arabs had been marrying Iberian women for 200 years – The great Caliph Abd er-Rahman III had blue eyes and red hair.

The Carthaginians were here: Hannibal took his elephants over the Alps, not from Tunisian Carthage, but from Cartagena down the road from Almería. The Greeks had trading colonies, and the Jews were here in numbers almost certainly long before the Diaspora, since the Prophet Obadiah in 600 BC refers to the 'captivity of Jerusalem that is in Sepharad'.

Then the Romans colonized the country. They had no bar of race, creed or colour. Their legions, which on retirement colonized Spain, were made up of men from every corner of their Empire, and may well have included your own great uncle Jack. Their greatest cities were Tarragona, Saragossa (Caesar Augusta) and Mérida (Augusta Emerita), but most of the major towns of Andalusia were Roman cities of the Province of Baetica.

The Germans then invaded. Of the first wave, only the Vandals reached Andalusia and gave it its name. But the beleaguered Romans asked those other Germanic people, the Christian Visigoths, for help and these people drove the Vandals over into Africa – and then occupied the country themselves.

At some stage after the seventh century but before the fifteenth, the Indian people we know as gypsies arrived and ceased wandering here. Then, in 711, Tariq crossed the straits with a raiding party, found the land ripe for conquest, and three years later the entire Peninsula belonged to the conquering Arabs (Yemeni and Syrian) and Berbers (from the Maghreb). This is not quite the end of the racial input. During three hundred years the Caliphs imported slaves from Russia and other Slav countries, to form their guards – so many of them that a Jewish philosopher of Al Andalus could write an open letter to the King of a Slav realm, a sort of tenth-century equivalent to Montesquieu's Persian Letters.

I mention elsewhere that the great Caliph Abd er-Rahman III had blue eyes and red hair. But the above should be enough to convince the reader that the Andalusians are a fair old racial mix.

Moslem Spain (Al Andalus) As soon as Tariq and his boss Musa, the Governor of Afrikiya, had conquered the Iberian Peninsula, the problem, inherent in all Arab peoples before and since, began to emerge, to wit their incapacity to stay united. Already, in the 620s, with his first disciples in Medina, Mohammed had thought up the Jihad, or Holy War, less for religious ends than to keep his followers united in a common cause of bashing (and plundering) the pagan tribes. So now the appointment of city governors in the newly conquered country set up jealousies between Kais and Yemenis (two confederations of Arab tribes), while the Berbers felt ill-treated by both. The supreme head of Islam was, in those times, the Caliph (or Successor) who was of the Umayyad dynasty ruling in Damascus.

In 755 a rival family, the Abbasids, took over power and murdered all Umayyads bar one. His name was (or rather became) Abd er-Rahman. He escaped and, profiting from rivalries and feuds in Al Andalus, got himself elected Emir in Córdoba. Thus began a dynasty that ruled Spain, and became a dominant power in much of

Africa and Europe, for the next 250 years. Córdoba grew to be four times its present size (a huge city for those times), and the splendour of the court there, and later in the vast city-palace of Medina az-Zahra, attracted scholars, architects, philosophers, mathematicians, geographers, doctors and poets from all round the Mediterranean.

From our distance it is only too easy to think in simplistic terms, and these cliché images have been reinforced by the history books of our childhood. So it may come as a surprise to learn of Moorish tolerance of Christians and Jews, or of the extent of diplomatic and cultural contact with other Northern and Eastern powers. We do not expect to see the great mosques at Córdoba and Seville surrounded by large and flourishing Jewish quarters; or to hear that the Rabbi Samuel ha Nagid was chief Visir and Marshal of the Army in Granada; or to learn that when Abd er-Rahman I wanted to build a great mosque he bought the Christians out of their church on that site and gave them another site to rebuild with the money he paid them.

On one hand, this is a simplification: only non-Moslems paid taxes, so that the Moorish potentates had little desire to cut off the revenue by forcible conversion, or by driving Christians out. But the truth remains that Christians and Jews were free to build their churches and synagogues, worship as they wanted, and keep their own customs and dress.

On the political plane, too, simple concepts are false: Abd er-Rahman III appointed Christian bishops in Granada; when Almansur sacked the pilgrimage city of Santiago, he had Christian lords with him among his forces, who took their share of the booty.

As for cultural contacts, the great first European Renaissance of the twelfth century owed much indeed to the philosophers of Al Andalus whose works, whether Moslem or Jewish, were written in Arabic and then translated into Latin or Hebrew. The Aristotelian scholar Ibn Rushd (Averroes) is cited by Chaucer as a model of learning; Avicebron's *Fons Vitae* was deeply influential on Christian thinking (he was a rabbi from Málaga called Solomon ibn Gabirol); Maimonides' *Guide to the Perplexed* made him of comparable stature to Averroes, though it must be said that he was active in the time of the intolerant Berbers and went to live in Egypt.

In the other direction, the Christian Emperor of Constantinople sent the Caliph mosaic artists and carvers, whose work and influence spread far beyond Córdoba. The Caliphate reached a peak of power in the tenth century under the able men Abd er-Rahman III and his son Al-Hakem II. But the latter's son succeeded as a child, power was taken by his visir Al Mansur ('the Victorious'), a brilliant, ruthless and power-hungry soldier and, within a few years of his death, the Caliphate collapsed.

Moslem Spain split up into a series of small kingdoms that often feuded with one another, and often called in the help of Christian 'allies' to the north in their feuds – usually to the territorial benefit of the Christians.

Almoravids and Almohads They then made the different mistake of calling in help from Africa. The Almoravids (or 'Frontiersmen'), who were warrior zealots, came, helped... and took over. Luckily they succumbed fairly soon to the good life of Al Andalus.

The next lot were not so easily softened. These were the Almohads ('Unitarians') who not only took over in the middle of the twelfth century, but considered Spain as a mere province of Africa, with their capital in Marrakech. To judge by the Giralda in Seville, they were more than just warriors: it is the work of an advanced and sophisticated art. But under them life began to be hard for Christians and Jews. But disunity, whether among Arabs or Berbers, helped the Christian advance from the north, which now, under Ferdinand III (the Holy) and his son Alfonso the Learned, began to look more like a crusade.

The Reconquest By the middle of the thirteenth century, the whole of Moslem Spain had been reconquered except for the kingdom of Granada which then covered a good part of present-day Andalusia: Granada, Almería, Málaga and parts of Cádiz. For the better part of 250 years it stayed that way. The kingdom of Granada saw a great flourishing, a final burst, of brilliant civilization, since artists, poets, thinkers, doctors flooded into this last Moslem enclave in Spain. Then came the end. The marriage of Ferdinand and Isabella united Aragon with Castile, he the sword, she the rosary. Or, for the Moors (and the Jews), he the butcher, she the bigot.

In 1485 Ronda fell; two years later Málaga, and Granada was cut off from Africa. Finally, in 1492, Granada fell, all Spain was in the hands of the Christians, and Isabella was released from her vow of months previously, not to change her body linen. The great fertile *vega* that the Moors had brought to fruition with their skills in irrigation and husbandry, was parcelled out as reward among the Castilian fighting nobility and began to revert to wilderness under the ignorance of its labourers and the absentee indifference of its new owners.

The civilization that gave us the Alhambra was, in its Mosques, razed to make way for Christian churches. Within the year, Isabella's Christianity, guided by the church, brought about the banishment (or forced conversion) of the Jews, and Spain was saved from almost total illiteracy only by those Jews who chose to keep their homes by renouncing their faith. The Inquisition was activated to make sure that these forced converts were either sincere or else burnt at the stake for the good of their souls. But Spain was now one, and Christian.

The Discovery of America This account aims only to help the visitor understand what he sees in Andalusia. The economic and social impact of the arriving treasure ships is beyond both aims and scope of such a sketch. Its visible impact shows only in Cádiz and Seville, and is mentioned in those sections.

The Patria Chica The accidents of marriage, inheritence and battle over the centuries have made Portugal another country while Catalonia, which also has a language and traditions of its own, is part of Spain. The same applies to other regions. Apart from these accidents of history, there is no reason why the boundaries of Spain should be where they are. The Aragonese feel nothing in common with their neighbours the Catalans, nor with their neighbours the Navarrese. The same applies to the other regions of Spain. Madrid was a dusty village when Seville and Valladolid were capital cities, and beyond its plateau it inspires no more feelings of allegiance than does Canberra to the man from Sydney or Melbourne, or Ottawa to the one from Toronto or Montreal.

The phrase *patria chica* means your little country as against your nation, the *patria grande*, and to the Spaniard of whatever region, it is more important. Thus, the man from Córdoba feels himself to be a Cordobés, first and foremost; only after that, an Andalusian; and only then a Spaniard. Scotsmen and Welshmen may understand this – possibly Yorkshiremen, too – but the rest of us

276

need to be made conscious of it if we are to understand these people and their recent background.

This phenomenon goes with – and has always gone with – a remarkable independence of mind. 'We, who are as good as you, accept you, who are no better than us, as our overlord.' So runs part of a declaration of some five hundred years ago. It might stand as a motto today.

The Background to Today When Castile gained hegemony over the other Spains, and above all when the first Bourbon king in 1707 made a decree abolishing all regional laws and privileges, it set up a tension between autocratic central control and regional independence that still affects Spain today. One more ingredient completes the picture: the vigorous sixteenth-century counter-reform to defeat Protestantism made Spain turn away from Europe as a contaminating influence.

Ever since then, the pendulum has swung back and forth. Every autocratic government has been centralist, and has turned away from Europe; every liberalizing trend has moved towards regional autonomy, and has turned towards Europe. 'The time has come for Spaniards to be governed in accordance with their history,' said one politician as he began a repression so savage it produced a revolution. 'If Spain is the problem, Europe is the solution,' said the philosopher Ortega y Gasset. Franco described the Spain shaped by nineteenth-century liberalism as '... Bastard, Frenchified, and Europeanizing' – the last word being the strongest abuse. Hence the name he gave his own party: Nationalist. Juan-Carlos in 1975, the year he came to the throne, said, 'We Spaniards are Europeans' – though few then seemed to notice the deep significance of that remark.

The Civil War The Republic that came in, in 1933, was the first, except for a one-year effort, in Spain's history. It was bumbling and disparate. It also represented Democracy, Regional Autonomy, Europeanism, and a strong element of Left-Wing Atheism. All of these were as red rags to the Army, the Church and the Falange (Spain's Fascist party, founded by José-Antonio, son of the 1920s dictator Primo de Rivera).

In the ensuing slaughter, approximately half a million died, less than half of them in battle. Executions and murders during, and continuing for years after the war, accounted for the rest. Added to this, some 300,000 went into exile. The country was scarred by traumatic hatreds and drained of resources.

We (Britain, France, and the USA) decided it was an internal matter and thus none of our business. A small number of volunteers went to help: George Orwell, André Malraux, Ernest Hemingway among them. But then, when we had finished our own affair with fascism, we decided that Franco was on the wrong side: Europe was picked up by Marshall Aid, but Spain was boycotted. Around 25,000 died of hunger, and these figures were only kept from catastrophic proportions by the intervention of Perón and the Argentine with a massive gift of food.

I was in Spain during the Falklands war, and avoided the television when the news was on, as the only gesture I could think of, in response to the deep courtesy of my Spanish colleagues who never mentioned the subject in my presence.

The Return to Democracy This was amazingly successful, rapid and complete. We in the West have been so preoccupied by communism over the last forty years, that few of us have taken note of the similarity between all forms of autocratic bureaucracy, whether left wing or right. Both communism and right-wing dictatorship have proved economically inept; both put the State before people, and enforce that precedence with police forces answerable only to the rulers. Yet few, if any, have noticed that what is now happening in Eastern Europe, happened fifteen years ago in Spain. And, unlike eastern Europe, Spain, with no more experience of democracy than Poland or Romania, has achieved democracy with astonishing success.

The return to democracy was dominated by weariness and wariness.

Weariness at the very thought of political strife may well account for the shrivelling of the extreme parties: Communists, the 40-year-long bugbear of Franco's rhetoric, dwindled to political nonentity. So did the parties of Francoist tendency: only in 1989 did the Partido Popular, founded by Fraga, the most 'liberal' of Franco's men, come into serious contention – and it is no further to the right than our own Conservatives. While Felipe Gonzalez's Socialist party is so pragmatic, so much at the centre of the spectrum, as to be unrecognisable as socialism. With hindsight (that exact science) it is easy to see that hunger brought about those extreme politics of sixty

It may be worth saying that Spaniards seem to show no inclination for chauvinism or even much consciousness of the nationality of others. You are extremely unlikely, whatever your country of origin, to have to overcome any prejudices. Politically, though not personally, there has been some animosity towards the USA which first boycotted Spain (together with the rest of us) on ideological grounds, but then shored up the Franco régime in exchange for air bases.

years ago. Or, as a taxi-driver said to me, 'I don't know right from left: I vote for my pocket, and at the moment that means Felipe.'

Wariness made tolerance and moderation necessary. The watchword was *convivencia* or living together; the idea was to let sleeping dogs lie – and go on lying until they died in their sleep. Thus, while the streets named after fascist or Nationalist leaders have been changed to such as Constitution Avenue or Velazquez St., the change has been gradual, and not insisted on; likewise, all monuments to the Nationalist dead in their glorious struggle against the 'reds' have been left untouched. The shrill fascist newspaper *Alcazar* continued to call for the return of morality and the lash until it went out of circulation two or three years ago – for lack of readers. There are still plenty of Spaniards who hanker for the days of Franco, censorship and prison without trial. They are referred to, with gentle tact, as *Los Nostálgicos*.

The greatest danger came from the army. With the loss of Morocco, Spain's last colony, the army's only possible mission might be seen as that of protecting Spaniards from themselves – shades of Pinochet, or of the Inquisition 'saving' people by burning them alive. And it so nearly happened.

23 February 1981 On this day a Colonel of the Guardia Civil marched into Parliament and held it at gunpoint, while one General marched on Madrid at the head of his troops, others prepared to do so, and others again dithered.

With hindsight this can be seen as a turning-point, both for Spain and for King Juan-Carlos. As titular head of the army, he rang all Generals Commanding and told them that to continue would be disloyalty. It was touch and go.

The next day the heads of the political parties, including both Fraga and the Secretary General of the Communist party, walked arm in arm through the streets of Madrid at the head of nearly a million people, to demonstrate their opinion of the aborted Putsch. The Generals seem to have got the message.

As for Juan-Carlos, appointed by Franco as his successor, to the indifference of the vast majority of Spaniards, his position is best expressed by quoting Santiago Carrillo, the Communist leader. When he acceded, Carrillo dubbed him 'Johnny the Brief'. After 23 February, Carrillo went public with the statement, 'If Juan-Carlos had not existed, we would have had to invent him'. As a declaration by a Communist about a Monarch, that says things about Juan-Carlos, Carrillo and Spaniards. Where else could it happen?

Andalusia, Regional Autonomy and Europe I hope the last few pages explain what is happening now. To the Andalusian, as to all Spaniards, the move into the European Community means the end of the swinging pendulum; it means not only democracy but, above all, stable democracy. And as for the British fear of loss of sovereignty, why should Andalusians fear that? They have been governed for centuries, and governed badly, by those Castilians in Madrid; Strasbourg, Brussels, the Hague are only stabilizing extensions. With their instinctive allegiance to their *patria chica,* they show little sign of nationalistic chauvinism.

As for interference 'from abroad', in 1982, Andalusia, together with 16 other regions, gained regional autonomy. For centuries they had been the poor cousins, on the fringes when it came to governmental support. The inequity of the *latifundio,* the huge estates owned by absentee landlords, with the peasants owning little or nothing, has led in our own times to massive emigration (to the industrial north or abroad). And yet this hungry land is one of the richest and most fertile in Spain.

Now it is their turn to manage their own affairs; my impression is one of energetic optimism. When we feel like complaining that the country is no longer cheap, it is well to remember that it is no longer poor.

The Sephardim – The Jewish People of Spain The Sephardim, or Jewish people of the Peninsula, lived in Spain for longer, in greater numbers, and played a more important role in the development of the country than is usually realized. Nothing is proved yet, but the balance of probability is that they were there in numbers many hundreds of years before Masada in AD 140, when Rome drove them out of Palestine into the 1,800-year-long exile that is called the Diaspora.

Jonah, when he fled in the eighth century BC found a ship going to Tarshish (Tartessos, in what is now Andalusia) so he paid the fare thereof... and only got as far as the belly of a whale. Obadiah, writing in 600 BC mentions the 'captivity of Jerusalem which is in Sepharad', which is the Hebrew name for Spain and Portugal, though it has been claimed that this could have been some other Sepharad. There exists a letter dating from approximately AD 140 from the Jews in Palestine, rebelling against the Romans, asking for help from those of Sepharad – which suggests numbers much higher than a few merchant groups.

Until the coming of the Moors in 711, the 'People of the Book' were virtually the only literate laymen in the kingdom which, whether the Visigothic or later Christian kingdoms, depended on them for their administration, not to mention for their doctors and lawyers. While the Visigoths had stuck to their original Arian heresy there had been no reason for animosity. The Arian belief that Jesus was man only, and not God, meant that to any but a theologian it was hard to perceive any difference between the faiths of Christian and Jew. It was only when the Visigoths converted to Catholicism that any persecution began. And even then, during the three hundred years of Visigothic rule, it is clear, from the frequency of the repetition of edicts forbidding marriage between Christian and Jew, that this is just what commonly happened. Persecution came from above; not from ordinary people.

With the coming of the Arabs in 711 there began a period of great prosperity, for it must be remembered that Islamic enmity to Jewry is a purely modern phenomenon. Both are Semitic peoples; both are 'the People of the Book'; and the Koran treats Abraham as a great forerunner of Mohammed. In Mohammed's lifetime, the Jihad, or Holy War, could only be fought against pagans; never against Jew or Christian.

Furthermore, Islamic Spain was characterized by racial and religious tolerance. Contrary to the old cliché image, persecution and intolerance were almost a Christian monopoly. But not quite: during two unpleasant periods, Moorish Spain was taken over by fundamentalist Berber fanatics from North Africa, who made life hard for Christian, Jew and Spanish Moslem alike. The first lot, the Almoravids (Frontiersmen), soon got softened by the good life of the peninsula; but the second mob, the Almohads (Unitarians) were nastier for longer.

Despite these, it was a golden age of great doctors, philosophers, poets, and religious figures. Hasdai ibn Shaprut was so renowned as a doctor that the Christian king Sancho the Fat came to Islamic Córdoba to be cured by him of his fatness. And Maimonides surpassed ibn Shaprut in renown. To Maimonides, together with the other great Aristotelian philosopher, the Arab ibn Rushd (Averroes), Saint Thomas Aquinas owed much of the knowledge that enabled him to gather Christian doctrine in Aristotelian form. Solomon ibn Gabirol, known to the West as Avicebron, wrote the *Fons Vitae*, a treatise that had considerable influence in the Christian West. He also wrote fine poetry: his religious poems are sung today as part of the Sephardic rite; secular poems such as his 'Night Storm' come across powerfully even in translation. Judah ha Levi and Samual ibn Nagrella are among the finest poets in the Hebrew language, the latter being also known as ha-Nagid (the Prince) because, as Chief Minister to the King of Granada, he was a very powerful man.

As for religious writing, the *Sefer ha Zohar*, the *Book of Splendour*, may even be the most widely read work ever to come out of Spain, since for several hundred years it ranked only after the *Torah* and *Talmud*, world-wide, as the most widely read work in Hebrew. Yet the *Zohar* is only one of the later among hundreds of Hebrew works written in Spain over the previous 200 or 300 years, most of which have yet to be read and edited by modern scholars, and which together make up one of the most remarkable mystical movements in the history of mankind. It was known as the Tradition (Kabbala). The word has some pretty silly connotations for those English readers who have come across Denis Wheatley. In fact, as the sheer number of written Kabbalistic works shows, it had nothing to do with the sort of secrecy of magic that Christian bigotry supposed. It merely shunned explicit teaching for the same reason that Saint Teresa recommended log-chopping and cold baths to an over-fervent disciple. All mystical forms of whatever religion – Christian, Jewish, Buddhist or Yoga – demand self-discipline and slow preparation. Except for the more medieval tricks of *Gematria* and *Notarikon*, the Kabbalistic books tend to read much like Dame Julian of Norwich or 'The Cloud of Unknowing'.

In the fourteenth century a paranoid Archdeacon of Ecija began preaching murder. While his Archbishop and King lived, he was kept in bounds. Both died. He became bishop with none to restrain him, and started to whip up an infectious lust to kill. On 1 June 1391 a horrific pogrom began, that in a mere matter of months had spread throughout the country. It was the virtual end of Jewish culture in Spain, though it was a hundred years later, in 1492, that the rest were given the choice: convert or go. No clear estimates are available of the numbers who opted to stay and accepted more or less sincere conversion to Christianity. The number must have been high for it was mainly after 1492 that the Inquisition really got to work. As for those who kept the faith and went into the second Galuth, or exile, the estimates vary widely. A number between 160,000 and 400,000 left the country that had been theirs for the better part of 2,000 years. And with their departure, together with that of the Moors at the same period, Spain was left a cultural near-desert.

This is not the end of the story. The rest is immensely ironic. Torquemada the Inquisitor, the very model of sadistic fanaticism, was Jewish, of a family of converts, and responsible for hounding and condemning thousands of his fellow-people. But even more ironic, in a period obsessed with racial purity, St Teresa and St John of the Cross, Spain's two best-loved (and most lovable) saints, are now known both to have been of Jewish stock.

Outside Andalusia little concrete trace remains of their millenial culture. The occasional church was recognizably once a synagogue (notably in Toledo and Segovia); the traces exist of an Aljama or quarter in Gerona, once the home of the great mystical movement, but there is little else. If there is more that survives in Andalusia, it is because here, under the Moors, they lived for centuries unpersecuted. Thus, we find the *juderia* in Córdoba, and the Barrio Santa Cruz in Seville, the one now crowded with tourists, the other the favourite evening resort of Sevillian students. There are, of course, many churches that started life as synagogues. Some, like Santa Cruz de Jerusalem in Seville, started as mosques, became synagogues, and have been churches since the massacres of June 1391 emptied them. In Lucena nothing remains of what was once a Jewish city, and probably had been so since Phoenician times, though the church of St James (Santiago) is known locally as the synagogue. But the synagogue in Córdoba only survived as such because it was (and is) part of a private house.

One more irony remains. In 1992 Spain celebrates the fifth centenary of the discovery of America with a great World Fair in Seville. That year is also the fifth centenary of the mass expulsion of one of the oldest peoples of the Iberian Peninsula, and of setting the Inquisition on to those who stayed. Israel is taking part in the Fair...

Horses In Andalusia, more than anywhere else in Spain, horses are important. The Andalusis are magnificent beasts, grey when young and white when mature. Their daily exercise in the Jerez Royal School looks to my ignorant eye like Olympic medal-winning stuff; while the Thursday performance of the equestrian ballet is such that if ever you had the urge to see the Lippizaners of the Spanish Riding School in Vienna, you really ought to include Jerez in your tour. This form of Haute Ecole has been going for a couple of hundred years, and seems to have been developed by Carthusian monks, of all people. I give more detail under Jerez, (*see* page 132).

But the Andalusian love of horses is not confined to such elevated stuff. The Spanish *gitanos*, like Gypsies everywhere, have always been horse copers. The owner of my hotel in Córdoba, a thoroughly urban gypsy of comfortable shape, amused me by his vehemence as he poured scorn on the idea that any hired horse such as the one I had ridden could possibly be a real Spanish horse. I felt it would be impolitic to tell him it had been named Gitana.

In the countryside, you still come across young men, neither gypsy or wealthy, who not only own a horse but give it the sort of care, and ride it with the same pride in their skill and its prowess, that in Britain is now more typical of the motorbike

Cádiar at dawn

enthusiast for his machine. And horses figure prominently, sometimes in hundreds, in some of the multitude of fairs and festivals that I list on page 311. Chief among them are:

The Horse Fair at Jerez in April/ May:

The great Feria at Seville two weeks after Easter (but before the end of April). This started life as a Horse Fair, and hundreds parade their horses, girlfriends (up behind) and costumes.

The Pilgrimage of the Virgen de la Cabeza at Andújar (Jaén) on and around the last Sunday of April:

And, massively, the Rocío Pilgrimage in Huelva Province, which involves up to a million people, coming from all parts of Spain, many of them by horse or ox-wagon. This means that in the week before Whitsun, riders with their women up behind, both in traditional colourful costume, will be crossing Andalusia from all points – the Granada brotherhoods, for example, set out from the city on the Sunday before.

But there are colourful lesser occasions, too, such as the cavalcade that is a strong feature of the Feast of Saint Eulalia at Almonaster la Real (Huelva) on the third weekend in May; or the Romería of the Virgin of Grace at Fuente Objeuna (Córdoba) on the Sunday nearest 25 April (for London theatre-goers this may have strong associations since Lope de Vega's moving drama about the townsfolk was played at the National Theatre with great success a couple of years ago).

Hiring

Aventura: Apartado 21, Orgiva, Granada. Tel: (9)58 78 52 53 – this is an English outfit. They do an 8-day and a 15-day trek in the Alpujarra. The latter takes you over the Sierra to the dry lands and to La Calahorra. It tempts me. They also organize a mule trek within the Alpujarra, for which you do not need any riding experience. I mention their 8-day trek in my section on the Alpujarra on page 219.

Bosler SL: Multicentro San José Real, 173, San Fernando, Cádiz. Tel: 88 23 53 – 'A galope por la costa: Chiclana to Bolonia'; this is a matter of staying at two places during the rides, and being transported to your horse each day. It is mostly beach and coast (*see* the Cádiz section, page 154, for the scenery). There is a 10-day ride extending to Algeciras: the terrain gets more hilly beyond Bolonia.

Ibérica Horse Tours SA: Calle Duque de Liria, 3, 28015 Madrid. Tel: (91) 242 31 25/242 45 57 – weekend and 8-day tours of the Sierra Morena from Aldeaquemada. You are based at a camp except for one trek to a hotel and back next day, and the emphasis seems to be on a little riding mixed with seeing bull-farms, bathing, etc. On the whole, the Sierra Morena is gentler terrain than the other Andalusian chains.

Rutas a Caballo SA: Calle Augustín de Aragón, 14–1° C, 28006-Madrid. Tel: (91) 402 95 00 – one of the oldest firms (going since 1975), they do tours in the Serrania de Ronda between Arcos and Zahara (*see* pages 107 and 113) and from Bosque to Ronda, which sounds good (*see* page 109). Their publicity emphasizes the comfort of Paradors and good food. Unfortunately, I must add a big caveat: I can confirm nothing about them, for they change address with every brochure and I have yet to get a reply from any.

Cavalry Tours: 14, Cromwell Crescent, London SW5 9QW. Tel: 071-602 8433 – they arrange riding holidays in many countries, including a couple in Andalusia. Estepona – Zahara, 1 week; this includes three nights spent at Almoraima, riding on what used to be a private estate; experienced riders only; £879 inc. flight. Also, 6 days' packhorse ride in the Sierra Nevada from £646.

Equitour: Calle Juan Güell 163, Barcelona. Tel: (93) 339 41 00 – tours start from Seville, and go to the white towns, the Sierra Morena, and Jerez and the Atlantic coast.

Aljibe Club de Viajeros: Calle Rui López 14, Jerez. Tel: (956) 32 26 25 – they have tours in the Alpujarra and in the hills east of Jerez, or they will organize one for your group.

Clearly, you will need to choose according to your own tastes and with more data from the firms than I have supplied. Personally, I would choose to return to Aventura, the trek where the purpose of the week's holiday is to make a journey on horseback, albeit a leisurely one, and where you have to look after your own horse and tack. This appeals to me as a more enjoyable and a more total break than a daily ride coupled with a visit to a local sight, before handing over your horse for whisky and tourist hotel.

If it sounds a bit tough, you should know that I am not young, not one who takes regular exercise, and had not climbed aboard a horse for many years. Yes, it was tiring; but by the end of the week it was so much less so that I was disappointed at having to stop. And, to my great surprise, no saddle sores.

I am also a fan of both Gerald Brenan and Penelope Chetwode (*see* Further Reading, page 319) and enjoyed using her transport to see his country. I was about to add 'and her sort of lodging' but, though we did use the old *posadas*, cleanliness, bathrooms and modern beds are now the rule, and I only came across one wall bracket that obeyed her immutable law by tilting when you hung your towel on it.

Both the English-run firms that I know of, want to know that you can cope and reserve the right not to accept you. And, of course, you must think about the terrain: there is no question of a gallop when riding the mountain tracks of the Alpujarras; if it is the pleasure of horsemanship you want, rather than a journey on a horse, then perhaps the Bosler, or else the Cavalry Tours Estepona trip, may suit you better.

Unhappy Postcript In early 1989 the dreadful horse plague crossed from Africa and affected a small area in the south of Spain. Immediately the equestrian events for the Spanish Olympics three years ahead were cancelled. Vets came down from all over the peninsula to help. In Africa they produced vaccination serum as fast as they could, and sent it over, together with their own experts. There was also a ban on the movement of horses.

Thanks to this ruthless reaction they managed in a matter of a few months to stop the disease, and to vaccinate all horses. But the plague is so deadly that the government is, probably quite rightly, maintaining the ban on the movement of horses even at the time of writing, a year after the last case. Thus, in 1990 the Jerez Horse Fair was held without horses, the wagons of the Rocio pilgrimage were drawn by tractors and the Seville April Fair was a pale imitation of itself.

The danger to the horse is now effectively over. So it is far more serious now that the ban, however wise and praiseworthy, has seriously put at risk the breeding of Andalusian stock, which is too expensive a business to survive easily without sales. And, of course, it is jeopardizing the livelihood of many smaller outfits that depend on the horse. I can only hope the ban can be lifted soon – at least, before you read this – and that the firms I name above will have weathered the storm.

Jerez wine festival

It is not certain that the sherry the Ancient Roman Columella wrote of, or Chaucer in the fourteenth century, is the same sherry as ours, though there is a ring of familiarity about Chaucer's:

This wine of Spain creepeth subtilly...
Of which there riseth such fumosity,
That when a man hath drunken draughtes three,
And weneth that he be at home in Chepe,
He is in Spain...

Sherry The English word 'sherry' and the French 'Xérés' are versions of the modern Spanish *jerez*, and both were adopted hundreds of years ago, for the making of sherry wine goes back a very long way.

Sherry, then called sack, was certainly drunk in the days of Henry VIII; and by the time of that miserly old killjoy James I it was so popular that he rationed the court to 'twelve gallons of Sacke a day, and *no more*'.

The sherry we know, really developed in the late eighteenth century, and its huge popularity in Britain resulted at least partially from the Prince Regent declaring it was the only stuff for him. In the latter part of the last century, the massive demands of the British market persuaded some shippers to supply inferior and even adulterated stuff, and this in turn brought about a virtual collapse in the market – at least for quality sherry.

I mention this because two things came of it. First, it made the sherry firms put their own houses very firmly in order. To protect its quality, the industry regulated itself – and did so very strictly – many years before similar controls were imposed on the other great wines such as claret and burgundy. And, secondly, the insatiable demand for sherry led indirectly to the production of British 'sherry' which now makes up more than 50 per cent of the British market. The Spaniards feel rather aggrieved that, while they obeyed immediately the Common Market injunction protecting other brand names such as Cognac, we were granted a ten-year delay before we must follow suit. So, for several years, while they lose trade, we can continue to call 'sherry' a liquid that bears no relation to sherry in composition and virtually none in taste. The Australian and South African versions are nearer to the real thing, but they still do not achieve it. Given the excellence of Australia's wines in other respects, this might seem surprising, but for two things: their success lies in varietal wines that are good in themselves, rather than in attempted imitations of others; and no amount of skill can reproduce the combination of climate, soil and other conditions that go to make a great wine. Notably the *flor*, that is so crucial to a *fino*, cannot be made to exist where it does not want to.

Sherry is unlike other wines in many different ways. The best grows on poor, chalky soil. This it has in common with champagne but, unlike champagne or any other great wine, it does so in a hot climate. This *albariza* soil, that gives its luminous quality to the landscape west of Jerez, absorbs the winter rains to a considerable depth and so makes the moisture available to the deep-rooting vines during the dry summers. The Palomino grape also grows well in the *arena* (sand) and *barro* (clay) soils of the area, though with less distinction.

A second big difference is that throughout its life, from fermentation and storage, right up to the moment of bottling, the wine must have access to air. So it is made and stored in airy bodegas, above ground, and kept in casks that are only loosely stoppered and not completely filled.

The *finos*, at least, develop under a film of flor, a form of yeast that may also grow in the Jura and in the Caucasus but nowhere else. It cannot be induced, but is easily killed, and it is essential to the quality of the wine. Hence the use of the *venencia* in sampling the wine: the *venenciador* lowers the long stalk with its narrow cup through the film of flor, and withdraws it with a minimum of disturbance. His skill in then pouring it a metre or so through the air into the glass is a feat demonstrated to every visiting group.

But perhaps the greatest difference between the making of sherry and that of other wines lies in the development of the various styles (*fino, palo cortado, oloroso*). For the strange fact is that you cannot tell which wine is going to emerge, no matter how skilful the *capataz* (foreman) or how good his 'nose'. (In parenthesis here, the foreman's palate is not needed, for nothing could be learnt from the taste of the 'must' in the earlier stages, only from the smell and the look.) Two barrels of must (as the grape juice is called), taken side by side from the same part of the vineyard, may develop, one into a delicate *fino*, and the other into a rich *oloroso*. Thus, at his first classification of the new wine, the *capataz* simply marks the potential quality of the butts.

After the lees have been racked off, the must, now usually called wine for the first time, is slightly fortified and a week or two later it is classified for a second time. The butts with wine breeding flor are marked as *palma* (Υ); those with a fuller wine with little or no flor are marked /; while // and # denote coarser and unusable grades, (the latter go to make brandy or vinegar). The butts are stored in the bodegas, three or four tiers high, each butt containing about 110 gallons, and left to develop as they will. For even now the character may change. Only when the wine is considered ready to be used in a *solera*, which may be after a few months or as much as three years, can it be classified definitively:

Υ *palma* a light and delicate *fino*.

Ⴘ *palma cortada*, a fuller *fino*, more like an *Amontillado*.

Ϯ *palo cortado*, a wine of a particular and delicate style, but which does not breed flor.

Ø *oloroso*, a fuller and darker wine.

/ *raya*, a coarser *oloroso*.

So far the butts are of single vintage (*añada*) wine. If they are left, they will go on developing in character and getting stronger for years. Indeed, there are single vintage sherries around, some of them of great age, though rarely, if ever, on the market.

The Solera System But it follows from the rather unpredictable way the wines develop and change, that the *solera* system is needed, for the buyers want a steady supply of sherries of known and constant taste. The system depends on the remarkable fact that if you top up a butt of older wine with up to a third of younger similar wine, the younger will take on the taste of the older, and become not similar but identical. So a *solera* is set up, consisting of a tier of butts of wine of one type, flavour and quality. The stocks for shipping are drawn from this, not more than a third at a time. The butts are topped up from a younger tier or 'scale'; and these are in turn topped up from a third scale, they from a fourth, and so on according to the number of scales in the *criadera* (nursery), the last of the scales being a new or newish wine of single vintage. Visitors, who see the massive butts stacked in tiers three or at most four high, are sometimes confused to learn that a *solera* may have up to nine scales in the *criadera*. The fact is, the tiers of butts that you see may well not even belong to the same *criadera*, whose scales may be found elsewhere in the building, or even in a different one.

Blending All these *solera* wines are dry, the *olorosos* as well as the *finos*. Now they are blended, to make the different brands we find on the shelves. Apart from blending from different *soleras*, this involves the addition of a variety of wines or wine syrups, some to sweeten and others to deepen the colour. The most notable of these special wines is from the other famous grape variety of the area, the Pedro Ximenes. It is made very sweet here in Jerez, but curiously, it makes a pleasant dry wine in the area south of Córdoba where it is called *Montilla* – or, more correctly, *Montilla-Moriles*.

Fortifying Apart from the slight fortifying to stabilize the wine, already mentioned, this may be done at later stages for a variety of reasons: to stop fermentation (in sweeter sherries); to kill any flor (in *olorosos*); to help a delicate wine to travel; to conform to import regulations of various countries which impose higher duty bands at differing strengths.

It is done by adding sherry brandy, but never much: natural sherries range from 15°–23°, whereas the (self-imposed) regulations say that sherry should never be less than 15.5° or more than 20.9°.

Types

Fino is the lightest, and usually the driest, but do not believe all you read on the label: dryness is a matter of fashion, and in Britain often of snobbery. So a lot of *finos* may be labeled 'Dry' to satisfy our Good Taste, yet in reality be medium to satisfy our palates.

Manzanilla is a variety of *Fino* made in Sanlúcar de Barrameda. The taste is distinct and delightfully fresh: I am told its slight tang comes from the sea air and the fact that Sanlúcar is a fraction cooler than Jerez. Whatever the cause, it tends to be slightly less alcoholic, and to my mind altogether delicious in the hot climate.

Amontillado. Some *finos*, given many years in the *solera*, may begin to develop into a true *Amontillado*, a wine with a rich nutty flavour, so named because of a family resemblance with *Montilla* wine. It is rare – and therefore expensive. It follows that the quantities of *Amontillado* sold in Britain are unlikely to be the real thing. Usually it is blended from a *fino*.

Palo cortado is, with *fino* and *oloroso*, one of the three ways a new wine may develop. Like *oloroso*, it breeds without flor and has a rich bouquet; like *fino* it has a certain crispness; like true *Amontillado*, it is rare. And so, like *Amontillados* in Britain, it is often not the real thing, but concocted from a blend of other wines, for the Spanish market goes for *Palo Cortado*, as we do for *Amontillado*.

Oloroso is a richer wine from which our sweet dessert sherries are blended. But in its natural form it is completely dry, though with a smooth finish. I was at first surprised when, of an evening in Jerez, I found that locals offering me a *copa* invariably handed me an *oloroso*. But I had been unused to it in its dry form, and was converted: a dry *oloroso* in a bar at midnight seemed as naturally right as a *manzanilla* in the heat of noon. Dry Sack is an example of a dryish *oloroso*. *Oloroso* starts life almost as pale as a *fino*, but soon grows darker in colour.

Montilla is not a sherry, and is made from the Pedro Ximenes grape. But I list it here because it has a similar taste, and because in other parts of Andalusia, the barman may well serve it, if you ask for a *fino*.

Drinking it Except traditionally with consommé, we in the UK have almost always used sherry as an aperitif. Indeed, a chilled *fino* makes a good one. But sherry goes excellently with food, as the Jerezanos know. And the combination of sherry and Jabugo ham is an experience not to be missed.

But even as an aperitif, UK consumption has gone down over the past few decades. This is surprising when you consider the remarkable boom in wine drinking over the same period. Perhaps already, before we could tell our Chardonnay from our Sauvignon, sherry had been getting a stuffy image as the drink Aunty keeps. Or else there are memories of Cyprus 'sherry' six months in the decanter, which is like judging Hock from a bottle of Yugoslav Riesling opened two days before. Yet any list of the world's great wines would include sherry high on it. And, what is more, a good one costs less than a good claret, or burgundy, or champagne. Nor do you have to make a pilgrimage to St James' Street to find it as there is quality drinking to be had from the High Street stores: San Patricio, Don Fino, Tio Pepe, Dry Sack, or an Amoroso such as Character, to name (quite unfairly) but a few.

The *copa* in which sherry is always served, and has been so for many years, is identical with the so-called Chauvet glass, more recently adopted elsewhere as the official wine-tasting glass – proof, if proof were needed, that the Jerezanos know what they are doing.

Fino and *manzanilla* taste best chilled, and keeping them in the fridge also makes them last longer: about 10 days in the fridge or about 3 days at room temperature, after which they begin to lose their subtlety. Decanting makes them go off even quicker. If you are not going to drink up the bottle in a couple of days, the tip is to pour half into an empty half-bottle and cork it tightly. Even sealed in the bottle, from the supplier, a *fino* begins to deteriorate after about three months.

Dry *oloroso* and *Amontillado* taste best cool; sweet sherries at room temperature. The sweeter the sherry the longer it will keep.

A *fino* will taste drier in Britain than it does in Jerez. So if you usually find Don Fino or La Ina too dry for your taste, try again when in Andalusia.

Bin Ends (Or bits and pieces of possible interest); ★Sherry in the barrel evaporates at a rate of something like 5 per cent per year. This is known as 'the angels' share'. Given the total stock of one million butts (or 110 million gallons), my pocket calculator tells me the Andalusian angels drink more than 5 million gallons of sherry per year. What is good enough for the angels… .★Sherry (and Madeira) get stronger with age. A very old, single vintage wine will have a splendid bouquet, but to taste, it would screw your mouth up. Such wines can only be drunk when diluted with younger wines.

★On the other hand, given the evaporation rate, a butt, if not topped up, would virtually disappear in 70 years.

★Unlike most wines, and except for *fino* under its flor, sherry improves with travel. The rolling of a ship helps the blend, and artificially increases the age. Hence, the old 'East Indian' sherries, shipped out and back in ballast.

★Oak casks must be used. New oak, strong in tannin, is needed for fermentation; after 10 years the cask is right for maturing the wine in the *solera*. The casks used for shipping the wine are bought by whisky distillers for maturing their raw spirit.

★*Tapas* were invented for sherry. In the 1920s waiters in the Rinconcillo bar in Seville (Calle Gerona) started serving each copa of sherry with a slice of mountain ham on it (*tapa* means 'lid'). The bar is still there and the décor unchanged. But today you pay for the ham.

★Gypsum plaster (*yeso*) is added to the grapes at the pressing. It reacts in the must to produce a precipitate that helps clarify the wine, and tartaric acid that helps the fermentation. The habit has probably been going on since Roman times – at least, the

Romans knew the trick – yet recent analysis (made by the current Honorary Foreman of the Sherry Industry, Professor Quiros) has shown that it also helps the wine in a good half dozen other ways, most of them previously unsuspected.

★Sherry and human beings take about the same time to reach maturity. But after that, sherry goes on slowly developing.

★When Señor González was going to receive a royal visit he got very excited and ordered from Germany a gigantic butt holding some 3,600 gallons. As this is the equivalent of 33 standard sherry butts, or the number of years in the life of JC, it came to be called *El Cristo*. Eleven ordinary butts were placed on either side, known as the *Apóstoles*. The twelfth, *Judas*, is in the vinegar cellar…

Bullfighting is not a sport; indeed, only the English word calls it a fight (*corrida* means a 'run'). It has something of the tragedy: you do not go to see Hamlet wondering who will win, or suggest that Othello would be better if the Moor were given a fair chance of coming out the winner. But then, in tragedy, death is only simulated: the hero dies; not the actor. Nor is it everyone who chooses to see Shakespeare. The closer comparison would be with the Ancient Greeks, for whom tragedy had an element of ritual, and was attended by people of all sorts – and, one assumes, appreciated in its finer points by them. Going to see a *corrida* for the first time is rather like going to see your first tragedy – acted in a language you do not understand. Yet a bullfight is clearly not a play and the comparison is not enough.

It has something of the championship tennis match: as it develops, the spectators can sense that one of the protagonists is gradually gaining dominance. You can feel this, and the attendant excitement and pity, even if you have no appreciation of the subtlety and skills of the players. At my first *corrida* one of the Matadors could not dominate his bull, made more and more daring passes to bend it to his will until, almost inevitably, he was gored; whereupon the number three, an old routiner long past the chance of stardom, came on, mastered the bull and despatched it with a minimum of show. As drama it was unforgettable. But in tennis it is like against like, with physical strengths matched as well as skills. In a *corrida* only courage is matched; otherwise it is massive strength against skill. And again, tennis, unlike the *corrida*, is a sport – and neither protagonist dies.

The corrida

For the subtlety and skilful grace, it would have something of the ballet, if you could imagine a dancer having to make his leaps to the edge of a precipice – right to the edge. For to keep at a safe distance, even by a matter of inches, would not help force the mastery of the bull, nor be well received by the crowd.

In fine, a *corrida* is a spectacle, in highly ritualized form, of violence and elegance, fear, courage and danger, a ritual with death at its centre.

If you intend to go to a *corrida*, it is important to make your first one a good one. The sort of so-called *corrida* that is laid on for tourists, or even a *novillada*, that uses younger bulls, are likely to prejudge the issue by disgusting without giving you a chance to experience what has gripped so many people for so many hundreds of years. After a *corrida* of quality you will have had a glimpse of skills and complexities, guessed at if not appreciated, and your verdict will be a fair one. The best *corridas* are likely to be the ones given during fairs or festivals such as the Seville April Fair, the Jerez Horse Fair in May, or major saints' days. By the same token, these occasions are likely to need booking in advance.

The Spanish fighting bull is only the remotest cousin of the fellow you keep an eye open for in an English pasture. It is not only bred to be fierce, it is probably descended from an African cousin of the fearsome aurochs, now otherwise extinct. It was large, quick, black and so nasty that for a man to hunt it was considered the biggest test of courage, lions not excluded.

Nowadays, the *toro bravo* (the word means wild, not brave) is bred not for size, or even endurance, but for the courage that makes it try to get its horns into everything in sight, and go on doing so, on and on until it tires and dies. The second quality the breeders aim for is one they call 'nobility', as a result of which it charges strong and straight. From the torero's point of view, the ideal bull is the *toro de carril*, which might be translated as 'tramline bull'.

In every *corrida* three Matadors take part, each killing two bulls and each supported by his team (*cuadrilla*). The occasion starts with ceremony. It also starts punctually – the saying is that in Spain only the mass and bullfights start on time – so be there in good time, for the gates are shut on last-minute arrivals. The President takes his seat, the band plays and all officials parade round the ring: the three Matadors side by side, each followed by his cuadrilla. What follows is like a rigidly ritualized play in three acts (*tercios*), each act heralded by the trumpet, sounded at the President's order.

Act I (The *suerte de varas*) Scene 1 – The bull charges into the empty arena. From the protection of the alley (*callejón*) that surrounds the ring, members of the team emerge cape in hand, one at a time, to provoke a charge, and duck back. The purpose is to enable the Matador to study the bull. Does it charge impetuously or with seeming deliberation? (If it is impetuous it can look terrifying to you: half a ton of very fast sharp-horned malevolence. But the torero knows that it will be easier to master: the cunning bull that considers its target before attacking is the more dangerous one because less predictable.) Does it hook right or left in the attack? How good is its eyesight? Will it see and charge from a distance or will he have to provoke it from close to?

These are not mere questions of aesthetics, or even of technique. Once he has provoked the charge, the tradition of his art demands that he keep his feet still – and the public will notice if he holds the cape away from his body, or if he leans over to keep the bull's horns that little bit further from his body. So he

296

must judge to the inch the line of charge. From a distance, that is harder; yet from closer to, the bull will be slower and there may be more chance of it switching its thrust from cape to body. The ability to achieve this is one of the three main attributes of the top-class Matador, but already from this sketchy preliminary outline you may perhaps see why the great names are so admired.

Scene 2 – Enter the Matador. He will normally take on the bull with a series of *verónicas*. The *verónica* is a simple-looking and elegant pass: it starts with the cape not fully open; as the bull comes on to him, the opened cape steers it past and round him in a graceful sweep; the bull's impetus carries it past, but each successive charge starts from closer to, until the fighter ends the series with a pass (usually one called a half *verónica*) that closes the cape and leaves the bull stopped short, at a loss.

The purpose of this episode is two-fold. Partly it enables the Matador to study the bull's ways more closely. But, more importantly, it begins his process of psychological domination, of making the bull do as he wishes. As spectacle it can be a high moment. The bull is still at full strength: its courage and desire to kill never flag. At the start of this first encounter, if it were a human opponent, it would be full of confidence. But if these first passes have been successful it is now beginning to be bewildered and frustrated. It needs something less elusive, something more solid to attack in order to renew its aggression. It gets it.

Scene 3 – The picador comes on with lance and horse. The wild bull has an imposing hump on its back behind the head. This is the massive muscle that enables it, not only to hold its head high, but to pick up and toss anything it can get its horns into or under,

A bull breeding farm near Cadiz

whether man, horse or rival in the herd. Before it can be killed, this muscle must be so weakened that the head is lowered, presenting an opening straight to the heart for the Matador's sword.

After its bewilderment and frustration at the hands of the Matador, it finds in the (heavily padded) horse something more solid to attack. The Matador alone would like the bull to toss the horse: anything that tires it helps him. The picador's whole skill and strength is geared to preventing this happening: his right leg is armoured, which makes it hard for him to pick himself off the ground without help, should he fall; and on the ground he is in danger both from the weight of his horse and from the bull's horns. So he thrusts his lance (*vara*) into the hump of muscle with all his weight behind it and tries to hold the bull off, damaging the muscle in the process.

This is the moment in the *corrida* that you are most likely to find distressing. I do not consider it my business here to take a stance or to persuade you one way or the other; merely to tell what happens, above all to explain why it happens, and try to convey a bit about the skills and dangers involved, so that you shall have as fair and informed a basis as I can manage, for making up your own mind.

Scene 4 – At this point all three Matadors enter together and use the cape to draw the bull off, so that the picador and his horse can leave. The process (and each pass of the cape) is called the *quite*. It is the only stage when the Matadors take part together, and it can give rise to some skilful rivalry and spectacular passes with the cape.

On the President's order, the trumpet signals the end of this first *tercio*, and the start of the second.

Act 2 (The *suerte de banderillas*) This *tercio* is short, balletic, and reminds one most of those Minoan pictures of bull dancing. The *banderillas* are barbed darts. The banderillero strikes a pose and walks slowly to provoke the charge, then runs to meet it, usually in a curve that avoids the charge, and plants the darts, two at each run, in the hump of back muscle. Sometimes the Matador takes over this job himself. There are many techniques, each with its name, but they are all of them spectacular.

Act 3 (The *suerte de faena y estocada*) This is the final stage and involves the Matador working with the *muleta* (a square of red cloth) and sword. The *faena*, or work with the *muleta*, is the stage in which the Matador's quality is given most play, the stage in which he has most opportunity to display mastery and art. And courage, for the *muleta* is smaller than his own body, and the bull has the opportunity to learn. But the final act, the sword thrust that kills the bull, is the culmination of everything else, the end for which everything else has been preparing. To look at it in any other light, to think, for example, of the duel with the *muleta*, as rather splendid and the following death as as a sorry ending to it, would be a misunderstanding and wishful thinking.

The faena – at the start of it, the Matador salutes the President and asks permission to kill. If he is pleased with his bull he is likely also to dedicate it to someone; if he thinks it outstanding he will probably dedicate it to the whole audience, in which case you may well be in for a memorable experience.

The Matador's purpose throughout this stage, which usually lasts about ten minutes but may go on for as many as fifteen, is to put together and orchestrate a series of passes that establish his dominance over the bull, bring it to a point of fatigue and submission, and provide a brilliant spectacle for the public. He will end each sequence of such passes with one (called a *remate*) that either stops the bull in its tracks or turns it to bring it back towards the centre of the arena if he is running out of space. The most classic pass of all, and the one you will see most often, is the left-handed *natural*, which draws the bull to the fighter's left side in a slow sweep: it is the least histrionic and the most elegant. This quality of slowness, if he can achieve it, marks the top class torero.

The estocada – the Matador has brought the bull to the moment when he finishes it with a sword thrust. If the bull's legs are square, and if its head is held at the right height, then there is an area about three inches across into which the sword will go for a clean kill. These 'ifs' give the measure of the judgement that needs to be shown throughout by the Matador and his team. Too much or too little tiring the bull, weakening its neck muscles, dominating it, and the bull has not been brought to the right point. However good the Matador's previous work with cape or *muleta*, his reputation will suffer unless the sword thrust is clean and the animal dies quickly. Sometimes the thrust is clean and mortal but the bull is slow in going down. In this case, a special weapon that severs the spinal chord is used.

The measure of the crowd's approval or disapproval is self-evident, but if they start whistling it may well not be in disapproval of the Matador but of the President, for not awarding any honour (such as an ear or both ears). In such cases, the President is usually swayed by the crowd's verdict.

Going to a Bullfight Use the local Tourist Office for advise on where to find tickets. Contrary to widespread belief, bullfights do not always start at 5 p.m. It may be any time from 4.30 to 7 p.m. It will last for two and a half or three hours.

Tickets are not cheap, and the prices vary widely between the best seats in the boxes (*Palcos*) or in the front row (*Barrera*) on the shady side (*Sombra*), and the cheapest seats in the back tiers (*Gradas*) on the sunny side (*Sol*). In between are the *Sol y Sombra* seats where the sun burns into your eyes for the first part of the fight before being masked by the roof opposite. The lower tiers, excluding the front row, are called the *Tendido*. Your ticket will show you which entrance to use, and your row (*Fila*).

Flamenco If you have seen a drunken Greek get up and dance in a bar in the Plaka, and as he does so, seem to go back inside himself and become a somebody; or if you have watched, when a Cobla comes to town in Catalonia, a group of young office workers and shop girls totally absorbed in the *Sardana* as they dance it with serious grace; then you will need no convincing that dance has been (and sometimes still is) something far removed from a giggle and a jolly social.

The difficulty with flamenco is that it is noisy and spectacular and seems akin to the tinsel of Lloyd Webber theatricals. You feel (usually quite rightly) that you are watching an act put on for the tourist trade. And yet flamenco is there and genuine, an absorbtion quite as real as the Greek or Catalan dance: sometimes, if you are lucky, you come across it as a spontaneous thing, akin to a New Orleans jam session, a *juerga* (or party) in circumstances that are quite clearly spontaneous, and then you need no convincing. Personally, the only thing I find hard to take about it is its gushing fans.

Flamenco is clearly a very old form of dance. The theorists and experts are mostly agreed on one thing, that although today the gypsies have almost monopolized it, its roots are not gypsy – or, at most, only so in part. Jewish music, Arabic forms, perhaps even

Flamenco dancers

older origins, possibly even going back to the Iberians, all these are under scrutiny. But for us, the visitors, the fact today is that we are going to find it performed by gypsies.

I shall not attempt an explanation of forms, meanings or techniques. No article or chapter that I have read has managed to do this usefully. The subject is too complicated to achieve more than subjective impression, or else a mere catalogue of names and terms. Indeed, I have come across no book that deals helpfully with the subject – by which I mean one that explains what happens, and shows the differences between the various forms without falling into grinding polemic or poetic gush. I would be grateful to learn of one.

But a word about the sevillanas, which have recently become popular with the general public, which you will see at any festival or even in bars such as the one I describe in Granada, and which are fun and graceful to watch.

It is common today for people to sneer a bit at their popularity. You hear that it is all very well for Andalusians to dance them but not Madrileñas; or else that the sevillanas is not real flamenco. This last point was put on television to a famous flamenco singer, an elderly gypsy woman, who told her respectful and disconcerted interviewer: 'That's a load of rubbish: any music that has *duende*, that sends a shiver down my spine and makes me want to dance, is flamenco.' What the old lady was expressing, was that even the commercialized music of the sevillanas can take a dancer in that absorbing grip which seems like a power from outside ('*duende*'). If the performer is good, this can happen whether the dance is spontaneous, or a commercial performance, or part of a competition.

The purists want to put flamenco in a museum, which is to say a mausoleum: the fact that sevillana music is pumped out by groups on cassette, may by a pity for the purists, but it is a sign that it is at least alive, and to that extent something genuine. The nicest proof of this point was provided by three of those little gypsy urchins, already tough-faced and hard-eyed at seven and eight years old. They came in to Machacos in Granada to sell flowers – the standard ploy is to put a carnation in your pocket and then demand wealth. (It was nice to see that several customers bought a carnation: never mind the rip-off, gypsies have to live, too.) But after a bit the sevillanas were too much for them, they dashed outside, flung their posies to the ground and started dancing. They danced very badly, but it was heedless of the belting they would get if their mothers saw what they had done to the flowers. It was certainly genuine. So if it is alive, what is wrong with Madrileñas or anyone else dancing it? When sevillanas are played nobody looks glum, and the dancers seem to come alive: they are authentic and real because people want to dance them.

A word on Tourism and Pseudery: you can miss out on a lot if you stay aloof because you suspect that what you are seeing is phoney or that you are being taken for a ride. Gypsies push to sell things, just as tourist shops push to sell things; some of the tourist shops have good bargains in them. If you see something you like, then think what you would think good value for it, and if you do not like the price then do not buy it; if you do think it of value, haggle for it – for fun and because with vendors that is what they will expect.

Likewise with flamenco. What you will see will not be the equivalent of the drunken Greek in the Plaka. It will be a commercial spectacle, regularly performed, however dead the audience and its reactions. Just so did Louis Armstrong or Bix Beiderbecke perform. In their day there were still, no doubt, plenty of people who, feeling down, expressed their mood by going off on their own and singing Blues. That fact did not make Louis Armstrong less authentic or worth listening to. I mention a few places where you can see flamenco performances in the sections on Seville and Granada – *see* pages 50 and 187 – (and deliberately omit others I know to be rip-offs). But I suggest you also use the advice of the local Tourist Office on this, as on most things.

Flora and Fauna For botanists and bird-watchers especially, Andalusia is one of the high spots of Europe. The variety of soils and conditions from the semi-desert of Almería to the rains of the Grazalema hills, from the lowlands of river and shore to the 11,000 feet heights of the Sierra Nevada, from the salt marshes of the lower Guadalquivir to the mountain streams at its source in the Cazorla range, from the Atlantic coast to the Mediterranean – these factors make for an astonishing profusion of plant life even to my uninitiated eye. After his *Wild Flowers of the Mediterranean*, Oleg Polunin turned to a study of specific areas in south-west Europe of which no less than eight are here in Andalusia (*see* Further Reading, page 319).

The bird life is no less rich. Some 125 different species of bird live and breed in the Coto Doñano National Park in the province of Huelva. But its fame comes at least as much from the fact that, with the Camargue, it is the major staging post for migrant species in their journeys between Europe and Africa, a matter of some 150 species more.

I am as ignorant of birds as of flowers, but the raptors are always exciting to see, and here are three sorts of eagle, various vultures including the Lammergeyer to which the Spaniards give the splendid name *Quebrantahuesos* ('Crunchbones'), kites, harriers, buzzards and falcons that I have seen and no doubt others that my ignorance has made me miss.

In one or another of the Nature Reserves it is possible to see the Cabra Montés or Spanish Mountain Goat, with its huge buffalo-like horns, boar, mongoose, and even the lynx – although you would have to be lucky: the wardens working the Reserves reckon it is dying out.

Spanish interest in the natural world is a relatively recent phenomenon but, as in so many other fields, they are catching up

Wayside flora

fast. It seemed to typify what has been happening all over Spain that a senior receptionist at my hotel in Ronda, when asked about the birds nesting just below the hotel terrace, should reply 'Aguiluchos' (literally a harrier, but in his case meaning 'some bird looking rather like an eagle'), whereas his young assistant, taking me tactfully out of earshot, specified that they were Peregrines and Lesser Kestrels.

There are various National Parks and Nature Reserves in Andalusia. Apart from the great Coto Doñana in the province of Huelva, there is the superb Nature Park of the Sierras of Cazorla and Segura in the province of Jaén; and the Sierra de Grazalema where the Pinsapo pine survives from before the Ice Age. The Torcal de Antequera (Málaga province), La Pata del Caballo (Huelva province), the Lugar Nueva (Jaén province) – all these are lesser but pleasant Reserves to explore.

The main authority and source of information on these palces is: ICONA (Instituto Nacional para la Conservación de la Naturaleza), Gran Vía San Francisco, 35, 28005 Madrid. Tel: (91) 266 82 00.

Some Architectural Terms

Caliphal Art The word is not exact since the Umayyad rulers did not declare themselves Caliphs until the tenth century. The term refers to the art developed in the Mosque at Córdoba, which was built between AD 750 and 1000. It includes the rounded horseshoe arch (the pointed horseshoe came later); the alternation of red (brick) with white (stone) in the make-up of the arches; the decoration of wall surfaces with arabesque plaster moulding or carved marble; and the patterning of wall surfaces with an inlay of brick and stone such as you see within the *alfiz* or rectangular surround to the heads of doorways and windows.

You recognize the style in the Palace of Medinat az-Zahra, near Córdoba, and in parts of the Alcazares at Seville.

Nasrid Art The Nasrid kings who built the Alhambra gave their name to this style, which flourished in the fourteenth and fifteenth centuries. The materials used were mainly brick, cedar wood, ceramic tiles (*azulejos*), marble and, above all, plaster, made of gypsum or of powdered alabaster, either moulded in arabesques or carved. The doors have pointed arches but the outline is broken by the elaborately carved surfaces.

304

The ceilings, when domed, can be of breath-taking richness. To fit a round dome on the square base of a room, they used the squinch, which is a small series of projecting arches across the corners that turns the base from square to octagonal. These were covered in plasterwork with pendant or stalactite forms that then extended over the entire dome.

Mudéjar This was the name given to Moorish craftsmen working under Christian rule. You therefore find the style as early as the thirteenth century and continuing right up to the end of the Middle Ages and even into the sixteenth century, for the work of the Moors was, not surprisingly, much admired.

The main characterisitic of the style is the use of brick, for decorative surfaces as well as construction. The wooden ceilings, richly coffered and painted, known as *Artesonado* did not originate with the Mudéjares – they can be found in the twelfth century (in Sicily, for instance) – but they were much used and developed in Mudéjar building and are a memorable part of one's experience of Spanish architecture.

Fernandine When the Christians first conquered major parts of what is now Andalusia, in the 1230s and 1240s, they built churches in the new Gothic style. The style here has been named Fernandine after the king, Ferdinand (Fernando) III the Holy. Its main point of interest, within the Gothic style, lies in the plain façades: after five hundred years of a civilization that considered images of man or animal blasphemous, it is probable that not only the Moslems but the Christians living here for so long (the so-called Mozárabes), would have found statuary offensive.

Isabelline At the very end of the Gothic period, in the times of Flamboyant (French) or Perpendicular (English), the word Isabelline is often used for the Spanish equivalent. As with our own Perpendicular – in the Henry VII Chapel in Westminster, for example – one of its chief characterisitics is the use of lines (as against forms or masses), in delicate tracery, either free-standing or applied to surfaces.

Renaissance (i) Plateresque It was almost a constant in Spanish architecture that surfaces were covered in rich and complicated decoration, from Islamic building right the way through to the end of the Baroque period in the late eighteenth

305

century. Plainer styles (Fernandine, Herreran, neo-classical) stand out as exceptional and almost foreign to the spirit of the country.

Platero means 'Silversmith'; the Plateresque style, apart from features such as flattened arches, is characterized by surface decoration that resembles the chased work and patterns in beaten relief that you find on silverware. The most famous examples in Spain are further north in the University buildings of Salamanca and the Cathedral of Santiago. But you will constantly come across examples in Andalusia in palaces and cathedrals, the old Cabildo in Jerez, the City Hall (Ayuntamiento) in Seville, and many other places.

Renaissance (ii) Herreran Seeming to run counter to the national genius are some massive and austere buildings of the Renaissance, such as the archives in Seville built by Herrera, the architect of that gloomy and immense monastery the Escorial. The finest example of the plainer Renaissance style is the palace built by Machuca for the Emperor Charles v within the complex of the Alhambra. Perhaps the strangest, for its site as much as anything, is the Calahorra Palace in the province of Granada, near the semi-deserts of inland Almería.

Baroque and Churrigueresque Baroque architecture developed all over Europe in the seventeenth century and seems to have been specially suited to Spain, where it continued right through the eighteenth century. It is characterized by compositions that are spatially complex and exuberantly decorated, by curving forms and, usually, a sense of mass, although latterly (when, for example, North European architecture had moved into rococo) it became lighter. The Charterhouse of Granada presents what amounts to an anthology of Baroque, but it is the style most commonly found throughout Andalusia, especially in its cathedrals and churches.

Churrigueresque is the word applied to its more exuberant and excessive examples, where the decoration seems a natural, though perhaps less pleasing, successor to Plateresque and Moorish plasterwork. The name is unfair, since Churriguera himself did not over-egg the pudding: he built the Plaza Mayor in Salamanca which must be one of the most beautiful squares in Europe.

Andalusian Cathedral Architecture Cutting across these periods and styles, the cathedrals of Spain from Toledo southwards and, indeed, in many other places so differ from the styles you may be familiar with from England or France that you may well feel slightly baffled by them. They contain the same elements as ours, but placed and proportioned differently. The architects never aimed at clear vistas, neither vistas of length as in our English cathedrals, nor vistas of height as in the French ones.

The form of the Spanish cathedral is usually either square or nearly so. In the case of almost every Andalusian example, this is because they replaced the mosque and occupied its rectangular site. But stranger still to our eyes, the High Altar, together with attendant canons' choir and bishop's throne, were almost always placed in the middle, leaving no more space (and sometimes less) to the west than behind the High Altar to the east. As there was always a *retablo* or altarpiece behind the High Altar, as well as a wall surrounding the choir, the effect is of one rectangular building placed within another and blocking our view of the whole from every standpoint. This central block or chamber is called the *capilla mayor*. Behind it, to the east, is usually another important altar and chapel. Thus, even in the mighty cathedral at Seville, lack of vista makes it hard for us to perceive its size.

The fact that the builders and users of these buildings never thought in terms of vistas, either blocked or open, may in part account for the dreadful Philistinism of those responsible for the Cathedral inside the Mosque at Córdoba: It may be that it simply did not occur to them that they were destroying something unique, since what they built was not a cathedral indeed, but just such a *capilla mayor* as they put in the centre of Seville Cathedral (or almost all others except Granada).

Some Other Terms you may Encounter

Ajimez –	(Moorish) an arched double window, usually with an *alfiz* or rectangular moulding around it
Alameda –	avenue of trees
Alcazaba –	castle
Alcázar –	palace, usually fortified
Aljama –	place of meeting, city quarter, of Moors or Jews, Mosque, Synagogue
Aljibe –	cistern
Artesonado –	Mudéjar-style wooden ceiling, painted and coffered

Ayuntamiento –	Town Hall
Azulejo –	coloured glazed tile
Barrio –	city quarter or district
Bóveda –	vault
Cabildo –	old word for Town Council and Town Hall
Capilla mayor –	the High Altar in a cathedral.
Carmen –	(in Granada) country cottage now in centre of town
Cartuja –	Charterhouse (Carthusian monastery)
Cortijo –	Andalusian farmhouse complex, the descendant of the Roman villa that housed owner and workers
Coro –	choir of Spanish cathedral, walled in and placed in centre
Ermita –	hermitage
Judería –	Jewish quarter, usually next to the mosque
Lonja –	exchange (corn, etc.)
Maqsura –	area reserved for potentate in mosque
Medina –	Moorish word for town
Mezquita –	mosque
Mihrab –	niche in Mecca-facing wall of mosque
Mirador –	belvedere, balcony, look-out point
Mocárabe –	plasterwork on ceilings that looks like stalactites
Mozárab –	Christian living under Moslem rule. The word means 'He who would be an Arab'
Mudéjar –	Moor living under Christian rule; his style of building
Patio –	central courtyard
Plaza –	square. Plaza Mayor – enclosed and arcaded square in some cities (e.g. the Corredera in Córdoba.)
Posada –	old style of Inn, with stables the main part
Puerta –	gate or door
Reja –	iron grille, protective or decorative
Sala Capitular –	chapter house
Retablo –	altarpiece

Some Arabic Words that Explain Place-Names

Alcalá –	fortress
Alcántara –	bridge

308

Alhama –	baths or hot springs
Atalaya –	watchtower
Bab, bib, viv –	gate (e.g. Bibrrambla in Granada = 'Sandy Gate')
Dar –	house (Daraxa = 'the house of Ayesha')
Gib, Jeb –	rock or mountain (Gibraltar, Tariq's Hill)
Guadi –	river (Guadalquivir, 'Great River' or Rio Grande)
Janet –	garden or Paradise (Generalife, 'the Garden of the Architect')
Rambla–	sandy stretch, dry river bed (Guadarrama, 'Sandy River')
Suq (Spanish version Zoco) –	market

Essential Addresses

London *Spanish Embassy*, 24 Belgrave Square, London SW1X 8QA. Tel: 071-235 5555.

Spanish Consulate, 20 Draycott Place, London SW3. Tel: 071-581 5921.

Spanish Tourist Office, 57–58 St. James's Street, London SW1A 1LD. Tel: 071-499 0901. Fax: 071-629 4257.

Spanish Tourist Offices in Other Countries:

Canada: 60, Bloor St West, Suite 201, Toronto, Ontario M4W 3B8. Tel: 416 961 3131.

USA: 665 Fifth Ave., New York NY 10022. Tel: 212 759 8822;

Water Tower Place, Suite 915 East, 845 N Michigan Ave., Chicago IL 60611. Tel: 312 944 0215;

San Vicente Plaza Building, 8383 Wilshire Boulevard, Suite 960, Beverly Hills, CA 90211. Tel: 213 658 7188;

5085 Westheimer, 4800 The Galleria, Houston, Texas. Tel: 713 40 74 11.

Consulates

Britain: Calle Fernando el Santo, 16, 28010 Madrid. Tel: (91) 419 0200;

Plaza Nueva 8 Duplicado, 41001 Sevilla. Tel: (954) 228 875;

Avenida de las Fuerzas Armadas 11–1°, 11014 Algeciras. Tel: (956) 661 600;

Edificio Duquesa, Calle Duquesa de Parcent, 8, 29001 Málaga. Tel: (952) 217 571.

Canada: Calle Nuñez de Balboa, 35, 28001 Madrid. Tel: (91) 431 4300;

Plaza Malagueta, 3–1°, 29016 Málaga. Tel: (956) 223 346;
Avenida de la Constitución, 30, 1°–4, 41001 Sevilla.
Tel: (954) 229 413.
Australia: Paseo de la Castellana, 143, 28003 Madrid.
Tel: (91) 279 8504.
United States: Calle Serrano 75, 28006 Madrid.
Tel: (91) 276 3600.

Tourist Offices in Andalusia These are listed with the
addresses given for each town. Others are:
Algeciras, Avenida Marina s/n. Tel: 60 09 11.
La Linea, Avenida 20 de Abril s/n.
Huelva, Calle Vásquez López, 5.
Jaén, Avenida de Madrid, 10.
Málaga Airport
Torremolinos, Bajos de la Nogalera, local 517.
Marbella, Avenida Miguel Cano, 1.
Benalmádena Costa, Carretera Cádiz–Málaga, km 229.

Some Tour Operators
Serenissima, 21 Dorset Square, London NW1 5PG.
Tel: 071-730 9841.
Swan Hellenic, 77 New Oxford St, London WC1A 1PP.
Tel: 071-831 1234.
Cox and King's, St James' Court, 45 Buckingham Gate, London
SW1E 6AS. Tel: 071-834 7446.
The above all operate tours of Andalausia.

Holidays of Special Interest
Golf: *Eurogolf Ltd*, 3b London Road, St Albans, Herts AL1 1LA.
Tel: 081-202 4744.
Longshot Golf Holidays, Meon House, Petersfield, Hants GW32
3JN. Tel: 0730 68621.
Walking: *Waymark Holidays Ltd.*, 295 Lillie Road, London SW6
7LL. Tel: 081-385 5015.
Riding: I list these in the section on Horses (*see* page 284).
Spanish Festivals: Mundi Color or Marsans may be helpful:
Mundi Color, 276 Vauxhall Bridge Road, London SW1V 1BE.
Tel: 071-834 3492.
Marsans Travel Ltd., 7a Henrietta Place, London W1M 9AG.
Tel: 071-493 4934.
Nature Study: Try Mundi Color or else:

Voyages Jules Verne, (address as for Serenissima).
Ramblers Holidays Ltd., Box 43, Welwyn Garden City, Herts AL8 6PQ. Tel: 0707 331133.

Events Calendar The Andalusians work as hard as anybody on earth. But when it comes to celebrating, enjoying themselves, letting off steam, no-one else can come near them.

Fiesta means 'festival'. Most of them are Church Holy Days (holidays), but in a land that never suffered the Puritans, that is no reason why devotion should not be also the most tremendous occasion for whoopee. Many festivities go back to pagan origins, just as do our pagan Easter eggs and Christmas tree.

Feria means 'fair'. Most started life as cattle- or horse-fairs, and some still are. To buy and sell cattle you have to come together, and that is enough for an Andaluz: it means dropping the daily grind, eating and drinking in company away from home. From there to the week of the Seville Feria, day and night non-stop, is a step – even if a giant one.

Romería means a sort of pilgrimage that often has the atmosphere of a picnic-cum-celebration. Humble village ones may be just a village outing; the one to the shrine of the Virgen de la Cabeza at Andujar is a four-day affair involving hundreds of horses and thousands of visitors, a horse and cattle-handling contest, a reception for everyone, the trek up the mountain to the Sanctuary, singing and dancing through the night, a procession, and general merrymaking afterwards. The Rocío, with its million participants, its covered, flower-decked wagons crossing all Andalusia, and its bars and clubs of enthusiasts singing the hymn to the Virgin of the Dew every night of the year, all over Andalusia, is a phenomenon unique in the world. It is not only the Andalusians' capacity for celebrating that amazes, but their sheer stamina.

Apart from the big fiestas just mentioned, the most important are Holy Week (especially in Seville or Málaga) and Carnival (especially in Cádiz), the Horse Fair in Jerez and, perhaps, the May Fair in Córdoba. To visit any of these you would have to book your hotel a long way ahead. Some others are pretty big: the Assumption in mid-August and St John or midsummer's night (23–24 June) everywhere, and the wine harvest festivals, especially in Jerez, are also big. But there are lots of lesser ones that are still an unforgettable experience, and can be the more enjoyable for being less overwhelming.

The following list of Saints' days and other jollifications is by no means complete: every parish celebrates its patron saint; in the cities many *barrios* (City Districts) will have their own Fiesta; and every self-respecting Andalusian village runs to anything up to half a dozen fiestas, ferias and romerías a year. So I list some of the more local or popular saints with no comment, in case you find yourself near a church of that name. For instance, I came across the Fuensanta in Córdoba by chance and much enjoyed it. But the Tourist Office does not mention it, and the police were annoyed when I happened to mention that I had taken an American family, because, while the shrine and festival are old, the place is a high-rise working-class suburb notorious for its drug problem and consequent petty crime. Yet for every thief there were at least a hundred family folk in the crowd, and when Sevillanas were being danced on stage, the children with me were riveted, not by that, but by the swirling in the crowd as dozens of groups of kids, punk hair-cut, leather jacket, jeans and all, danced Sevillanas themselves. 'Mom', said the younger one, 'this is where it's at!' And as for any thieves, with my wallet tucked safely in my shirt, and with my companions persuaded to leave handbags, cameras, necklaces and earrings in their hotel, we could be carefree. This consideration applies only to cities: village and country folk are honourable.

Perhaps the most nearly complete list is published by the Andalusian Government (Junta de Andalucía) in a booklet entitled *Fairs and Festivals of Andalusia* obtainable free from any Tourist Office. It lists, by Province and by village rather than by date, more than 600 celebrations – fairs, fiestas and romerías. Many of them are included in the following calendar but, clearly, with both to hand you should have little difficulty in finding colour, fun, noise, flamenco, horses, ritual, music, ceremony, bonfires, eats, exuberance, pageantry, fireworks and general *joie de vivre*.

Since Easter is celebrated on the Sunday following the first full moon after 21 March, and many feast days depend on that, I have placed these in the approximate month and marked them Movable Date (MD).

Major festivals are described in a bit more detail under the town concerned, and some of them under Horses (*see* page 284).

Do not forget that any of these may mean the closing of banks and, while on that subject, you should not forget public holidays that are not fiestas: 1 January, 19 March, 1 May (Labour Day), 6 December (Constitution Day).

January

1–9   *Winter Festival:* ALMERÍA.

6   *Reyes* (Kings), *Epiphany*, or *Twelfth Night*. The Three Kings bring children presents (as in Britain they get them at Christmas). It is a day of processions and general celebration all over Andalusia. In GRANADA and MOTRIL a parade of the Three Kings. In SEVILLE and HIGUERA DE LA SIERRA (Huelva) the processions are mounted.

10–15 ALMERÍA: *Romería de Torre Garcia.*

17   *San Antón* (popular because he, too, was tempted). Bonfires or processions or both, often on the eve. In ARQUILLOS (Jaén), the Tempter chases locals with an espadrille.

20   *San Sebastián.* In some parts of Almería (LUBRIN and GERGAL) he is associated with battles of Moors and Christians, though these pop up on many occasions: 10 June in CARBONERAL (Almería), and 13 in TREVELEZ (Granada); 1 August in BENAMAHOMA (Cádiz), 4 in BENLAURIA (Málaga), and 27 in BENADALID (Málaga); 12 September in ALCAUCIN (Málaga), 26 in TURRE (Almería) and 15 in VALOR (Granada).

February

1   *Saint Cecilia:* GRANADA and others.

2   *Candlemas* (Candelaria) Purification of the BVM: ALCAUCIN (Málaga) and others.

3   *St Blaise* (San Blas – invoked for sore throats and sick animals).

MD   Carnival i.e. The week leading up to Shrove Tuesday. Celebrated most famously in CÁDIZ.

March

MD   Holy Week: SEVILLE and MÁLAGA notably, but also ARCOS DE LA FRONTERA, BAEZA, UBEDA, JAEN, HUERCAL-OVERA (Almería), GRANADA. In BAENA (Córdoba) there is a drum-roll from Wednesday to Friday continuously; Easter Day, in various

313

places is a bit like Guy Fawkes: Judas is burnt with fireworks. Every town and village has its own ceremony: the *Coria Embrace* at CORIA DEL RIO (Seville); the *Toro Embolao* at VEJER DE LA FRONTERA (Cádiz) where mutton broth and dry sherry are distributed. Everywhere, the Andaluces show their genius for enjoyment.

11   *St Eulogius* (San Eulogio).

MD   4th Sunday in March. *Sword Dance:* OBEJO (Córdoba).

25   *Annunciation.*

April

4   *St Isidore of Seville.*

MD   *Feria:* SEVILLE: usually 2 weeks after Easter, but always within April.

MD   Last Sunday in April (including Friday and Saturday, *Romería de Nuestra Señora de la Cabeza:* ANDUJAR (Jaén). One of the biggest celebrations and pilgrimages, with horses and carriages.

MD   Sunday nearest 25th, FUENTE OBEJUNA: (Córdoba) *Romería de la Virgen de la Gracia* (carriages and horses).

25   *St Mark.* Outdoor festivals; blessing fields; cakes and buns.

May

EARLY MAY (sometimes starting 30 April). Mayos and Cruces: the *Mayos* or Maydays celebrate with singing. For the *Cruces* (Holy Crosses), families decorate each their own cross, often splendidly; as ever, much singing and dancing withal. The Andalusian love of flowers comes into its own here; and nowhere more than in CÓRDOBA, where it is followed by the *Fiesta of the Patios* when householders compete for the most beautiful patio.

1–7   *Jerez Horse Fair* (may be end of April).

1–2   *Romería Nuestra Señora de la Estrella:* NAVAS DE SAN JUAN (Jaén).

1–4   *Romería: Santo Cristo of the Almoraima Mountains.* CASTELLAR (Cádiz).

5–12   CÓRDOBA: *Fiesta de los Patios,* and *Cruzes de Mayo.* The *Cruzes* may be in many places.

MD   *Whitsun* (and the Saturday and Monday) *Rocío* pilgrimage and fiesta: ALMONTE. Up to a million *rocieros* (regular participants belonging to clubs and brotherhoods) and spectators from all over Spain, take part in this, the most colourful of all pilgrimages. *See also* under Almonte in the Huelva section (page 255).

Whit Monday *Romería of Sts Alodia and Numilón:* HUESCAR (Granada).

MD   Third weekend. ALMONASTER LA REAL (Huelva): *Feast of Saint Eulalia.* Cavalcade, etc.

17   *Romería San Isidoro* SETENIL (Cádiz).

21–24 MONTILLA (Córdoba): *May Fair.*

27–31 *Manzanilla Fair:* SANLUCAR DE BARRAMEDA (Cádiz).

June

MD   *Corpus Cristi* (Thursday after Trinity Sunday): many places. The Host is paraded through the streets in magnificent Monstrances: but notably at CÓRDOBA, ZAHARA DE LA SIERRA (Cádiz); and SEVILLE where, in the cathedral, six boys (*los seises*) dance before the high alter in red silk costume, with their hats on, and then lead the cortège. Often the procession involves Carnival-like masks and grotesques.
GRANADA: a *music festival de Falla and Cante Jondo.*

13   *St Antony of Padua* (invoked for lost objects, a category that includes future husbands). Fair in his honour at CHICLANA de la FRONTERA (Cádiz) 10–14 also at EL BOSQUE (Cádiz).

23   *Eve of St John Baptist* (Víspera de San Juan). Not unlike our Hallowe'en. Bonfires and much else.

24   *St John Baptist.* All sorts of celebration of the summer solstice, and its pagan origins show: I cannot vouch personally for today, but late March used to show an appreciable surge in the birth-rate.

29   *St Peter.* Important as a fisherman in a land of such.

July

9–14 *San Francisco Solano:* MONTILLA (Córdoba): Fair and Fiesta.

16   ADRA (Almería): *Romería de la Virgen del Carmen.*

18   *Fiesta of the Tethered Bull:* GRAZALEMA (Cádiz).

22   *St Mary Magdalene.*

25   *St James* (Santiago). He of the mighty Pilgrimage to Compostela in Galicia, but also as Matamoros, the Moorslayer. Battles of Moors and Christians, notably in GRANADA, the ALPUJARRAS, ALMERÍA, CÁDIZ, JAÉN.

26   *St Ann.* Especially in the Triana district in SEVILLE.

29   *St Martha* (Santa Marta).

August

5   *Romería Virgen de las Nieves:* TREVELEZ (Granada). Nieves means 'snows' – it goes up Mulhacen, the highest peak in Spain.

7   *St Dominic* (Santo Domingo).

10 *St Lawrence* (San Lorenzo).

15 *Assumption.* This is one of the biggest days of church celebration in the year, dedicated not only to the Virgin but many other saints as well, and it is a national holiday in Catholic countries (Ferragosto, le quinze août, etc.). Not a day to be looking for a hotel, or provender but, if you have them, a good day to be in Andalusia.

16 *San Roque* (St Rock, or Roach: invoked if ill).

18–21 Celebration *Fiesta of the Guadalquivir:* SANLUCAR DE BARRAMEDA.

19–21 *Vendimia* (Harvest Festival): MONTILLA (Córdoba).

22–25 GRAZALEMA (Cádiz): *Fair.*

24 *St Bartholomew* (San Bartolomé).

28 *St Augustine* (San Agustin): MOJACAR.

September

6   *Battle* between GUADIX and BAZA (Granada): A representative of Guadix (the Cascaborras) tries to get to Baza perfectly clean. If he does so he wins the statue of the Virgin of Piety. A robust occasion, not for the dainty.

6–10 ADRA (Almería): *Fiestas of the Patron Saints* (Virgen del Mar and St Nicholas Tolentino).

7–14 *Moscatel Fiesta* CHIPIONA. A good place for flamenco; a sizeable gypsy population.

8   *Birth of the BVM.* Hence many festivals such as:

4–8 *María Santísima de la Sierra:* CABRA (Córdoba);

6–8 *Nuestra Señora de la Fuensanta:* CÓRDOBA;

8   *Romería de NS de los Angeles:* ALAJAR (Huelva);

8–10 *Feria y Fiesta NS de la Consolacion:* UTRERA (Sevilla).

14 *Santa Cruz* (Holy Cross). Everywhere.

MD *Royal Fair and Wine Harvest Festival:* PALMA DEL CONDADO (Huelva). Three days of Feria.

15–20 approx: JEREZ: *Sherry Harvest Festival.*

21 *St Matthew.*

29 *St Michael and all Angels.* Therefore, the Archangel Raphael,

patron of CÓRDOBA. Also a *Romería to St Michael* in the ALBAICIN at GRANADA. *Fiesta and Feria* in UBEDA (Jaén).

October

4   *St Francis* (San Francisco).

6   *El Santísimo Cristo del Paño pilgrimage:* MOCLIN (Granada).

7   *La Virgen del Rosario:* MOJACAR (Almería).

15   *St Teresa of Ávila.*

18   *St Luke.*

19   *St Peter of Alcántara.* In the town of that name on the Costa del Sol.

3rd Sunday. *Romería Virgen de Valme:* DOS HERMANAS (Sevilla).

Last but one Sunday RUS (Jaén): *young people's Sunday.*

November

1   *All Saints' Day:* largely gastronomic, and family.

2   *All Souls' Day:* not celebration: day for visiting graves.

24   *St John of the Cross.*

30   *St Andrew.*

December

8   *Conception of BVM.*

14   *St John of the Cross* (San Juan de la Cruz). Especially in UBEDA (Jaén) where he died. (His official day is 24 November, however).

21   *St Thomas.*

24   *Christmas Eve* (Nochebuena). Carols after Midnight Mass.

24–28 VELEZ BLANCO (Almería): carolling every night.

25   *Christmas* (Navidad).

26   *St Stephen* (San Esteban).

27   *St John the Apostle.*

28   *Holy Innocents.* Some churches have the Festival of Fools and little Bishops: a child is made bishop for a day.

28   VENTA DEL TUNEL (Málaga): *Verdiales,* i.e. a sort of singing match between a mountain group and a sort of home team.

30–1 Jan *Cart Festival:* COGOLLOS DE GUADIX (Granada). Especially 31st evening, huge bonfire.

31   *St Silvester.* HUESA (Jaén): Castillos del Santo, sort of bonfire with dancing and singing.

31   *New Year's Eve* (Año Nuevo). Common tradition: you have to pop a grape in your mouth at each chime of midnight. Just thought I would warn you – it's not as easy as it sounds…

Children on Car Journeys Children on car journeys often get bored. The following list of car numbers may help, used with or without a map of Spain. They might simply collect provinces; or autonomous regions (e.g. CC and BA both counting as Extremadura); or simply find out where the car comes from.

Car Matriculation Nos.

Alava	VI	Lérida	L
Albacete	AB	Logroño	LO
Alicante	A	Lugo	LU
Almería	AL	Madrid	M
Avila	AV	Malaga	MA
Badajoz	BA	Melilla	ML
Baleares	PM	Murcia	MU
Barcelona	B	Navarra	NA
Burgos	BU	Orense	OR
Caceres	CC	Oviedo	O
Cádiz	CA	Palencia	P
Castellon	CS	Pontevedra	PO
Ceuta	CE	Salamanca	SA
Ciudad Real	CR	Santander	S
Córdoba	CO	Segovia	SG
Coruna	C	Sevilla	SE
Cuenca	CU	Soria	SO
Gerona	GE	Tarragona	T
Granada	GR	Tenerife	TF
Gran Canaria	GC	Teruel	TE
Guadalajara	GU	Toledo	TO
Guipuzcoa	SS	Valencia	V
Huelva	H	Valladolid	VA
Huesca	HU	Vizcaya	BI
Jaén	J	Zamora	ZA
León	LE	Zaragoza	Z

To these should be added:

ET   Ejército de Tierra (Army)

EA   Fuerzas Aereas (Air Force)

FN   Fuerzas Navales (Navy)

MOP   Obras Públicas (Ministry of Public Works)

PGC   Parque de la Guardia Civil (Police Motor Pool)

PMM   (Ministries)

Further Reading
General

Gerald Brenan *South from Granada*. **His best: His life between the wars in the remote Alpujarra.**
The Face of Spain.

Richard Ford *Handbook for Travellers in Spain*. **A great work, written in 1845. His name is famous in Spain, not in England. It has recently been republished by Centaur... at £65.**
Gatherings from Spain. **A shortened version, now out of print. May be obtainable.**

John Hooper *The Spaniards* (Penguin). **An excellent introduction and a good read, though no topical book can stay up to date.**

Nicholas Luard *Andalucia* (Century). **Good when on people, flora and fauna.**

A. Boyd *The Road from Ronda* (Collins)

R. Fraser *The Pueblo – A Mountain Village on the Costa del Sol* (Allen Lane)

Recent History

Gerald Brenan *The Spanish Labyrinth* (CUP). **His attempt to make sense of the Civil War. Moving and honest.**

Raymond Carr *Spain 1808–1975*

Raymond Carr and Juan Pablo Fusi
Spain, Dictatorship to Democracy (Allen & Unwin)

Hugh Thomas *The Spanish Civil War* (Penguin). **1,000 pages, but accepted in Spanish Universities as the best account.**

George Orwell *Homage to Catalonia* (Penguin). **Personal experience of the Civil War.**

Ian Gibson *The assassination of Federico García Lorca* (Penguin) 1984. **He has received honorary Spanish nationality for this.**

Other History

J. Elliott   *Imperial Spain* (Penguin)

C. Petrie   *A short History of Spain* (Sidgwick & Jackson)

W.H. Watt and P. Cachia
A History of Islamic Spain (Edinburgh UP) 1977

Special Interests

Oleg Polunin and B.E. Smythies *Flowers of South West Europe* (Oxford Paperbacks)

Peterson Mountford and Hollom
Field guide to the Birds of Britain and Europe (Collins). **Still the best. The Spanish edition (Pub: Omega) gives the names in English and all Peninsular languages, and adapts the work for Spain. I use the two in conjunction.**

Julian Jeffs *Sherry* (Faber & Faber)

Marimar Torres *The Spanish Table* (Ebury Press). **The daughter of the famous wine maker shows it is not all gazpacho and paella.**

Nicholas Butcher
The Spanish Kitchen (Macmillan) 1990. **An English restaurateur living in Spain. Extensive section on Tapas**

Jesus Pelaez del Rosal
The Jews in Cordoba, trans. Patricia Sneesby (Almendro). **From the Sepharad bookshop, Cordoba.**

Golfing in Europe (Ashford Press)

Horse Riding in Europe (Ashford Press)

John Reay-Smith *Living in Spain* (Robert Hale)

Holiday Reading

Penelope Chetwode
Two Middle Aged Ladies in Andalusia (Century). **One of them being her horse. Highly recommended.**

C.S. Forester *The Gun* (Penguin)
Death to the French (Penguin). **Set in Portugal but true for Spain in Wellington's day, and a very good yarn.**

Georgette Heyer *The Spanish Bride* (Pan). **Also set in the peninsular war, and she is a competent historian.**

Elizabeth Longford
Wellington, the years of the sword (Panther). **The striking thing about these two books is how good a yarnspinner the historian is, and how scrupulous with fact the romantic novelist is.**

Ted Walker *In Spain* (Corgi). **A travel writer, personal and chatty, who writes well. Two of the chapters cover Andalusia.**

Laurie Lee *As I walked out one Midsummer Morning*
   A Rose for Winter
   I Can't Stay Long
You like him or – like me – you can not stand him.
Washington Irving
   Tales from the Alhambra. **Early Romantic stuff (1829), but if the style shows it, the yarns are good. And without him, the Alhambra might now be a mere ruin. Easy to find in Granada, not in the UK.**

Language Guide If you learn to pronounce Spanish well, you will be doing yourself a great disservice: your phrase-book question will draw a barrage of incomprehensible gabble in reply. Remember this – the worse you pronounce, the more likely you are to get a slow and clear answer, aided by gestures, that you can actually understand. Even if you do not understand it, both parties will probably get a laugh out of it, which is not a bad thing to happen, on holiday. Furthermore, Spaniards have been at least as bad as us at learning languages, which means you need not bother about any linguistic inferiority feelings. On the other hand, they are now dead keen to learn English, which means that you may well be doing them a kindness to let them try out their halting skills. I recommend you learn by heart one phrase that could turn out to be the most diplomatically productive of all:
'*No se preocupe: Su inglés es mejor que mi español.*'.' ('Don't worry: Your English is better than my Spanish.')

   However, it will not do any harm if you can get near enough to the Spanish sounds to be comprehensible.

   Vowels The are all clipped, and always pronounced the same way: none of your English Cat, Kate, Cart

a – as in But, or an Irishman saying Father

e – as in Met

i – as in Feet

o – roughly as in Hot (or perhaps Bought)

u – as in Book (but never as in Rebuke)

u is only ever silent in que, qui, gue, gui. Thus, the first sound in *queso* (cheese) is like the first sound in Kettle, not as in Quest. In the same way, *qui* (who) is like a tersely spoken Key, *gue* as in Game, *gui* as in Guitar.

'As soon as we got there, my wife and I started taking lessons . . . I mean, it's not as if you were doing them a favour by learning the language, is it?' Gary Lineker, quoted by Simon Barnes (The Times 28/12/1988).

321

Otherwise, even in pairs or groups, all vowels are always pronounced as above. Thus, Huelva will sound rather as in 'Well, for heaven's sake!'; Jaén rather as in 'High entry fee'.

Consonants Only a few give any trouble.

j – is a cinch to Scotsmen and a pain to Sassenachs; you pronounce it as the *ch* in Loch. If you find that hard, try to make a more audible h than the English one – you will be understood, and what else matters?

g – is as in Gat, Got, Gutenberg Bible. BUT before e or i it is like the j.

c – is as in Cat, Cot, Couturier. BUT before e or i it is like the th in Thin. Brook no interference from people who know all about Andalusian speech. They will tell you I have got it all wrong and that for Andalusians the ce and ci are sibilant. But just you try hearing it! Stick to the lisped cin = Thin. People will understand you, and you may have a chance of understanding them.

d – make it half-way between English d and the th in Then. You will be understood but you may not recognize places like Cádiz (cathee).

h – is always silent

ll – as in Million

ñ – as in Canyon

r – is rolled in Spanish; Easy forrr Scots again. If you rrreally can't, then somehow it must always be hearrrd.

s – always as in Missing, never as in Miser. The English z sound does not exist in Spain.

z – like the lisped c, as in thin.

Stress is important. There are only two rules (and there are two things you can do about them):

A word ending in any vowel, or -n or -s, is *normally* stressed on the last syllable but one; any other word is *normally* stressed on the last syllable. Simple. Now comes the rub. A lot of words do not beháve in this nórmal way: with these the stress is marked with a written áccent.

Those are the two rules and here are the two things you can do about them. Either, you can get hold of these two rules (which have no exceptions) and practise them on city names, shop signs and wine bottles until you know them. Or else, you can throw them out of the window, and cunningly pronounce all words *with equal stress.* Do not say Trfalg' sqa', as we do; do not say Tra-fal-garr as the Spaniards do; say trá-fál-gár with equal weight, which is what the French tend to do – and get away with murder.

Basics and Courtesies

Yes – sí

No – no

Please – por favor

Thank you – gracias

You're welcome – de nada

Excuse me – perdón

It doesn't matter – es igual

Good morning – buenos días

Good afternoon – buenas tardes

Good evening / Good night
   – buenas noches

I'm English – soy inglés, inglesa
   escocés; irlandés; galés;
   canadiense, (no change,
   man or woman);
   Americano, – a; etc;

I don't know – no sé

Do you speak English?
   – ¿habla inglés?

Hello – ola

Goodbye – adiós; hasta luego

How are you?
   ¿Como está usted?
   (or) ¿Qué tal?

Very well, and you?
   – muy bien, y ¿usted?

OK, All right, fair enough
   – vale

Where – donde

When – cuando

How – como

What – qué

Who – quien

Which – cual

Leave me alone – déjame

Good – bueno

Bad – malo

Time, Days, Dates

What time is it? – qué hora es?

At what time? – a qué hora

One o'clock – la una

Half-past two – las dos y media

A quarter to four – las cuatro
   menos cuarto

Today – hoy

Yesterday – ayer

Tomorrow – mañana

Tomorrow morning – mañana
   por la mañana

Tomorrow afternoon – mañana
   por la tarde

Now – ahora

Later – más tarde

Earlier – más temprano

Monday – lunes

Tuesday – martes

Wednesday – miércoles

Thursday – jueves

Friday – viernes

Saturday – sábado

Sunday – domingo

Getting About

Where is… – ¿dónde está?

X street – la calle x

The station – la estación

The road to – la carretera de

To the left – a izquierda

To the right – a derecha

Go straight ahead – sigue recto
(or) adelante

The traffic lights – el semáforo

Up(wards) – arriba

Down(wards) – abajo

After – después

Before – antes

Is it far? – ¿lejos?

Is it near? – ¿cerca?

Fast - rápido

Slow – despacio

Shopping

I would like – quisiera

How much – cuánto?

Where is… – dónde está?

A bank – un banco

A chemists – una farmacia

A little food shop – una tienda
de comestibles

A supermarket
– un supermercado

A telephone – un teléfono;
la telefónica

Open – abierto

Closed – cerrado

Expensive – costoso

Cheap – barato

Something – algo

Nothing – nada

More – más

Less – menos

For a (young) person
– para una persona joven

Elderly – de edad

1 uno

2 dos

3 tres

4 cuatro

5 cinco

6 seis

7 siete

8 ocho

9 nueve

10 diez

11 once

12 doce

13 trece

14 catorce

15 quince

16 diez y seis

17 diez y siete

18 diez y ocho

19 diez y nueve

20 veinte

21 veinte y uno

30 treinta

40 cuarenta

50 cincuenta

60 sesenta

70 setenta

80 ochenta

90 noventa

100 cien

500 quinientos

1000 mil

1.000.000 un millón

Hotel

I should like – quisiera

Do you have… – tiene?

A double room – una habitación doble

A single room – una habitación individual

Breakfast included – desayunado incluído

Air-conditioning – aire condicionado

With bathroom – con baño

To book – reservar

For (such and such) a date – para la fecha (tal)

For (three) days – para (tres) días

Until – hasta

We'll arrive – llegaremos

We are leaving – nos vamos

Restaurants Remember that the humbler restaurants will usually give you a *plato compuesto* (a made-up dish, i.e. that includes protein and veg.) if you ask for it. And that restaurants of all categories are usually happy to accomodate you with something not on the *carta* if they can.

Sopas

Gazpacho (of course!)

Salmorejo – Córdoban version of gazpacho

Sopa de…

… ajo – garlic soup

… verduras – vegetable soup

… garbanzos – chick peas

… arroz – rice

… pescado – fish soup

Caldo – broth

Migas – soup made with breadcrumbs, garlic, oil and water

Entremeses y Huevos – Hors d'Oeuvres and Eggs

Entremeses variados – assorted.

Fiambres – cold meats

Jamón Serrano – smoke-cured ham

Jamón de York – boiled ham (English style)

Aceitunas – olives

Huevos flamencos – with spiced sausage and tomato

Huevos revueltos – scrambled

Tortilla (española) – Spanish omelette, i.e. with potatoes

Pescados y Mariscos – Fish and Seafood

Anchoa – anchovy
Atún – tuna
Bacalao – cod
Baila – bass
Besugo – sea bream
Una freiduría – fry-up
 of small fish
Lenguado – sole
Merluza – hake
Mero – grouper
Mojama – salted tuna
Pez Espada – swordfish
Rape – monkfish
Sardina – sardine
Salmón – salmon
Salmonete – red mullet
Trucha – trout
Urta – delicious but no one has
 been able to identify it for me

Almeja – clams
Boquerones – whitebait
Calamares – squid
Cangrejo – crab
Chipirrones – small squid
Gambas – prawns
 (and shrimps)
Langosta – lobster
Langostina – crayfish
Mejillones – mussels
Percebes – barnacles
Pescadilla – small whiting
Pijotas – even smaller whiting
Pulpo – octopus
Puntillitas – even smaller
 squid
Sepias – cuttlefish
Zamburiñas - baby clams

Aves y Caza – Poultry and Game

Faisán – pheasant
Pato – duck
Pavo – turkey

Pollo – chicken
Conejo – rabbit
Jabalí – boar

Carnes – Meat

Cabra – goat
Carne de vaca – beef
Cerdo – pork

Cochinillo – suckling pig
Cordero – lamb
Ternera – veal

Cuts

Chuleta – chop
Chuletón – T-bone
Filete – fillet

Lomo – loin
Solomillo – sirloin, tenderloin
Rabo de Toro – ox-tail

Ways of Preparing

Cocidos
Estofados
Fabadas   } All various
Cazuelas   sorts of stew
Caldereta
Asado – roast

A la plancha – grilled
A la parilla – grilled
A la brava – with a hot sauce
Frito – fried
Al horno – baked
Cocido – baked

Hervido – boiled

A la inglesa – boiled

Bits and Pieces

Albóndigas – meatballs

Chorizo – highly seasoned sausage

Salchicha – sausage

Salchichón – big one (like salami)

Morcilla – blood sausage

Morcón – black pudding

Verduras – Vegetables

Aguacate – avocado

Ajo – garlic

Alcachofa – artichoke

Arroz – rice

Berenjena – aubergine

Cebolla – onion

Espárragos – asparagus

Espinacas – spinach

Habas – (white) beans

Judías (verdes) – French beans

Drinks

Vino tinto – red wine

Vino blanco – white wine

Clarete – rosé wine

Un vaso – a glass

Media botella – a half bottle

Una botella – a bottle

Cava – Spanish champagne-style

Vino de mesa – table wine

Vino de la casa – the house wine

Cerveza – beer

Una caña – a small draught beer

Una clara – shandy

Agua natural – tap water

Agua con gas – fizzy mineral water

Agua sin gas – flat mineral water

Zumo de naranja – orange juice

Limonada – lemonade

Pasado por agua – boiled (for eggs)

Mollejas – sweatbreads

Callos – tripe

Criadillas – mountain oysters

Higado – liver

Riñones – kidneys

Sesos – brains

Palmitos – palm hearts

Patata – potato

Pepino – cucumber

Pimientos – pimentos

Rábano – radish

Setas – mushrooms (boletus)

Champiñones – mushroom (white)

Tomates – tomatoes

Zanahorias – carrots

Chocolate – chocolate

Leche – milk

Un batido (de leche) – milkshake

Horchata – soft drink from powdered nuts

Té – tea: con limón, con leche, sin leche

Café – coffee

Café largo or americano: more water in

Café solo – black

Café con leche – large white

Café cortado – small, with a touch of milk

Andalusia Index